ISBN: 9781314494273

Published by:
HardPress Publishing
8345 NW 66TH ST #2561
MIAMI FL 33166-2626

Email: info@hardpress.net
Web: http://www.hardpress.net

THE SOUTH VINDICATED

LONDON
PRINTED BY SPOTTISWOODE AND CO.
NEW-STREET SQUARE

THE SOUTH VINDICATED

BEING A SERIES OF LETTERS WRITTEN
FOR THE AMERICAN PRESS DURING THE CANVASS FOR THE
PRESIDENCY IN 1860, WITH A LETTER TO LORD BROUGHAM ON THE JOHN BROWN
RAID, AND A SURVEY OF THE RESULT OF THE PRESIDENTIAL
CONTEST, AND ITS CONSEQUENCES

BY

THE HON. JAMES WILLIAMS

LATE AMERICAN MINISTER TO TURKEY

WITH AN INTRODUCTION BY JOHN BAKER HOPKINS

From the Second American Edition published at Nashville, Tenn., Confederate States of America,
by the Southern Methodist Publishing House

LONDON
LONGMAN, GREEN, LONGMAN, ROBERTS, & GREEN
1862

PREFACE

TO AMERICAN EDITION.

THE following letters were written at Constantinople during the canvass for the Presidency of the United States in 1860, and forwarded at the time for publication in a political journal. In deference to the desire of a number of intelligent gentlemen, they have been collected together and are now reissued in their present form, as a single atom in the history of that great struggle which terminated in the election of a President by the united votes of the Northern States, to be speedily followed by the dismemberment of the Confederacy.

It is a remarkable fact that the only intelligent observers of the events which were transpiring in the United States, who were surprised at the immediate success of the 'Republicans,' were those who were themselves the instigators or actors in that great political crusade against the South. These seem, in their calculation of consequences, to have ignored alike the existence of that great body of earnest fanatics whose passions they had aroused to madness, while invoking their necessary aid, and of that natural instinct of self-preservation, which would teach the freemen of the South, while fathoming the hostile intentions of their enemies, that although it might be swift destruction to resist, it would be but an ignoble life and a lingering death to submit! They alone seemed blind to the consequences which would follow, as a necessary sequence upon the heels of their victory. They alone seem not to have considered, that whilst the multitude of their mad followers would not be content to postpone gathering the fruits of their victory, and would press forward at once to reach the promised goal, the SOUTH would, AS ONE MAN, gird on his armour for defence, and by accepting the challenge to immediate combat, make 'gradual emancipation' for ever impossible.

While it was universally believed throughout Europe that the only question at issue in the struggle for the Presidency was that of slavery in the Southern States, and that the result would involve the destruction of that institution, or the dissolution of the Confederacy, in the event of the success of the 'Republican party,' the greater number believed that the only result would be the ultimate emancipation of the slaves. So active and successful have been the enemies of the South, in misrepresenting the character and qualities of the Southern people, there were but few who supposed that they could offer any serious resistance to the encroachments of their powerful neighbour. The events of the last few months have not only dispelled this delusion from the public mind, but they have created a revulsion in the sentiment and opinion of the civilised world, as startling in its magnitude as it is just in its conclusions. Europe is at length beginning to discover, as passing events are developing with a rapid movement, the true merits of this life-and-death struggle for supremacy over the soil of the South; how egregiously it has been deceived by the persistent misrepresentations of the Southern people by their unscrupulous enemies.

That the war in which the gallant sons of the South are now engaged will end in securing their independence, cannot be questioned; that its prosecution will be attended with heavy sacrifices is equally true. But amidst all the evils which may accompany it, or the blessings which will succeed its successful close, not the least gratifying of the results achieved will be, the vindication of the character of the Southern people before the civilised world, against the aspersions and misrepresentations which have been so unjustly and so profusely heaped upon them by those who claimed to be their fellow-countrymen.

CONTENTS.

INTRODUCTION.

Posterity will be amazed at the attitude of Europe in reference to the Second War of Independence in America. The apparent apathy respecting the crucial struggle of a gallant people for national existence will be inexplicable to future generations, especially when it is considered how strongly interest as well as duty dictated a policy of avowed and hearty sympathy. The complete and abundant records of the contest will enable the historian of 1900 to state the problem accurately and minutely, but not to give a satisfactory solution thereof. Sovereign States, wisely or unwisely, secede from a Federal Union, and amongst the seceding States are some of which Europe has distinctly and formally recognised the individual sovereignty. The non-seceding States choose to call this rebellion, and to go to war for the purpose of reconstructing the Union, or rather of subjugating the South. The North makes the contest as injurious as possible to foreign nations, by needlessly paralysing a great industry and a principal branch of commerce. Europe, though smote on either cheek, not only abstains from intervention, but refuses to recognise a *de facto* Government chosen by nearly eight millions of people inhabiting a country of 800,000 square miles. After two campaigns, in which the South has gallantly and, by the favour of Heaven, most effectually maintained her independence, we still refuse to recognise the Confederate States. And this we do contrary to all precedent, and especially contrary to the theory and practice of the United States. We have recognised new Governments notwithstanding the opposition of powerful minorities, as was lately the case in respect to Italy, and notably when France acknowledged the independence of the revolted colonies of Great Britain. In the Southern States there is no Union party, not a vestige of Union feeling, but on the contrary a manifest and unparalleled unanimity; yet from them we withhold recognition. Why? Is the cause of the anomaly inscrutable?

How, for example, can we explain the conduct of England? Our Government is the chief obstacle to recognition, yet we have such a great, such an imperial stake in the termination of hostilities, that the Continent, though suffering much from the American war, waits for us to give the signal for a combined action, that will eventuate in peace. The blockade of the Southern ports has pauperised the working population of Lancashire; and the cotton famine, if it continues, will prove more costly to us than would be a war with one of the Great Powers. The suggestion of Northern emissaries that the present struggle will so weaken the Northern States as to make our tenure of Canada more secure, is equally specious and fallacious. No one believes that the United States can conquer Canada, though they may attack it; and however exhausting this war may be, it will not, cannot, secure Canada against attack; on the contrary, a ruined nation, a nation bankrupt in means and reputation, is at all times a dangerous neighbour. The loyalty of the Canadians is unquestionable; but if they desired to separate from the mother-country, they would be permitted to do so without the necessity of waging war or seeking the aid of the Northern States; and we may be sure that fire and water would sooner unite than Canada and the North. The Canadians have a deep-rooted and ever-growing antipathy to the institutions and policy of the United States. Besides, if Canada were really endangered, is not the establishment of the Southern Confederacy a strong defence against our enemy? Nothing will so curb the license and ambition of the North as having a powerful neighbour bound to Europe by the adamantine chains of mutual interests. If the late United States had been one in theory as well as in fact, if there had not been a severance of races and interests, the peace of the world would have been in jeopardy; but in America as in Europe there is happily a providential disunity which generates an international balance of power, the only guarantee of national independence. Yet though a divided America is undoubtedly good for England, for Europe, and for the people of America, we must not conclude that any advantage is derivable from a weakened America. A weak nation is a bad customer, her productiveness and consumption being small. The division of America is a subject of congratulation, not because it diminishes her aggregate strength, but that it makes it less menacing.

France has the strong motive of the welfare of her manufacturing industry and her commerce to urge her to welcome the Confederate States into the family of nations; and certainly she has nothing to fear from the hostility of the North, for none of her territory is vulnerable to Northern vengeance or ambition. France, moreover, has fought for the right of a nation to choose its own form of government, and has gained so complete a victory that when the monarchy of July was replaced by a republic and the republic by the empire, Europe on each occasion hastened, as in duty bound, to acknowledge and recognise the new state of affairs; and France, too, has lately set the example of recognising the Kingdom of Italy, the existence of which is greatly due to her armed intervention. The French nation could not then display an unwillingness to acknowledge the independence of the Confederate States without ignoring her past history; and France has not been unwilling, but has anxiously awaited the concurrence of England.

The merest tyro in politics knows the advantage that will result to Spain from the formation of the Southern Confederacy; and a very slight acquaintance with commercial affairs will enable any one to appreciate the enormous gain to Germany from the existence of a free-trade Government in the Southern States. Indeed it is impossible to point to any nation that will not be benefited by the secession of the South, excepting the North, but not the West, of the United States.

Europe cannot plead that she is actuated by her opposition to the institution of slavery. The North did not enter upon the war to emancipate the slaves, and has loudly repudiated the charge. The cry of emancipation now raised is a cry of passionate vengeance. If the South cannot be conquered, let her, if possible, be desolated. Remembering the bitter hatred, the inexpressible loathing felt for the negro in the North, that he is there regarded as an accursed leper not fit to worship God in the same church, or to ride in the same carriage, or to walk in the same street, or indeed to live in the same country, it cannot be denied that even if slavery in the South, instead of being as it is, is as abolition fanatics represent it, still it is inconceivably better for the negro than that he should have any connection with the people of the North. The independence of the South will not, *per se*, put an end to slavery, neither will the subjugation of the South do so, but the latter would enslave the white race and leave the condition of the black race unchanged—except, indeed, that the negro would pass from the dominion of those who treat him kindly to the dominion of those who would, but for his labour value, deny him a home and a country; who mock him with the name of brother and treat him as a reptile.

What, then, is the cause, for there must be an adequate cause, for the peculiar conduct of Europe? I do not hesitate to say, it is mainly, if not entirely, the prejudice engendered by a quarter of a century of Northern calumniation.

Of the many wonders connected with America and American history, the general ignorance and misconception with respect to the Southern States is the most astounding. It has been produced by persistent and malignant Northern vilification; but seeing that the South was open to and visited by Europeans, that Southerners have mingled freely in European society, it is marvellous that the slanders of fanatics, demagogues, and designing politicians have so successfully blinded and prejudiced intelligent nations. Moreover there are, and have always been, indisputable statistics and incontrovertible facts, accessible and palpable, which completely refute the atrocious calumnies. The war of independence now raging has done much towards correcting grievous errors, for surely those errors are very grievous that have inspired us with an antipathy and prevented a deep-rooted sympathy for a noble and kindred race. It is manifest, even to the most prejudiced, that a people cannot be enervated who fight as the Confederates have fought, for the sanctity of their homes and the inviolability of their country, and who being cut off from foreign supplies, and having no arsenals of their own, construct vessels of war and prepare military equipments, to oppose an enemy nearly three times as numerous, and to whom the European markets are open. Europe has been regretfully, I firmly believe, but in consequence of the blockade, inevitably, the active ally of the North. A people, heretofore devoted to the pursuits of peace, that can on an emergency form well-disciplined armies, instead of being lawless, must be thoroughly imbued with the spirit of obedience as well as of command. Whilst the North has found it necessary to abolish the freedom of the press, and to suspend the right of *habeas corpus*, in the South the press has remained perfectly unmolested, and personal liberty has not been assailed. The manner in which Southerners have sacrificed their property without a sigh of regret, shows a people imbued with that excellent disposition which, without despising wealth, esteems honour far more precious; and upon such nobility of character national greatness and even national prosperity is founded; for commerce and riches will not linger in the land from whence has departed honour and supremacy. The women of the South have signally and gloriously vindicated their country; for where there are such noble mothers, wives, and daughters, the men must be noble. During the terrible trial they have combined with the tenderest solicitude for their husbands, fathers, and sons, a grand antique heroism in their cheerful submissions to deprivation and sufferings. The stern virtue of patriotism has ennobled, but not impaired or diminished, the graces of womanhood. Anyone who knows a tithe of what Southern women have done with alacrity and borne without a murmur for their country's sake, will not think I am eulogistic, but rather confess such deeds inspire a veneration that must be felt but cannot be expressed.

Nor can we fail to perceive how utterly false are the oft-repeated charges brought against the Southerners of ill-treating their slaves. Certainly it was passing strange that a Christian people should find such gratification in being cruel to an inferior race as to sacrifice their property to indulge their malignant propensity; for, unless the negro is cheerful and happy he is not well and cannot work, but the last year has afforded a proof, stronger than the strongest inferential argument, that the accusation is not true. If the negroes were so hardly dealt with, and were ripe for revolt, they have had their opportunity; but they have not revolted, they have never given a tittle of information to the enemy, their loyalty is unimpeachable; they have been left alone with the women and children, and to till the fields, and they have approved their faithfulness, and discharged their duties. In the midst of this fiery ordeal, it is not the negroes but the invaders, such men as Butler, Mitchell, Turchin, and their brutal and mercenary soldiery—and whose conduct, be it observed, has been endorsed and even applauded by the press, people, and Government of the United States—who have made war on defenceless women and who have outraged humanity.

Still the war has in many quarters extorted as it were an unwilling grudging admiration, and the leaven of Northern detraction is very perceptible. No one denies the barbarity, imposture, and falsehood of the North, but, on the other hand, many hesitate to give their full and frank sympathy to the South, because the utter groundlessness of Northern slander is not understood. Indeed, it is almost incredible to those who have not studied the question, that, amongst others, Northern ministers of the Gospel, who have been foremost in traducing the South, should so atrociously transgress the divine command, 'Thou shalt not bear false witness against thy neighbour;' though it must be confessed that the incredulity is somewhat diminished, when we find these same ministers using the same pulpits to incite the people of the United States to commence a war with England, upon pretexts the most false and frivolous. Under these circumstances I doubt not the publication of Mr. Williams's book on this side the Atlantic will be eminently useful. Sooner or later, Europe will have to acknowledge the independence of the South; and the character of a new nation, of one that cannot fail to be intimately associated with foreign nations, is a matter of grave importance. Besides, civilised and Christian communities are bound to do the South justice. It is unrighteous to condemn her, even in thought, upon the testimony of an enemy whom we know to be unscrupulous and malignant. Let us seek the truth, and endeavour to form a calm, dispassionate judgement; and when we find, as all such enquirers must do, that the South is worthy of profound esteem and cordial amity, we shall be ready to proffer the right hand of fellowship to a people upon whose prosperity, to some extent, depend the prosperity and happiness of the industrial communities of Europe. Justice, like charity, is twice blessed; and in the case we are discussing, the nation that does justice will be as much blessed by the act as the nation to which the tardy tribute is rendered.

Mr. Williams's book is the first entered according to the Copyright Act of the Congress of the Confederate States of America. With the exception of the concluding part, it was published during the canvass for the last presidential election in the late United States, and so before secession became inevitable. In this respect it is a remarkable and conclusive reply to those who assert that secession was a surprise, whereas the North was loudly warned that, if the political independence of the South was overthrown, the South would unhesitatingly secede. It is worthy of notice how earnestly Mr. Williams, who is an uncompromising Southern patriot, strove to preserve the Union. Unfortunately for the South, she did not think that the North would be mad enough to drive her out of the Union; and when that was accomplished by the election of Mr. Lincoln, there was no thought that secession would lead to hostilities, and therefore the South was unprepared for war, and by her unpreparedness encouraged the Northern attack. Mr. Williams addressed himself to Americans, not to Europeans, for the purpose, if possible, of averting the threatened catastrophe by showing the North the true position and condition of the South. The effort was in vain, for Northerners had so long and habitually belied their neighbours that at length, despite the most conclusive evidence, they half believed their monstrous inventions.

For the title of the English edition, 'The South Vindicated,' I alone am responsible. No Southerner could, without a forfeiture of self-respect, condescend to answer the absurd charges brought against his country. If Englishmen were accused of using the skulls of their dead for drinking cups, and the bones of their dead for children's toys and ornaments, or if Frenchmen were accused of torturing and ill-using their dependents from inherent malice and savage ferocity, such charges would pass unanswered; yet the calumnies uttered against the South are not less extravagant and diabolical. Even now the European press is issuing books about the South in which the truth is perverted in an extraordinary manner, and the most infamous and unfounded slanders coolly stated. But though the South will not stoop to enter the lists with such unworthy antagonists, Europe may with the utmost propriety join issue with the North and vindicate the South; or rather Europe is bound to do so, and the more because she has believed the evil report.

Mr. Williams mainly confines himself to the question of slavery, though some of his letters are historically valuable for the light they throw on the causes that produced the separation of the North and South. From a long residence in Europe, it is but natural that the author should discuss slavery in the Southern States as though he had been replying to European and not American adversaries. With the abstract right or wrong he does not in this volume concern himself. He treats slavery as it is, refers to its origin, compares it with other systems of labour, and reminds us, that the Anti-slavery party is of recent date, and that until within the last sixty years slavery was encouraged and used by Christian men, and Christian nations, without a thought of its being opposed to the spirit of Christianity. Whether or not the European reader adopts the author's conclusions as to the question of morality and philanthropy involved in the issue, he cannot peruse this volume without having a clear view of the case, and perceiving that to anathematise the Southerners on account of the institution of slavery is indirectly to anathematise our forefathers, and indeed the whole Christian world prior to the beginning of the nineteenth century. My editorial labours have been confined merely to revision of the proof sheets. A sense of fairness impels me to produce the work without the slightest curtailment or modification. It is an exact copy of the second American edition, with a few additional notes by the author; and I think the value of the book is enhanced by being an unabridged exposition of Southern views, by a Southerner, but not written as an appeal to Europe. Some passages will doubtless be looked upon as rather strong denunciations of English Abolitionism and English policy; but Englishmen do not shrink from a free discussion, and, considering the greatness of the provocation, every reader must be struck with the courteous tone of Mr. Williams's remarks, and with the absence of any approach to vituperative recrimination.

Having thus briefly given an account of *The South Vindicated* and of the reasons that seem to me to make its republication expedient, I propose to conclude this introduction by presenting some statistics in reference to the South, which dispose of the allegations of Southern degeneracy, and of the demoralising influence of Southern institutions, and which show the productiveness of the South, and the interest Europe has in the free developement of Southern resources. Statistics are generally shunned as dry and tedious, but when they are adduced to vindicate the character of a whole people, they surely deserve careful attention and ought not to be esteemed wearisome. My figures are taken principally from the United States Census of 1850, the census of 1860 not being completed or published.

The following is a comparative table of the population in 1840 and 1850, and, according to the published returns, in some of the States since 1850, the ratio of increase has not been less favourable to the South:—

	White Population		Free Coloured		Slave	
	1840	1850	1840	1850	1840	1850
Alabama...	335,185	426,514	2,039	2,265	253,522	342,844
Arkansas...	77,174	162,189	465	608	19,935	47,100
Florida ...	27,943	47,203	817	932	25,717	39,310
Georgia ...	407,695	521,572	2,753	2,931	280,944	386,682
Kentucky..	590,253	761,413	7,317	10,011	182,258	210,981
Louisiana ..	158,457	255,491	25,502	17,462	168,452	244,809
Mississippi.	179,074	295,718	1,366	930	195,211	309,878
Missouri ...	323,888	592,004	1,574	2,618	58,240	87,422
N. Carolina	484,870	553,028	22,732	27,463	245,817	288,548
S. Carolina	259,084	274,563	8,276	8,960	327,038	384,984
Tennessee ..	640,627	756,836	5,524	6,422	183,057	239,459
Texas	—	154,034	—	397	—	58,161
Virginia ...	740,858	894,800	49,852	54,333	449,087	472,528
Maryland..	318,204	417,943	62,078	74,723	89,737	90,360
	4,543,312	6,113,308	170,335	210,955	2,519,087	3,112,806
Other States of the Union	9,615,534	13,347,780	215,968	223,248		

	1840	1850
Southern States total population	7,232,734	9,527,437

From this return it would seem as if the white population increased much more rapidly at the North than at the South, but it happens that in 1850, out of 2,240,585 born in foreign countries, only 283,503 resided in the Southern States, and 1,957,032 in the other States of the Union. The excess of increase in the North, then, is due to immigration.

The free-coloured return is significant. In the South, from 170,000 the number increased in ten years to 210,000, being an increase of 40,000. In the North, the increase upon 215,000 was only 7,500. The free-coloured do not find a welcome home in the North.

The traducers of the South constantly refer to 'mean whites' or 'white trash.' They say the majority of the whites are semi-savage, that they are idle lawless vagabonds thoroughly despised by a small ruling minority. A Northern advocate, in a work recently published, estimates the 'mean whites' or 'white trash' at 'five millions of human beings—about seven-tenths of the whole white population.' Four millions of slaves cruelly oppressed by their masters, and seven-tenths of the white population consisting of thieves and ruffians, is the picture presented to our view. It is loaded with falsehood, for on such terms no community could exist, and the property and lives of the ruling minority would not be worth a month's purchase. But not only are these statements about 'mean whites' and 'white trash' monstrously absurd, but there is not a vestige of truth in them.

The chief pursuit of the South is agriculture. In 1850, according to the census of the United States, the total free population was 6,300,000, of which about 3,200,000 were males, and of these not more than 1,700,000 were above twenty years of age, and not making any allowance for those who were unfitted for labour, either by reason of infirmity or old age, we must admit that 1,700,000 is an over-estimate of the number of free males in the South who could labour in 1850. Of these 1,700,000 there were employed in agriculture:—

Virginia	108,364
North Carolina	81,982
South Carolina	41,302
Georgia	83,362
Florida	5,977
Alabama	68,635
Mississippi	50,284
Louisiana	18,639
Carried forward	458,545
Brought forward	458,545
Texas	25,299
Arkansas	28,942
Tennessee	118,979
Kentucky	115,017
Missouri	65,561
Maryland	28,588
Total	840,929

Thus 50 per cent. of the free male working population was entirely engaged in agriculture. The number of farms in the Southern States, together with their average acreage and their average value, is thus given:—

	No. of Farms	Average Acres	Average value $
Alabama	41,964	289	1,655
Arkansas	17,756	146	950
Florida	4,304	371	1,622
Georgia	51,759	441	1,964
Kentucky	74,777	227	2,142
Louisiana	13,422	372	6,511
Mississippi	33,960	309	1,782
Missouri	54,458	179	1,234
North Carolina	56,963	369	1,261
South Carolina	29,967	541	2,889
Tennessee	72,735	261	1,419
Texas	12,198	942	1,533
Virginia	77,013	340	2,901
Maryland	211,860	212	1,222
	563,138		

Thus, out of 840,929 free males engaged in agriculture, 563,138 were farming on their own account; and, allowing for family and other partnerships, we must conclude that the whole of the free agricultural population of the South consists of farmers, and not of farm servants. Where are the seven-tenths of 'white trash?' Further, we are told these five millions, or seven-tenths of white trash, are 'too poor to keep slaves and too proud to work.' Let the United States census answer.

In 1850 the number of families, white and free coloured, in the Southern States—and, according to the United States census, 'a family in the census is either one person living separately in a house or part of a house, and providing for him and herself, or several persons living together upon one common means of support,' so that every one occupying separate apartments is counted as a family—was as follows:—

White and Free Coloured families in 1850.

State	Families	State	Families
Alabama	73,786	*Brought forward*	529,498
Arkansas	28,416	Missouri	100,890
Florida	9,107	North Carolina	105,451
Georgia	91,666	South Carolina	52,937
Kentucky	132,920	Tennessee	130,004
Louisiana	54,112	Texas	28,377
Maryland	87,384	Virginia	167,530
Mississippi	52,107		
Carried forward	529,498	Total	1,114,687

The number of families owning slaves were as follows:—

State	Families	State	Families
Alabama	29,295	*Brought forward*	178,626
Arkansas	5,999	North Carolina	28,303
Florida	3,520	South Carolina	25,596
Georgia	38,456	Tennessee	33,864
Kentucky	38,385	Texas	7,747
Louisiana	20,670	Virginia	55,063
Mississippi	23,116	Maryland	16,040
Missouri	19,185		
Carried forward	178,626	Total	345,239

The following was the classification of slaveholders throughout the United States:—

Holders of	1 Slave	68,820
"	1 and under 5	105,683
"	5 " 10	80,765
"	10 " 20	54,595
"	20 " 50	29,733
"	50 " 100	6,196
"	100 " 200	1,479
"	200 " 300	187
"	300 " 500	56
"	500 " 1,000	9
"	1,000 and over	2

Thus, it appears that one family out of three own slaves, and if we allow for single persons being taken for families, the number of families owning slaves becomes much greater. No less than 174,503 families own one or less than five slaves. But besides slaves owned, thousands are hired. What becomes of the 5,000,000 or seven-tenths of 'white trash,' too poor to own slaves? The writer who makes such a statement either consciously slanders the South or he damages the reputation of a people struggling for freedom by writing without enquiring as to their actual condition. I know not which is the more culpable. Yet he is, after all, a fair representative of Southern detractors, and his fabrications are not more gross than those of his colleagues.

Ignorance and irreligion are said by the Northern advocates to prevail in the Southern States. Is it so? The following is a return of the educational establishments in the South in 1850:—

COLLEGES, ETC.

	No. of Colleges.	Public Schools.	Private Schools.
Alabama	5	1,152	169
Arkansas	3	353	190
Florida	—	69	34
Georgia	13	1,251	219
Kentucky	15	2,234	330
Louisiana	6	664	143
Mississippi	11	782	171
Missouri	9	1,570	204
North Carolina	5	2,657	272
Carried forward	67	10,732	1,732

	No. of Colleges.	Public Schools.	Private Schools.
Brought forward	67	10,732	1,732
South Carolina	8	724	202
Tennessee	18	2,680	264
Texas	2	349	97
Virginia	12	2,930	317
Maryland	13	898	223
	120	18,313	2,835
Other States	118	62,649	3,247

The South, in 1850, had absolutely more colleges than the North, though her free population was more than 100 per cent. less. The proportion of public schools was smaller, but the proportion of private schools was greatly in excess.

The white population at school in 1850 was:—

Alabama	62,670	*Brought forward*	434,324
Arkansas	23,332	Missouri	91,991
Florida	4,638	North Carolina	100,041
Georgia	76,914	South Carolina	39,993
Kentucky	129,667	Tennessee	145,963
Louisiana	29,576	Texas	18,768
Maryland	58,770	Virginia	109,500
Mississippi	48,757		
Carried forward	434,324	Total	940,474

This sufficiently refutes the implication of ignorance; for the number of scholars, as given above—being one-third of the population under twenty years—is equal to the number of children of an age to attend school. Below are the returns of illiterates over twenty years of age, in 1850, which, though creditable to the North, is honourable to the South, when we consider her large free-coloured population:

State	Number
Virginia	88,520
North Carolina	80,423
South Carolina	16,564
Georgia	41,667
Florida	4,129
Alabama	33,992
Mississippi	13,528
Louisiana	24,610
Texas	10,583
Arkansas	16,935
Tennessee	78,619
Kentucky	69,706
Missouri	36,778
Maryland	41,877
Total	557,931

State	Number
Maine	6,282
New Hampton	3,009
Vermont	6,240
Massachusetts	28,345
Rhode	3,607
Connecticut	5,306
New York	98,722
New Jersey	18,665
Pennsylvania	76,272
Delaware	10,181
Columbia	4,671
Illinois	41,283
Indiana	72,710
Ohio	66,020
Michigan	8,281
Wisconsin	6,453
Iowa	8,158
California	5,235
Total	469,440

With regard to religion, I shall quote a return of the number of churches, and it is fair evidence that neither absolutely nor relatively is the South an irreligious nation:—

NUMBER OF CHURCHES.

Maine	945
N. Hampshire	626
Vermont	599
Massachusetts	1,475
Rhode Island	228
Connecticut	734
New York	4,134
New Jersey	813
Pennsylvania	3,566
Delaware	180
Columbia	46
Illinois	1,223
Indiana	2,032
Ohio	3,936
Michigan	399
Wisconsin	365
Iowa	193
California	28
	21,521

Virginia	2,383
N. Carolina	1,795
S. Carolina	1,182
Georgia	1,862
Florida	177
Alabama	1,373
Mississippi	1,016
Louisiana	306
Texas	341
Arkansas	362
Tennessee	2,014
Kentucky	1,845
Missouri	880
Maryland	909
	16,445

The population of the North in 1850 was 50 per cent. in excess of the population of the South, including the slaves; but the number of churches in the North was not more than 35 per cent. in excess of the number of churches in the South.

The returns I have given will bear comparison not only with the Northern States, but with the returns of any other nation. The number of persons owning farms is very remarkable, and perhaps in no other country is there such a large class of real property holders. 'Every man his own landlord' is not a state of things favouring the existence of 'mean whites' or 'white trash.'

Crime and pauperism are amongst the peculiar vices ascribed to the South, but these, like the rest of the articles of impeachment, are unfounded.

The following table gives the total number of convictions in 1850. As such a return is compiled solely from official documents, it is strictly and not merely approximately accurate.

Whole Number of Convictions within the Year:—

Alabama	122	California	1
Arkansas	25	Columbia	132
Florida	39	Connecticut	850
Georgia	80	Delaware	22
Kentucky	160	Illinois	316
Louisiana	297	Indiana	175
Maryland	207	Iowa	3
Mississippi	51	Maine	744
Missouri	908	Massachusetts	7,250
Carried forward	1,889	*Carried forward*	9,493

Brought forward	1,889	*Brought forward*	9,493
North Carolina	647	Michigan	659
South Carolina	46	New Hampshire	90
Tennessee	81	New Jersey	603
Texas	19	New York	10,279
Virginia	107	Ohio	843
		Pennsylvania	857
		Rhode Island	596
		Vermont	79
		Wisconsin	267
Total	2,789	Total	23,766

In order that the reader may thoroughly appreciate this table, I give the aggregate populations of the respective States for 1850, including the slaves, who are included in the above returns :—

Aggregate Population in 1850.

Alabama	771,623	California	92,597
Arkansas	209,897	Columbia	51,687
Florida	87,445	Connecticut	370,792
Georgia	906,185	Delaware	91,532
Kentucky	982,405	Illinois	851,470
Louisiana	517,762	Indiana	988,416
Maryland	583,034	Iowa	192,214
Mississippi	606,326	Maine	583,169
Missouri	682,044	Massachusetts	994,514
North Carolina	869,039	Michigan	397,654
South Carolina	668,507	New Hampshire	317,976
Tennessee	1,002,717	New Jersey	489,555
Texas	212,592	New York	3,097,394
Virginia	1,421,661	Ohio	1,980,329
		Pennsylvania	2,311,786
		Rhode Island	147,545
		Vermont	314,120
		Wisconsin	305,391
	9,521,237		13,568,141

With a population of 9,500,000, the number of criminals in the South was 2,789, and therefore, with a population of 13,500,000, the number of criminals in the North should have been rather less than

4,000; but the number of criminal convictions in the North was 23,767, being 19,000 above the average, or nearly six times as numerous, even allowing for the difference in population. Admitting that to a limited extent the petty offences of the slaves are punished by their masters, this is a startling result to those who have believed the maligners of the South. But the foregoing is not more surprising than the returns of the confined in gaols on June 1, 1850:—

	Black Population	No. in Gaol	One in
North	150,142	478	312
West	46,852	87	540
South	3,442,788	323	10,000
Total	3,639,782	888	

	White Population	No. in Gaol	One in
North	8,342,938	2,710	3,000
West	5,413,039	760	7,000
South	6,222,418	1,288	5,000
Total	19,978,395	4,758	

Thus with the black population in the North the crimes were 1 in 310, in the West 1 in 542, and in the South 1 in 10,000. According to this table the black population in the North is nearly twice as criminal as in the West, and more than thirty times as criminal as in the South. But I shall be reminded that the slaves are under the jurisdiction of their owners, and are punished by them; but this does not account for the difference. Nor are we left to conjecture. In 1850, of the free blacks in the South in gaols there was 1 in 800, but in the North 1 in 310. At all events the free coloured are not under the jurisdiction of the slave-owners. Further, in the census of 1850 there is a table of the 'State Prisons and Penitentiaries for 1850,' giving the number of inmates in each prison and the ratio of inmates to 10,000 of the population, from which I take the following estimate:—

In every 10,000 Coloured Persons, excluding Slaves:—	
Slaveholding States	·938
Non-Slaveholding States	28·743

Now what becomes of the demoralising effect of the institutions of the South? It appears that the influence of Southern institutions upon the coloured race is 2,800 per cent. better than the influence of Northern institutions.

I do not wish to make an exaggerated charge against the North. That the social condition of the North should be worse than that of the South was to be expected. In the former there is an incongruous assemblage of races, a perpetual immigration of the most discontented and least orderly classes of Europe, and an insane passion for getting money by sharp dealing. In the South the dominant race is singularly united, the immigration is small, and being an agricultural community, there is a spirit of individual independence, and the dollar, though not despised, is not deified. Like personal, national morality or immorality is mainly the result of circumstances, favourable or unfavourable, and the United States has much to plead for her demoralisation, but no excuse can be found for her infamous vilification of the South.

Without denying the blessing of mental culture, there is no doubt that poverty, much more than ignorance, is the parent of crime. We must confess that in Europe, with the increase of schools there has not been a commensurate diminution in the number of criminals, and the principal effect on the criminal returns produced by the spread of education is to increase the number of criminals who 'can read and write;' and we expect one reason that so small a percentage of our criminals are of 'superior education' is, that persons superiorly educated are not often in such poverty as to be homeless and foodless. Thus, then, much and deeply as I value education, I would rather take the returns of pauperism than the returns of education as a test of the criminality of a nation. Do the returns of pauperism in the United States' census endorse the criminal returns? Below is a table of the 'whole number of paupers supported in whole or part within the year ending June 1, 1850:'—

State	Paupers	State	Paupers
Alabama	363	California	no return
Arkansas	105	Connecticut	2,327
Florida	76	Delaware	697
Georgia	1,036	Illinois	797
Kentucky	1,126	Indiana	1,182
Louisiana	423	Iowa	135
Maryland	4,494	Maine	5,503
Mississippi	260	Massachusetts	15,777
Missouri	2,977	Michigan	1,190
North Carolina	1,931	New Hampshire	3,600
South Carolina	1,642	New Jersey	2,392
Tennessee	1,005	New York	59,855
Texas	7	Ohio	2,513
Virginia	5,118	Pennsylvania	11,551
		Rhode Island	2,560
		Vermont	3,654
		Wisconsin	668
Total	20,563	Total	114,199

The cost of pauperism in the South in 1850 was $565,159, and in the North $2,389,647. Thus the pauperism coincides with the criminality. One cause of Northern pauperism is the immigration of paupers; but I have to deal with results, not causes, and the returns I have presented prove that in respect to crime and pauperism the much abused South occupies an immensely higher position than the calumniating North.

As to the internal improvements of the country, it will be sufficient to glance at railway enterprise. The following table is corrected up to the end of the year 1859:—

State	Length	In operation	Cost
inia	2,058·5	1,525·7	43,069,360
h Carolina . . .	1,020·0	770·2	13,998,490
h Carolina . . .	1,136·0	807·3	19,083,345
gia . . .	1,617·2	1,241·7	25,687,223
da . . .	730·5	289·8	6,368,699
ama	1,822·4	798·6	20,975,639
issippi	445·1	365·4	9,024,444
siana	1,160·0	419·0	16,073,270
s	2,667·0	284·6	7,578,943
nsas	701·3	38·5	1,130,110
ouri	1,337·3	723·2	31,771,116
essee	1,434·4	1,062·3	27,348,141
ucky	698·4	468·5	13,852,062
	16,828·1	8,794·8	235,960,842

his return is still more satisfactory when we re-nber that in the South the great rivers are to some ent natural substitutes for railroads. Between 1855 1859, the length of road completed in the United tes measures 11,248 miles, of which 6,822 miles ngs to the North, and 4,426 to the South; and according to the relative populations, the latter built in those years a greater length of road than former.

n unerring test of the social and moral condition country is its productiveness. Where there is istry and order, even sterile soils yield an increase; re there is idleness and anarchy, the most fertile ntries are barren. What of the Southern States? Northern advocate says seven-tenths of their te population are thieving vagabonds who will work; but this is false, as we have seen by the istics of population and property, and an estimate he products of the South will convince the most sceptical that the Southern people are preeminently energetic and industrious.

The Southern States do not grow cotton and little else, as is very generally surmised. In 1850, the South produced grains which constitute food to the value of 307,328,112 dollars; of other produce (not including cotton) 46,305,950 dollars; value of slaughtered animals, 54,398,015 dollars; giving a total value of 408,030,077 dollars. The North and West produced in grains which constitute food to the value of 305,769,963 dollars; that is, 1,557,149 dollars less than the South; but, allowing for the difference of population, the North and West produced of grains which constitute food nearly 50 per cent. less than the South. The consumption per head of breadstuffs in the North and West is equal to, if not rather in excess of, the consumption per head in the South. What, then, becomes of the surplus of the South, or how is the Northern deficiency supplied? Why, instead of the South being dependent on the North, the latter section receives enough from the former to supply its deficiency for home consumption, and to enable it, assisted by the prolific West, to do a considerable export trade in grain and flour.

Of other agricultural products, the North and West raised, in 1850, to the value of 178,904,527 dollars, being 132,600,577 dollars more than the South, which we must admit, even allowing for the difference of population, is a large excess. But hay is included in this return, of which the Northern and Western production was valued at 127,008,580 dollars, and the Southern at 11,377,846 dollars. At the same time, the number of head of live stock in the South was 40,823,727, and in the other sections, 36,409,134. That is, the value of hay in the North exceeded the value of hay in the South by 132,600,577 dollars, whilst the South had 4,414,000 head of live stock more than the North. Animals in the South do not eat less than in the North, but in the South there is no need to make hay, in consequence of the comparative mildness of the seasons and the unceasing verdure. The necessity of haymaking is a heavy tax upon Northern labour, which the South escapes. Deducting, then, from both sides the value of hay crops, the agricultural produce (excluding grains which constitute food) of the South (excluding cotton) was 34,426,104 dollars, and of the North and West 46,303,950 dollars. Correcting these results by population, it makes the return of North and West deficient by about 16,000,000 dollars. The value of animals slaughtered in the North and West was 56,990,237 dollars, being 2,592,222 dollars more than the South. Correcting these returns by population, the North and West show a comparative deficiency of about 21,000,000 dollars. Thus the total value of the agricultural products of the South (not including cotton), was 408,030,077 dollars; of the North and West, 541,663,717 dollars, being nearly a dollar per head of the population in favour of the South. But these returns are inaccurate until we have deducted the returns for hay, or allowed an equivalent for the perennial grass of the South. Less the hay, the returns are:—for the South, 396,652,231 dollars; for the North and West, 409,063,140 dollars, giving for the latter an average of thirty dollars per head, and to the former forty-two dollars per head.

The United States exports, in 1859, amounted to 278,392,080 dollars. The following were of Southern origin:—

	Dollars
Cotton	161,434,923
Tobacco	21,074,038
Rice	2,207,148
Naval Stores	3,695,474
Sugar	196,735
Molasses	75,699
Hemp	6,227
	188,693,496

Leaving the exports of Northern origin equal to 89,698,584 dollars.

But the most convincing proof of Southern energy and industry is the developement of the cotton production. And be it observed, that no cultivation requires so must industry and skill as cotton. The cotton farmer must be on the alert from year's end to year's end; he must have, too, a supply of labour at command, to seize the right moment for picking, for if he neglects that, his crop is spoilt. Instead of being jealous of the efforts made to grow cotton in India and elsewhere, the Southerners neither fear nor shun the competition. Many intelligent planters are of opinion that the South might, by growing less cotton, produce other crops that would yield a larger profit. This may be true to some extent, but my own impression is, that the Southern States are the destined cotton field of the world.

In 1790, Mr. M'Culloch says, the export trade of the United States in cotton commenced, though it is thought that small quantities were exported in previous years. The following admirably-arranged table, showing the growth, exports, and export value of the United States cotton, from 1790 to 1835, together with estimates of the total cotton produce of the world, was communicated to the United States' Congress in 1836, by Mr. Woodbury, the then Secretary of the Treasury: —

GROWTH AND EXPORT OF COTTON.

	IN THE WORLD.	UNITED STATES.		
Years	Growth lbs.	Growth lbs.	Exports lbs.	Ex value dols.
1790	—	1,500,000	250,000	—
1791	490,000,000	2,000,000	200,000	—
1792	—	3,000,000	143,000	—
1793	—	5,000,000	500,000	—
1794	—	8,000,000	1,667,000	500,000
1795	—	8,000,000	6,000,000	2,000,000
1796	—	10,000,000	6,000.000	2,000,000
1797	—	11,000,000	3,500,000	1,000,000

GROWTH AND EXPORTS OF COTTON.

Years	In the World. Growth lbs.	United States. Growth lbs.	Exports lbs.	Ex value dols.
1798	—	15,000,000	9,000,000	3,000,000
1799	—	20,000,000	9,000,000	4,000,000
1800	—	35,000,000	17,000,000	5,000,000
1801	520,000,000	48,000,000	20,000,000	9,000,000
1802	—	55,000,000	27,000,000	5,000,000
1803	—	60,000,000	41,000,000	8,000,000
1804	—	65,000,000	38,000,000	8,000,000
1805	—	70,000,000	40,000,000	9,000,000
1806	—	80,000,000	37,000,000	8,000,000
1807	—	80,000,000	66,000,000	14,000,000
1808	—	75,000,000	12,000,000	2,000,000
1809	—	82,000,000	53,000,000	8,000,000
1810	—	85,000,000	93,000,000	15,000,000
1811	555,000,000	80,000,000	62,000,000	9,000,000
1812	—	75,000,000	29,000,000	3,000,000
1813	—	75,000,000	19,000,000	2,000,000
1814	—	70,000,000	17,000,000	2,000,000
1815	—	100,000,000	83,000,000	17,000,000
1816	—	124,000,000	81,000,000	24,000,000
1817	—	130,000,000	95,000,000	22,000,000
1818	—	125,000,000	92,000,000	31,000,000
1819	—	167,000,000	88,000,000	21,000,000
1820	—	160,000,000	127,000,000	22,000,000
1821	630,000,000	180,000,000	124,000,000	20,000,000
1822	—	210,000,000	144,000,000	24,000,000
1823	—	185,000,000	173,000,000	23,000,000
1824	—	215,000,000	142,000,000	22,000,000
1825	—	255,000,000	176,000,000	39,000,000
1826	—	250,000,000	204,000,000	25,000,000
1827	—	270,000,000	204,000,000	29,000 000
1828	—	325,000,000	210,000,000	22,000,000
1829	—	365,000,000	264,000,000	26,000,000
1830	—	350,000,000	298,000,000	30,000,000
1831	820,000,000	385,000,000	277,000,000	25,000,000
1832	—	390,000,000	372,000,000	32,000,000
1833	—	445,000,000	324,000,000	36,000,000
1834	—	460,000,000	384,000,000	49,000,000
1835	—	—	—	61,000,000

It will be noticed how steady, as well as rapid, has been the increase in the exports. From 1821 to 1835, there was an uninterrupted annual increase. In 1790 the quantity of cotton consumed in the United States was 1,250,000 lbs., and in 1834, 70,000,000lbs., being fifty-six times as much. The cotton export of the United States in 1790 was 250,000 lbs., and in 1834, 384,000,000 lbs., being 1536 times greater. But in 1834 the cotton trade was still in its infancy. The exports were 384,000,000 lbs. in 1834, and in 1849, 1,026,000,000 lbs., being nearly a threefold increase in fifteen years. Further, according to the returns of the United States' Treasury Department, the crop of 1850 was 2,796,706 bales, the quantity exported was 635,318,604 lbs., and the export value was $71,984,616; and in 1859 the crop was 3,851,481 bales, the quantity exported 1,386,468,542 lbs., and the export value $161,434,923. I should remark that the official export value is always below the actual value. But taking the returns as they are presented to us, they show that in nine years (from 1850 to 1859), the crop had increased 50 per cent.; that the exports had increased more than 100 per cent.; and that the export value had increased at a still greater ratio.

An inspection of the table we have given above will dissipate the impression that the Southern planters have enjoyed a monopoly of price. How could they? They could not regulate demand, and they could only compete with other markets by the quality of their material and its cheapness. In 1834 the quantity exported was twenty-three times greater than in 1800, while the export value was only tenfold. By comparing the estimates of the world's growth, which are carefully prepared, it will be seen that the total increase of cotton production is from the Southern States, and that the rest of the world has remained nearly stationary. Not that in all other parts of the world there has been a lack of enterprise and capital, but it has been found impossible to compete with America in supplying the increased and increasing call for cotton. Cotton-growing countries have considered it cheaper to import fabrics of American cotton rather than increase the area of their own cotton culture. Before the introduction of American cotton the increasing demand was supplied from other places, as the following return of cotton imports into England shows: —

Years.	Imports
1781	5,101,920 lbs.
1782	11,206,810
1783	9,546,179
1784	11,280,236
1785	17,992,888
1786	19,151,867
1787	22,600,000

That we may observe how the progress of the English cotton manufacture has been concurrent with the production of American cotton, we will quote the state and value of our cotton trade in 1787. In that year there were in England and Scotland: —

143 water mills, valued at	£715,000
550 mules jennies, of 50 spindles each, valued at	19,250
20,070 hand jennies, of 80 spindles each „ .	140,490
Buildings, carding machines, &c. . „ .	125,260
	£1,000,000

The number of persons employed in spinning was about 60,000. The imports of the raw material into England for that year were 22,600,000 lbs., from the following places:—

British Islands	6,600,000
French and Spanish Settlements . . .	6,000,000
Dutch Settlements	1,700,000
Portuguese Settlements	2,500,000
East Indies	100,000
Smyrna and Turkey	5,700,000
	22,600,000 lbs.

Not a pound from the United States, and the East Indies contributing only a 226th of the entire quantity. Even allowing for the then comparatively circumscribed dominion of British India, it must be confessed it was a very small portion. It seems as if it had not been possible for India to compete for the supply of European markets before America entered the field; and that instead of checking, American rivalry has rather stimulated Indian production.

The following is a statement of the crops, exports, and export values, from 1836 to 1850 — dates which embrace the most interesting period of the history of the American cotton trade:—

Years	Crop in bales	Exports in lbs.	Export Value
1836	1,422,930	423,631,367	$71,284,925
1837	1,801,497	444,211,537	63,240,102
1838	1,360,532	595,952,277	61,556,811
1839	2,177,835	413,624,212	61,338,982
1840	1,634,945	743,941,061	63,870,107
1841	1,683,574	530,204,100	54,330,341
1842	2,378,875	584,717,017	47,593,644
1843	2,030,409	792,297,106	49,119,086
1844	2,394,503	663,633,455	54,063,501
1845	2,100,537	872,905,996	51,739,643
1846	1,778,651	547,555,055	42,767,341
1847	2,347,634	537,219,958	53,415,847
1848	2,728,596	814,274,431	61,998,294
1849	2,096,706	1,036,602,296	66,396,967
1850	2,355,257	635,381,601	71,984,717

A comparison of the quantities and export values proves how much more the consumers of cotton have benefited by the developement of the Southern cotton cultivation than the producers. I am not claiming any quixotic generosity for the South, but merely direct attention to a striking and important fact.

The British exports of cotton manufactures have been developed concurrently with the increase of the United States exports of the raw material; but our exports do not afford an exact criterion of the increase of our manufactures, as our home consumption has become larger and larger, until it has been brought up to 9 lbs. per head of the population, whilst in France the consumption is 4 lbs. per head of the population. The declared value of our exports of cotton manufactures were:—

1820	£16,516,748
1834	20,513,586
1850	28,257,401
1859	48,208,444

It will be seen by a reference to the table on page xlv, that the increased production of cotton during the present century is from the Southern States, and that other countries have remained stationary. This great increase has only been limited by the demand; that is to say, the Southern planters have been conducting their operations legitimately, not increasing the growth on speculation, or seeking to glut the market. The Cotton Planters' Convention has published the following interesting table as to the production and consumption of cotton throughout the world:—

	Production. Bales per annum	Consumption. Bales per annum
Average from 1825 to 1830	1,231,000	1,187,000
" 1830 to 1835	1,450,000	1,540,000
" 1835 to 1840	1,919,000	1,943,000
" 1840 to 1845	2,561,000	2,414,000
" 1845 to 1850	2,791,000	2,869,000
Average production for five years	9,592,000	9,953,000

Thus in twenty-five years the whole production was 49,760,000 bales, and the total consumption 49,765,000, being an excess of 5,000 bales, equal to an excess of 200 bales per annum. So far from striving to discourage other growths by glutting the market, the Southern planters have always evinced an anxiety not to jeopardise prices by making the supply exceed the demand. Indeed, small crops have frequently yielded a better return than large crops; not that we should infer that small crops are therefore desirable, for cheapness and a fully satisfied demand encourages and increases consumption, and so ultimately benefits the producer.

It will not, I trust, be considered out of place if I add a few observations upon the capabilities of the Southern States for an increased production of cotton.

In England there has been a chronic panic lest the supply of the raw material should fail. With regard to the increasing consumption of cotton fabrics, no doubt has been entertained. With the advance of civilisation this consumption of cotton increases, and, indeed, the consumption of cotton is an unerring test of national wealth and national progress. India and China would multiply our cotton trade, if the consumption in those countries should equal 20 per cent. of the present consumption per head of the population of the United Kingdom

The average annual consumption of cotton from 1850 to 1860 may be thus estimated :—

Country	Population	lbs. consumed	per head
England	29,000,000	260,000,000	9 lbs.
France	36,000,000	140,000,000	4 lbs.
United States	28,000,000	315,000,000	11 lbs.
Other European countries	213,000,000	1,096,000,000	1 lb.
Other parts of America	29,000,000		
Asia	775,000,000		
Africa	200,000,000	—	—
	1,310,000,000	1,811,000,000	

To make the general consumption equal to 2 lbs. per head, even at the above under-estimate of population, it would require nearly double the quantity of cotton at present grown; but, unless the progress of civilisation is a chimera, 2 lbs. per head is a low and inadequate average. The above table is based partly upon statistics collected nearly four years ago; and during the last four years the consumption of cotton has greatly increased.

It has, then, never been with us a question of finding a market for our manufactures, but whether we could rely on obtaining a sufficient supply of the raw material. On the other hand, the planters of the Southern States have been fully persuaded of their power to produce any quantity of their staple that might be called for; but they have always been anxious concerning the possibility of the demand being limited. There will always be fluctuation in consumption, values, and prices, but hitherto there has not been any over-productiveness of staple; that is, the bounty of the Creator has not been found a useless gift. Nor hitherto has the production of cotton proved inadequate to the wants of man. The increase of demand has gone hand in hand with the increase of production. To show that the planters were, from facts within their own knowledge, justified in feeling confidence in being able to supply any possible demand, I will quote from the census of 1850 the acres of improved and unimproved land in farms in the States in which cotton may be profitably cultivated.

	Improved	Unimproved
North Carolina	5,453,975	15,543,008
South Carolina	4,072,651	12,145,049
Georgia	6,378,479	16,442,900
Florida	349,049	1,246,240
Tennessee	5,175,173	13,808,849
Arkansas	781,530	1,816,684
Alabama	4,435,614	7,702,068
Mississippi	3,444,358	7,046,061
Louisiana	1,590,025	3,399.018
Texas	643,976	10,852,363
	32,324,830	90,002,240

Thus, in 1850, only 37 per cent. of the farm land in the Cotton States was improved. What an enormous margin does this leave for increased production; particularly when we consider how, during the last ten years, agricultural science has facilitated and cheapened the improvement of land.

According to the census of 1850, there were 113,032,614 acres of improved land, of which 17,247,614 acres were not in actual cultivation.

We must, therefore, make an allowance of about 3 per cent. for the improved land that may be cultivated. Further, in 1850 the number of acres in cotton cultivation was 5,000,000 throughout the United States; so that not quite a sixth part of the cultivated land in the Cotton States was used for the production of cotton. If, then, the demand for cotton renders it expedient — that is, profitable — there is land ready to receive cotton seed, or the South could limit its growth of other agricultural produce, or the unimproved lands could be brought into cotton cultivation.

But I have not yet disposed of the question of area. The acres of farm land in the ten cotton-growing States are 122,327,110; but the total area of those States is equal to 452,000,000 acres; and persons acquainted with the country, and having a knowledge of the kind and climatic position of land necessary for cotton cultivation, estimate that half this immense territory may be used as cotton fields. It is surely needless to further press the point of there being sufficient available land in the Southern States to grow as much cotton as can be consumed. As a proof that an increasing area has been sown with cotton, we may observe that the total product in 1850 was 2,796,706 bales, and in 1860, 4,300,000 bales, and that this increase was not merely the result of improved farming; but that, whereas in 1850 only 5,000,000 acres were in cotton cultivation, in 1860 there were not less than 8,000,000. With such immense resources in the way of land, it is not surprising that the planters should have directed their attention more to the improvement of quality rather than to the quantity to be obtained per acre.

Besides the suitable land, and the demand for the produce, capital and labour are needed. Will the productiveness of the Southern States be limited for lack of these indispensable agents? With regard to capital, assuredly not. We always find abundance of money forthcoming to foster enterprise that has a prospect of returning a profit. The West Indian proprietors refuse to advance the means for growing cotton on their estates, but are ready with capital for the cultivation of sugar. As an instance of the anxiety of capitalists to find a promising investment, we may recall a fact revealed by the crash of 1847—that London houses had advanced on sugar crops to be grown three or four years after the date of the advance. In British India capital for cotton growing cannot be procured, but there is a superabundance of capital for public works, indigo and opium cultivation, and all other pursuits that yield a profit. The competition for capital is not greater than the competition for investment.

If, then, it became necessary, European capital

would be furnished to the Southern planters; but it is improbable such a necessity will arise. Hitherto the increased crops have been brought to market without any unusual assistance. The capital of the Northern States increased with the increase of the cotton cultivation, and the advances made to planters were profits arising from the cotton trade However, without considering special circumstances, the question of capital is disposed of by the canon—that where there is suitable land, suitable labour, and a profitable demand, capital will be attracted. Having satisfied ourselves as to the land and the demand, and the needful capital, it remains to enquire whether the Southern States will be able to find the increased labour necessary for the increased supply. That they have hitherto done so we know. What are their prospects of so doing in the future?

The following is a return of the labour population in the cotton-growing States for four decades:—

	1820	1830	1840	1850
North Carolina	205,017	245,601	245,817	288,548
South Carolina	258,475	315,401	327,038	384,984
Georgia . .	149,656	217,531	280,944	381,682
Florida .	—	15,501	25,717	39,310
Alabama . .	47,439	117,549	253,532	342,844
Mississippi .	32,814	65,659	195,211	309,878
Louisiana .	69,064	109,588	168,452	244,809
Arkansas .	1,617	4,576	19,935	47,100
Tennessee .	80,107	141,603	183,059	239,459
Texas . .	—	—	—	58,161
	844,189	1,233,009	1,699,705	2,336,775

From 1820 to 1830 the growth of the black population was 50 per cent.; from 1830 to 1840, 25 per cent.; and from 1840 to 1850, 40 per cent. From this we gather that the labouring population of the South is increasing with a rapidity that will be equal to the additional demand for labour.

We have, then, an increasing demand for cotton, an almost indefinite extent of land in the Southern States fit for the profitable growth of cotton; there is no lack of capital, and the supply of labour is abundant, and constantly becoming larger. In seventy years, from producing only a few bags, America has become the cotton grower for the world, and has created that industry which has attained such gigantic proportions in England. We have seen how the whole growth of the cotton trade, from the close of the last century until now, is due to the Southern States, and that the Southern States, so far from being exhausted, are in a position to yield more and more cotton, according to the exigencies of mankind. England ought especially to rejoice in the prospect of the continual developement of her cotton manufactures, for it is through her agency that India, China, and Africa are to be clothed. A great deal is said about breaking up the American monopoly. What monopoly does the South enjoy? She must sell as well as the world must buy. The strength of the South consists in the special fecundity of her soil and climate; and such a patent of monopoly can neither be bestowed nor destroyed by man. America was the last to enter the cotton market, and at a single bound she outstrips all her competitors. The American cotton crop in 1790 was 1,500,000 lbs.; in 1860 it was 2,250,000,000 lbs. As in the past, so in the future, the Southern States will be the main source of the cotton supply, and when from war or any other catastrophe that supply is cut off, the commerce in cotton must dwindle.

Since the establishment of Christianity, the event which has had the greatest influence on the civilisation of mankind is the discovery of America. The New World was a vast, timely, and splendid addition to man's heritage. There is not a labourer or peasant in the civilised nations of the Old World, who is not better clothed, better fed, and richer, than he would have been if the New World had not existed, or had not been discovered. The advance of civilisation is the result of the growth of modern commerce, and without the cotton, not to speak of the tobacco, of America, how comparatively small would be its proportions. We have realised some of the ills that result to Europe from a war between the United States and the Confederate States, but it is impossible to imagine, much less to express, how commerce would be dwarfed and the condition of mankind be deteriorated if the whole country should become semi-barbarous—a huge Mexico. Such a contingency is happily beyond the range of possibility, though we might reasonably dread an approximation to it, if there was a chance of the wild and unscrupulous ambition of the Northern States becoming dominant. The disintegration of the late Union, and the formation of the Southern Confederacy will make the New World more than ever a source of profit and prosperity to the Old World. This consummation will be hastened and insured by a cordial alliance between Europe and the Confederate States of America; but a cordial alliance is impossible until the prejudices instilled and fostered by Northern slanders are thoroughly eradicated by candid and patient investigation.

JOHN BAKER HOPKINS.

London: *September*, 1862.

THE SOUTH VINDICATED.

LETTER I.

Prefatory Remarks — Slavery established in North America by Great Britain — The New Republics obliged to adopt the existing Institution — Causes of Antagonism between the White and Black Races — M. De Tocqueville on Slavery in America.

THE American-born citizen, who has been called to reside for a time in a distant country, may, after the lapse of a few years, cease to feel any great personal solicitude in regard to the mere material out of which a Presidential ticket is composed; yet he is all the more deeply concerned in observing and noting the popular impulses, the sentiments, and the purposes which animate the electors, and which are supposed to be represented by their respective candidates. However intense may have been his feelings when at home, touching the local, sectional, or personal controversies, which are often turned to account by ambitious men, as auxiliaries to their personal aggrandisement, they are softened by continued absence, and soon become merged into that broad American sentiment, which embraces every foot of territory over which floats the flag of the Union! Not that he loves less the home and the friends which he has left behind him, or that the local attachments which have had their origin in education or association are less strong or active; for on the contrary, these feelings which spring from and encircle the heart, are only intensified by absence. But the expanded vision discovers more clearly the magnificence of that great confederacy, of which each particular part forms an essential element ; and in the contemplation of which the geographical lines which define these minute divisions, become fainter and more faint, until they are lost in the outline—the form—the dimensions—the aspect of that grand unit, which represents to the nations of the world the associated sovereignties of the several States.

I am sure that if these letters ever meet the eye of those for whom they are intended, they will not find therein the expression of a thought, or a sentiment, or a feeling, or an impulse, which is not reconcilable with that broad and comprehensive Americanism which embraces each and every member of the federal Union.

That the writer is a Southerner by birth and education, may be readily inferred. That he feels in every fibre of his heart an earnest and unchangeable attachment for the political institutions of the section in which he was born, which no time can eradicate, and which neither obloquy nor misfortune can abate, he is proud to declare; yet he trusts that this frank avowal will not close the eyes and ears of those who may have different local attachments, against the truths which he may enunciate. However unsuccessful he may be in implanting his own convictions in the minds of others, he only asks that they be considered with the same frankness, and under the influence of the same American feeling, which animates him in their utterance.

In order to arrive at just conclusions in regard to the merits of a question which enlists, to a greater or less extent, the passions and prejudices as well as the interests of those who are arrayed upon one side or the other, it is well to understand the relative positions of the parties to the controversy. A knowledge of the motives of human actions is essential to an understanding of the merits of these actions themselves, and we may reasonably distrust the arguments of those who have a great personal selfish interest behind the ostensible object which they propose to accomplish. The passions, the prejudices, the interest, or the ignorance of men often impel them to act unjustly towards their fellow-men; and no injustice is more common than that of condemning others for apparent or real faults—as tested by the standard of abstract right—without considering the circumstances of those against whom such censures are directed. In order to comprehend fully the true merits of the subject of controversy between the North and the South, upon which the respective sections have arrayed themselves in the now pending contest for the Presidency, it is necessary to begin at the beginning—to commence at the foundation, and to trace step by step the origin and progress of the causes that have produced a conflict within the heart of the confederacy, which may end in disaster to one or both. Many statesmen and wise men in the Old World, both the friends and enemies of the Republic, declare unreservedly their belief, that the Chief Magistrate now in the occupancy of the Executive Chair is the last of the line of American Presidents who will rule over the present confederacy of States. At home and abroad the danger is apparent; and as the writer of these letters cannot participate personally and actively in the conflict, he adopts this as the only means by which he may communicate with his countrymen. For it he offers no other apology or explanation than that he is an American citizen.

History and experience teach us that when nations, or communities, are engaged in a controversy, the real source of difficulty is scarcely ever allowed to play a prominent part. The effort of each is to stimulate the zeal of their own adherents, and to secure the approbation of mankind. Hence, whatever selfish or unworthy designs may actuate the leaders in such cases, they are often hid away beneath profuse protestations of a benevolent or philanthropic purpose. In truth, the multitude rarely fathoms the intentions of those who employ them as accessories to work out their designs. The fathers of the great American Revolution entered upon their struggle with the mother-country for the ostensible purpose of resisting a small tax imposed upon them by the Government of Great Britain. Their real object was independence, but it was not avowed until the public mind of the colonists had been sufficiently aroused by the conflict, in regard to the unjust taxation which it was sought to enforce upon them. The Crimean war was ostensibly based upon a controversy between the Latin and Greek priests, in regard to the custody of some rusty keys of an almost roofless church in Jerusalem. England, France, and Sardinia joined their forces to those of the Sultan of Turkey, and engaged in deadly strife with Russia; and after a bloody and terrible war made peace; but in the treaty which followed, the custody of the aforesaid keys remained an unsettled question. It is needless to say, that the real causes of this war had a much graver significance than the puerile question which was the ostensible origin of the conflict.

So it may be said, with equal truth, that the real causes of conflict between the North and the South were not in the beginning those which have been made prominent in the contest which is now progressing. It will doubtless be readily conceded, that if the manufacturing States of the North had never conceived the idea of enriching themselves by means of prohibitory tariffs, at the expense of the South, the passions of the multitude would never have been so excited as they have been against the domestic institution of slavery in the Southern States. This combined attack upon the South, by parties strong enough to overwhelm them at the *ballot-box*—the one stimulated by cupidity, and the other by fanaticism—is well calculated to arouse the most serious apprehensions of the Southern States. I propose, in this and in subsequent letters, to discuss briefly all the questions upon which the two sections of the Union are now arrayed against each other; but more especially and at greater length, the subject of African slavery, which has been made by the leaders of the Republican party the main issue which is to decide the result of their struggle, to obtain for the North the complete and undivided control of the Federal Government. To this subject my mind has been directed, not only by what I hear and read from America, but also by the erroneous opinions which are maintained in Europe, in regard to the Southern States, and the institution of domestic slavery ; and also by the prevailing delusion, that the only question at issue is that of slavery, and that the only interest which moves the North in this matter is founded in a philanthropic desire to eradicate that 'great evil' from the American continent.

It is necessary to a complete understanding of the subject of slavery in America, to trace it from its origin, through all its intermediate stages, to the present time. It would be manifestly unjust to set up a standard of abstract right, and by this to judge of the Slave States, which are now by their colleagues of the North placed upon their trial before the civilised world. The institutions of no nation would stand the test of such an ordeal. When an individual, a community, or a state is arraigned before the bar of public opinion, for an offence of whatsoever character it may be, the party accused has a right to defend the act by a reference to the circumstances under which the offence was committed. Killing is not murder if the doing thereof is necessary in self-defence, though the burthen of producing the proof rests upon the party accused.

Slavery, abstractly considered, is now regarded by the majority of the civilised world as a wrong; therefore it rests with the Southern States to show that they are right, under the circumstances existing, in upholding and continuing the existence of African slavery. If the Slave States fail in the effort to satisfy public opinion that their defence is conclusive of their innocence, they have still a right in fairness to test the value of their institutions by a comparison with those of their accusers.

In order to understand fully the merits of the question, it is necessary to consider the circumstances under which and by whom slavery was established upon the continent of America, and has been perpetuated to the present day, in the Southern States of the American Union.

The first African slaves who were introduced into what now constitutes the United States of America, but which at that time formed the larger part of the North American provinces of Great Britain, were transported thither under the sanction and by the authority of the British Government. The speculation was pecuniarily successful; and under the special patronage of this Power, slaves were imported in such large numbers as to alarm the European inhabitants for their personal safety. The colonists thereupon urged the British Government to abandon, or at least to suspend, the farther introduction of these barbarians, and seconded their request by a detailed statement of the evils which they believed they had reason to apprehend if the system should be continued.

But that Government was deaf to their representations and to their complaints, and the traffic in slaves was prosecuted with increased activity and effect. The trade was valuable to England in a double sense. First, the price paid for the slaves enriched the British subjects, who were either directly or indirectly interested in the traffic, while at the same time it gave profitable employment to her ships, and added to her power upon the ocean; and, secondly, the production of the colonies rapidly increased, stimulated by this augmentation in the number of her operatives.

The treatment of these captives was necessarily harsh and cruel; for besides being savages but just subjected to the galling and unaccustomed restraints of servitude under civilised masters, with no other feelings towards those by whom they had been enslaved and held in bondage but that of fear and hatred, they were formidable in numbers; and when added to the strength of the native races who were at enmity with the colonists, it will readily be seen that a lack of due circumspection or vigilance might have been attended with fatal consequences to the sparse population of European blood.

From that period up to the very moment when, after a long and sanguinary war, the American colonies achieved their independence and became one of the family of nations, the Government of Great Britain never ceased to encourage the importation of slaves. It constituted, up to that epoch, a most important branch of her commerce, and the great value which she attached thereto may be estimated by the fact, that at the end of a long and bloody European war of the last century, in which she figured as one of the chief combatants, she only claimed as her portion of the spoils of victory the exclusive privilege of supplying the Spanish American colonies with slaves.*

* The Assiento was a contract or convention between the King of Spain and other Powers for furnishing the Spanish dominions in America with negro slaves. The Spaniards, having destroyed the native Indian races in their American colonies, supplied the deficiency of labourers thus created by importing negroes from the coast of Africa. The Genoese first undertook to supply Spain with negroes at a stipulated price. They were succeeded by the Portuguese; and after them, the contract was transferred to France, and the trade yielded to that country enormous profits — insomuch that Great Britain coveted the contract. By the Treaty of Utrecht, Philip V. being declared King of Spain, at the close of a bloody war, in which all the great Powers were engaged, and in which England and her allies were the victors, it was one of the articles of peace between France and England that the contract referred to should be transferred from the former to the latter. Accordingly, a new instrument was signed in May 1713, to last thirty years, and the furnishing of negroes to Spanish America was committed by England to the South Sea Company — an enterprise in which numbers of the royal family of England, the chief nobility, and many of the leading statesmen, as well as other citizens in every rank of life, were stockholders. In virtue of this treaty, England agreed to furnish Spain with one hundred and forty-four thousand African slaves, for which it was to receive pay at the same rate which had been paid the French. A condition was added, that during the first twenty-five years only one-half the duty should be paid for such as they should import beyond that stated number. By the Treaty of Madrid, concluded on the 5th of October, 1750, the right of England to this traffic for the four years not yet

It may with truth be said, that of all the nations of the earth Great Britain has contributed most — first, towards the establishment of African slavery in America, and afterwards towards exciting against it the prejudices of the civilised world.

Scarcely had the American Revolution brought about a change in the immediate and probable future condition of slavery and the slave trade, than the British Government changed its policy, and caused her navy to institute a rigorous search after all vessels which were engaged in what she then denominated the 'infamous traffic in human flesh.' These, when found, were captured — carried into British ports — condemned as lawful prizes, and the proceeds thereof placed in the pockets of the captors.*

An enlightened and unprejudiced judgement might decide that this sudden conversion, and ostentatious

expired by former treaty was re-transferred to Spain, and all claims against the Spanish Government growing out of the same were surrendered upon the payment by Spain to the British South Sea Company the sum of 1,000,000*l.*— about five millions of dollars. For a more detailed account of these transactions, the reader is referred to Anderson's 'Commerce,' Robertson's 'History of America,' and other contemporaneous historians.

* The reader is referred to the case of the American brig Fortuna — Dodson's Adm. Reports, vol. i. page 95 — and of the American ship Arcadia — reported in Acton's Adm. Reports, vol. i. page 24. The capture of the former occurred in 1807, and of the latter at a period somewhat later. In both instances the American vessels were condemned as lawful prizes by the Lords of Appeal, and the products thereof divided among the crews of the vessels which had seized them.

horror of the institution of slavery, occurred at an epoch well calculated to create doubts in regard to the genuineness of that philanthropy which, however noisy in its demonstration, was painfully at variance with her practice, as long as she retained a controlling interest in the traffic in slaves, and in the fruits of their labour.

Upon the establishment of the independence of the United States about one-fifth of the population, in round numbers, were slaves, many of whom had been but recently brought from the shores of Africa. Thoroughly barbarous — without even the instincts of civilisation — they still formed a considerable portion of the population; and in the formation of the new government it was necessary to assign for them a position. The question arose, What shall be done with these wild and uncultivated savages? What rank shall they occupy in the State?

If these slaves had been at the time congregated together upon the neighbouring tropical islands, or if they had been isolated from the body of the European inhabitants in provinces more or less remote, there would have been allowed a much wider latitude in determining what should be their future condition. Their emancipation, either immediate or prospective, would have been a mere question of expediency, involving only a certain sum of money, as a remuneration to the owners. Great Britain, under like circumstances, abolished slavery in her West India possessions. Whether her measures were well taken, or whether the speculation has proven to be a profitable one, it is not my present purpose to investigate.

But the revolted colonists found themselves in a position in which no such alternative was presented to them, even if it would have seemed the part of wisdom to have adopted it. By the policy of Great Britain in establishing these slaves upon the American continent, they were intermingled with the white inhabitants in the greater part of the States of the new confederacy. They were employed as servants or farm labourers at almost every domestic threshold, and hence the questions involved in deciding upon their future position were of much graver significance, and the choice of means was much more limited.

The new government being a Republic, founded upon the principle of equality of rights, was bound in the beginning to confer *upon all whom she recognised as citizens* the same privileges under the Constitution. From this position there was no escape. To have conferred upon one class of citizens certain rights, which should be withheld from another, would have been not only absurd, but, in a Republic, impossible. The primary, the essential condition of a Republic, is the absolute political equality of the individual members composing it.

It certainly requires no argument to prove that these African slaves were totally unfit, by nature, habit, and education, to enter upon the discharge of the responsible duties of free citizens. To have created them such would, in the very act of inaugurating the government, have sounded its death-knell! Every instinct, every impulse, every feeling of the white race, would have revolted against the contaminating association, while the friends of the infant Republic would have had the mortification of witnessing its destruction, even before the erection of the corner-stone of that edifice which now stands in all its magnificent and complete proportions, the pride of every American and the wonder of mankind.

Wiser counsels prevailed. The African, unsuited to be a citizen, was continued in his condition of slavery, and the product of his labour and that of his descendants has enriched the world—has contributed largely towards bringing within the reach of the great masses of mankind the essential products of the warm latitudes; and last, though not least, Americans should bear in mind that it has been a principal element in developing the resources and increasing the power of the United States.

Soon after the establishment of the new Government, the Congress enacted a law fixing upon a period, not remote, after which no slaves should be brought from abroad into any State or Territory of the Republic. Of the nearly four millions of slaves now held as such in the United States, not five hundred have been introduced in contravention of that enactment. It is, in reference to this fact, worthy of especial remark, and English emancipationists at least should remember, that for the ancestors of the great body of Africans at this day held as slaves within the limits of the American Republic, the estimated value thereof was paid, under the sanction and approval of the British Government, to British subjects! For *nearly every drop of blood* which flows in the veins of the slaves of the United States, our mother *England has received the price in gold!* And yet this England shakes her gory locks at *us*, and says, 'the sin' is *ours!* She points to her desolated islands, with their famishing freed slaves, and tells us that her 'skirts are clear.'

The separate States which had secured their independence, although exercising sovereignty, each within its defined limits, delegated certain powers to a government, erected by themselves, which should be the representative of all. They established the Federal Union, but the sovereignty of each State remained entire, except wherein a limited power was surrendered specifically to the General Government, having reference almost exclusively to their foreign relations, and to their mutual intercourse.

The free inhabitants of the Slave States, constituting a large majority of the whole, being desirous rather to establish a firm, and lasting, and prosperous government, than to test in practice the merits of a doubtful theory, adapted their form of government to the exigencies of the circumstances by which they were surrounded. As before stated, they recognised in their Constitutions the political equality of all the European races. This was but the admission of an existing fact. But they denied to the African slaves the rights of citizenship. These were wisely left in the same relative position to the white races which they had occupied while the country was under the dominion of Great Britain. The change, therefore, in the form of the government was not attended by any violent changes in the habits or condition of the people. Had different counsels prevailed, and had the governments of these States sought to engraft upon their constitutions and laws the theoretical idea of universal equality, it must be admitted that they would have failed to secure the end proposed, and the experiment would, in all human probability, have resulted disastrously to the interests and the happiness of all. There would have been a perpetual conflict between the two races, or there would have been an amalgamation of them. Either would have been alike fatal.

This departure from the theoretical doctrines of visionary enthusiasts, who would change even the laws of Heaven itself, to make what they conceive to be a perfect government, has, from that period to the present, afforded for the adherents of this system a theme for unceasing denunciation.

It may here be said that the adversaries of slavery, beyond the boundaries of the Slave States, ask that something be done which is revolting to every feeling, or sentiment, or thought, or impulse of the dominant race. They demand that the free white citizens should not only disregard the prejudices of education, and the instincts of nature, but even set at defiance the apparent will of Omnipotence, which has marked with signs so unmistakeable the distinctions between the races. They demand that eight millions of freemen, of a race distinguished above all others for its rapid growth in greatness and power — the admitted representative of the highest order of civilisation to which man has ever attained — shall remove the political and social barriers which separate them from four millions of another and a distinct race; which of all others has proven itself least capable of advancement from the depths of ignorance and brutality, from which it has never at any period of its history emerged; and which is the acknowledged representative of the lowest grade of barbarism to which any of the races of man have fallen.

When we consider farther that these two races, as dissimilar in their physical aspect as in their intellectual capacity and endowments — the one *white*, the other *black* — both having been transplanted to the soil of America, from far distant countries, and from different continents by an overruling power—the one self-exiled from their native land under the promptings of necessity, the other by the application of physical force—having by the will of a common superior occupied towards each other the relation of master and slave; and having continued that relation from the day their ancestors first met face to face, as strangers in a strange land—who, but the enemy of both, would desire to witness the sudden disruption of those ties, to which both have become reconciled by habit, and under which both are living happily and contentedly together, while contributing far more than their due proportion to the welfare and happiness of mankind?

We may readily imagine a physical force competent to the destruction of the liberties of the freemen of the Southern States. We may conceive of a concentration of power, adequate to the purpose of enchaining their limbs, and consigning the bodies of the refractory and unyielding to loathsome dungeons. But in view of the feelings with which the Africans are regarded by the European races in America, we cannot imagine any possible exercise of human tyranny potent enough to compel them to admit in their hearts a political equality, or an amalgamation with the degraded race. However theoretical philanthropists may refuse to recognise in their systems of government the distinctions of colour, capacity, and race; still the ineradicable prejudice exists, and the testimony of the past, as well as the promptings of common reason, teach us that in establishing laws for the government of mankind, we cannot eschew the common and prevailing sentiments of the governed, except in the presence of an overwhelming force of bayonets.

In the case we are considering, the distinctions are so legible—the lines so ineradicable—the differences so indelibly stamped by nature itself, that the repugnance must be perpetual. Any withdrawal of the legal barriers which now keep the races asunder, would inevitably result in the destruction of one or both.

Let not the honest and well-meaning opponents of slavery delude themselves or others into the belief that there can be any important modification of the existing relations between the whites and the blacks, while they inhabit a common territory. Let them remember that an essential condition of a Republic is, that all who are recognised as citizens must be invested, under any given state of circumstances, with an equality of rights. Whenever the States of the Confederacy, or the General Government, recognise by their Constitutions and their laws, two sets or classes of citizens, invested with unequal privileges, and with different sets of laws for each, they violate the fundamental principle upon which a purely republican government is founded. In making laws, therefore, to be applied to the great mass of Africans, they must be regarded as either slaves or citizens. If as citizens, then must they be placed upon a political equality with the European races.

Even assuming, however, that in a Republic there could exist recognised classes of citizens, with different and unequal political rights, is it not plain that a change which would involve only a partial degree of liberty would render the condition of the African worse than his present state of servitude? Accomplish this change and it could only be perpetuated by an overwhelming power from without; and upon the instant when the external pressure should be removed, that instant would the conflict between the races commence—the one to free itself from all political inferiority, the other to reduce the African to his former condition of servitude—without considering the cost during its progress, this could only result in the complete subjection of one or the other.

Whatever may be the abstract merits of slavery—whatever its evils or advantages—it is manifest that when Great Britain introduced Africans into her American colonies, she designed that their enslavement should be perpetual. She never could have conceived it possible that they would occupy any other relation to the European races. No brazen collar around the neck of the slave was necessary to distinguish him from his master. The hand of Omnipotence, in characters broad, deep, and ineffaceable, had marked him as of a different and inferior race. The British slave-dealer sought in the traffic *present gain;* but the British Government, looking to the future, and anticipating no change in the sovereignty of the country, sought to enlarge the productions of her colonies in all time to come by transplanting a race with characteristics so widely distinct from the Europeans that, whatever might be the desire of the dominant race, they could not occupy towards each other any other relation than that of *master* and *slave.* In establishing African slavery, therefore, the British Government designed that it should be perpetual.

In regard to the existence of this natural repugnance, heightened by habit and education, even M. De Tocqueville, notwithstanding his theoretical and cultivated hostility to slavery, bears ample testimony. Anxious as he was to discover arguments adverse to the institution of slavery, and eagerly as he sought for and recorded the evils, real or imaginary, emanating therefrom, and indulging those prejudices as he did, to the great injustice of the American Slave States, he was constrained most reluctantly to admit, that any material change in the relative condition of the races would result disastrously to one or both.

M. De Tocqueville says:—

The abstract and transient fact of slavery is fatally united to the physical and permanent fact of colour. The tradition of slavery dishonours the race, and the peculiarity of the race perpetuates the tradition of slavery.

That the negro transmits the eternal mark of his ignominy to all his descendants; and though the law may abolish slavery, God alone can obliterate the traces of its existence.

The modern slave differs from his master, not only in his condition, but in his origin. You may set the negro free, but you cannot make him otherwise than an alien to the European. Nor is this all; we scarcely acknowledge the common features of mankind in this child of debasement, whom slavery has brought among us. His physiognomy is to our eyes hideous, his understanding weak, his tastes low; and we are almost inclined to look upon him as a being intermediate between man and the brutes.

If it be so difficult to root out an inequality which solely originates in the law, how are those distinctions to be destroyed which seem to be founded upon the immutable laws of nature herself? When I remember the extreme difficulty with which aristocratic bodies, of whatever nature they may be, are commingled with the mass of the people, and the exceeding care which they take to preserve the ideal boundaries of their caste inviolate, I despair of seeing an aristocracy disappear which is founded upon visible and indelible signs. Those who hope that the Europeans will ever mix with the negroes appear to me to delude themselves.

Hitherto, whenever the whites have been the most powerful, they have maintained the blacks in a subordinate or servile position; wherever the negroes have been strongest, they have destroyed the whites — such has been the only course of events which has ever taken place between the two races.

I see that, in a certain portion of the territory of the United States at the present day, the legal barrier which separated the two races is tending to fall away; but not that which exists in the manners of the country — slavery recedes, but the prejudice to which it has given birth remains stationary. Whosoever has inhabited the United States must have perceived that in those parts of the Union in which the negroes are no longer slaves, they have in no wise drawn near to the whites. On the contrary, the prejudice to the race appears to be stronger in the States which have abolished slavery than in those where it still exists; and nowhere is it so intolerant as in those States where servitude has never been known.

It is true that in the North of the Union marriages may be legally contracted between negroes and whites; but public opinion would stigmatise a man who should connect himself with a negress, as infamous, and it would be difficult to meet with a single instance of such a union.

In the South, where slavery still exists, the negroes are less carefully kept apart; they sometimes share the labour and the recreations of the whites; the whites consent to intermix with them, to a certain extent; and although the legislation treats them more harshly, the habits of the people are more tolerant and compassionate.

In the South the master is not afraid to raise his slave to his own standing, because he knows that he can in a moment reduce him to the dust at pleasure. In the North the white man no longer distinctly perceives the barrier which separates him from the degraded race, and he shuns the negroes with the more pertinacity, because he fears lest they should some day be confounded together. Thus it is in the United States that the prejudice which repels the negroes seems to increase in proportion as they are emancipated, and inequality is sanctioned by the manners, while it is effaced by the laws of the country.

I am obliged to confess that I do not regard the abolition of slavery as a means of warding off the struggle of the two races in the United States. The negroes may long remain slaves without complaining; but if they are once raised to the level of freemen, they will socn revolt at being deprived of their civil rights; and as they cannot become the equals of the whites, they will speedily declare themselves as enemies. In the North everything contributes to facilitate the emancipation of the slave; and slavery was abolished without placing the free negroes in a position which could become formidable, since their number was too small for them ever to claim the exercise of their rights. But such is not the case in the South. The question of slavery was a question of commerce and manufacture for the slave owners in the North: for those of the South it is a question of life and death.

When I contemplate the condition of the South, I can only discover two alternatives which may be adopted by the white inhabitants of those States, viz. *either to emancipate the negroes, and to intermingle with them, or, remaining isolated from them, to keep them in a state of slavery as long as possible. All intermediate measures seem to me likely to terminate, and that shortly, in the most horrible of civil wars, and perhaps in the extirpation of one or other of the two races.*

When the Europeans chose the slaves from a race differing from their own, which many of them considered as inferior to the other races of mankind, and which they all repelled with horror from any notion of intimate connection, they must have believed that slavery would last for ever, since there is no intermediate state which can be desirable between the excessive inequality produced by servitude and the complete equality which originates in independence. The Europeans did imperfectly feel this truth, but without acknowledging it even to themselves. Whenever they have had to do with negroes, their conduct has either been dictated by their interest and their pride or by their compassion. They first violated every right of humanity by their treatment of the negro, and they afterwards informed him those rights were precious and inviolable. They affected to open their ranks to the slaves: but the negroes who attempted to penetrate into the community were driven back with scorn.

If it be impossible to anticipate a period at which the Americans of the South will mingle their blood with that of the negroes, can they allow their slaves to become free without compromising their own security? And if they are obliged to keep that race in bondage, in order to save their own families, may they not be excused for availing themselves of the means best adapted to that end?—*Democracy in America*, p. 388, American edition.

These must be received as the conclusions of one who, entertaining strong prejudices against slavery, visited the Southern States with the view of finding proofs in corroboration of his theory. He permitted his enlightened and comprehensive mind to be biassed by a distorted conception of its evils, yet, with all his undisguised hostility, he is constrained to express his conviction, founded upon facts, reason, and observation, that any change in the relative condition of the European and African races in America would be fatal to both.

The prejudices of this distinguished author were *against slavery as a system of labour, not against the slaveholder*. Hence, while his opinions in reference to the former were moulded in conformity with these prejudices, he was not indisposed to do justice to the latter. His inclination was, *without crushing the slaveholder, to elevate the slave*—differing in this essential particular from modern abolition philanthropy, which, without any special desire to *elevate the slave*, seeks only to *reduce the master* to that standard.

LETTER II.

Historical and judicial records of Slavery—Reasons why Slavery could not be Abolished and proofs that it should not have been Abolished—Emancipation would make the condition of the Slaves worse—The Abolitionists cannot accomplish their purposes even with the assent of the Slaveholders—Slavery was Abolished in the North by selling the Slaves to the South.

HISTORY informs us that slavery existed in Great Britain, or in her provinces, by the authority of her laws, from the first dawn of civilisation to a period within the memory of all men who are now in the meridian of life. The same may be said in regard to almost every nation of the world, great and small. It is fair to assume from this fact that slavery has existed since man was created; and we have no reason to believe that it ever became unpopular or unfashionable until a very late period in the world's history. However that may be, it forms no part of my purpose to prove the wisdom or the folly of the world in its treatment of this question during the past half century. It is not my purpose to discuss abstract, but actual slavery; not what might be theoretically best under an assumed state of circumstances, but what is best under the actual circumstances; in short, not whether slavery is right or wrong under all circumstances, but whether it is right or wrong under the circumstances now existing in the planting States of America. To understand what those circumstances are, it is necessary to understand how they were brought about.

I have said that slavery existed in England as far back as we have records or the tradition of a Government; though that is not the term by which it was known. However, in substance, it was the same as now exists in a modified form in America. Villenage under the common law of England was thus described by that eminent lawyer Hargrave, in 1771 (see 20 Howell's State Trials): —

> The condition of a villien had most of the incidents which I have before described in giving the idea of slavery in general. His service was uncertain and indeterminate, such as his lord thought fit to require; or, as some of our ancient writers express it, he knew not in the evening what he was to do in the morning; he was bound to do whatever he was commanded. He was liable to beating, imprisonment, and every other chastisement his lord might prescribe, except killing and maiming. He was incapable of acquiring property for his own benefit, the rule being *quicquid acquiritur domino.* He was himself the subject of property; as such, saleable and transmissible. . . . The origin of villenage is principally to be derived from the wars between our British, Saxon, Danish, and Norman ancestors. . . . There were many bondmen in England before the Conquest, as appears by the Anglo-Saxon laws regulating them; and therefore it would be nearer the truth to attribute the origin of villiens as well to the preceding wars and revolutions as to the effect of the Conquest.

In the time of Elizabeth this form of slavery existed

in full force; but during the reign of that queen, certain measures were instituted which had the effect of finally eradicating white slavery from the territory of Great Britain. This result, however, was very gradually achieved; for it did not finally disappear until the reign of James II. In the appendix to 20th volume of Howell's State Trials may be found a commission issued by Queen Elizabeth to Sir William Mildmay and Cecil Lord Burleigh, authorising them to manumit her slaves in certain counties named, upon the condition, however, that the said slaves *should pay a reasonable sum of money for their liberty!* It may be inferred that in manumitting their slaves, the lords imitated the example of their sovereign, and surrendered to them their liberty only upon the receipt of their estimated value in money. The queen's commission is in the following language: —

Elizabeth, by the grace of God, &c. To our right trustie and well-beloved consellor, Sir M. Cecill, of the Garter Knighte, lord Burghly, and Highe Treasorer of England, and to our trustie and right well-beloved consellor, Sir Walter Mildmay, Chauncellor and Under Treasorer of our Exchequer, greetinge.

Whereas divers and sundrie of our poore faithfull and loyal subjects, being borne bonde in blode and regargaunt to divers and sundrie our manor and possessions within our realm of England, have made humble suyte unto us to be manumysed, enfraunchised, and made free with theire children and sequells, by reason whereof they, theire children, and theire sequells may become more apte and fitte members for the service of us, and of our commonwealthe:

We, therefore, having tender consideration of their said sute,

and well considering the same to be acceptable to Almighty God, do commytt and give unto you full power and authoritie by these presents to accepte, admitte, and received to be manumysed, and enfraunchised, and made free, such and so many of our bondmen and bondwomen in blood, with all and every their children and sequells, their goodes, landes, tenements, and hereditaments, as are now apperteynyng, or regardaunte to all or any of our manors, and within the said several counties of Cornwall, Devon, Somersett, and Gloucester, as to you shal seam mete and convenient, compounding with them for suche reasonable fines, or sommes of money to be taken and received to our use for the manumyssion and enfranchisement, and for the possessions, &c., &c., as you and they can agree for the same after your wisdoms and discretions.

We may reasonably conclude, however, that the abolition of this species of servitude — which is as fully described by the word 'slavery' as that which exists at the present day in America—did not have its origin in a belief that slavery was even abstractly wrong; for while white slavery was disappearing from England and France, all the Christian nations of Europe, with England, Spain, France, and Portugal at their head, were establishing black slavery over the entire continent of America. All America, North and South, was occupied or held by these Powers. Louis XIII. established slavery in all his colonies in America; Portugal established it in Brazil, and also in all her other colonies; Spain, by the advice of Las Casas, substituted African slaves for the native Indians, who had been nearly exterminated during the time they had been under subjection to the European

Powers; while England supplied her possessions in North America and the West Indies.

After England succeeded, in 1713, in wresting from France the contract with Spain for supplying her provinces with slaves, it was no uncommon occurrence for slaves to be sold — in fact, they were sold, almost daily — on the public Exchange, London (see 2 Haggard's Reports, page 105). The question having arisen as to the legal right to hold slaves in England, it was submitted for decision by the Crown to the twelve judges of the empire. Their judgement was rendered in the following words:—'In pursuance of His Majesty's Order in Council, hereunto annexed, *we do humbly certify our opinion that negroes are merchandise.*'

Subsequently, the merchants of London submitted the question to Sir Philip Yorke, the Solicitor, and Lord Talbot, the Attorney-General. They certified that 'a slave coming from the West Indies into England, with or without his master, doth not become free; and his master's property in him is not thereby determined nor varied; and the master may legally compel him to return to the plantations.'

In 1749, the Lord Chancellor, Lord Hardwicke, affirmed the doctrine above stated, by a decree in a cause in Chancery involving this issue. This ruling of the law was recognised until 1761, when it was decided by Lord Mansfield that the colonial laws could not be made to apply to England, and, therefore, that a slave-owner had no remedy. This decision, however, did not deny the right of the owner to property in his slave, nor did it assume that the slave by coming into England was thereby made free; he was only virtually so, because there were no laws in England by which he might exercise the rights of a master in case of resistance by the slave.

Lord Stowell, one of the most eminent and learned judges that England has ever produced, in deciding a case, in the year 1827, against the right of a slave to freedom, because she had once been carried into England, said:—

> The fact is, that in England where villenage of both sorts went into total decay, we had communication with no other country; and therefore it is triumphantly declared, 'once a freeman, ever a freeman.' But slavery was a very favoured introduction into the colonies; it was deemed a great source of the mercantile interest of the country, and was on that account largely considered by the mother country *as a great source of its wealth and strength.* Treaties were made on that account, *and the colonies compelled to submit to those treaties by the authority of this country.* This system continued entire. Instead of being condemned as *malus usus,* it was regarded as a most eminent source of its wealth and power. *It was at a late period of the last century that it was condemned in England, as an institution not fit to exist here, for reasons peculiar to our own condition;* but it has been continued in our colonies, favoured and supported by our own courts, which have liberally imparted to it their protection and encouragement.

In response to the legal argument, that a slave could not breathe the air of Britain, this distinguished jurist declared that, after painful and laborious research into historical records, he did not find anything touching the peculiar unfitness of the English atmosphere for respiration *during the ten centuries that slaves had lived in England!*

Now, since it is thus manifest by the highest judicial decisions, as well as by historical records, that slavery was established in America by Great Britain, and that her then 'colonists were compelled to submit thereto by the authority of the mother-country,'—that it took 'a thousand years' for her to discover the immorality of the institution and to apply a suitable remedy,—and that even then she only 'condemned it as not fit to exist in England, *for reasons peculiar to her own condition*;' may not we, the inheritors of that soil and of those slaves, ask with a modest confidence of our philanthropic cousins of the 'fast-anchored isle,' to allow us at least a hundred years of grace to decide whether the peculiar condition of *our* country would justify us in condemning the institution as unfit to exist upon American soil?

The institution of slavery, as we have thus seen, was a legacy, whether for good or evil, left to the United States of America by their former sovereign. As slaves, the Africans were transferred from the kingdom of Great Britain to the new Republics, and as slaves they were thereafter held. Whether or not slavery is right or wrong in the abstract, the slave

States found themselves in the presence of an existing contingency, which, as before said, left them no alternative but to adopt, and endeavour to make available to their interests, an institution which they might wisely direct, but which they could not abolish.

No one who desired to witness the successful establishment of the new Government could have regarded with any other feeling than distrust, any attempt to elevate these slaves to the condition of free citizens. The instinct of self-preservation, and a dawning perception of the sublime destiny which, in the not distant future, would attend the developement of that great country, alike forbade such an unhallowed amalgamation. The wisdom of that decision, without even considering the necessity which left them no other alternative, is already apparent. Where there is so much to admire, so much for which, as a people, we have reason to be proud, how can the true friend of America seek to plunge into that vortex of abolitionism from which we could only hope to escape through disaster and a sea of blood ?

Here the defender of American slavery might pause in the presence of that necessity which allowed no discretion or choice in regard to the continuance of slavery, and submit the question, without argument, to any unprejudiced umpire. Whatever might be the predilections of just men sitting in judgement, however their sensibilities may have been excited by works of fiction, by falsehood or by caricatured truth, the decision could not be otherwise than that slavery, inaugurated in the United States by its former sovereign, was perpetuated by the Republic under the ruling of an inexorable necessity.

But even this impregnable fortress of defence is weak in comparison with others which have been erected by the dominant race upon which the duty has devolved of directing and controlling the institution which they thus inherited.

Was slavery under European auspices a crime in its inception, and a curse in its perpetuation? America has converted it through the fruits of its labour into a blessing to mankind! Was slavery cruel? America has made it merciful! Did British cupidity drag the unhappy African from his native land, and consign him to eternal servitude? American practical philanthropy has given to the involuntary exile a home, better far than he or his ancestors had ever known. America found in the slave which she inherited a savage, and she has civilised him! She found him a heathen, and she has Christianised him! She found him naked and starving, and she has clothed and fed him! Slave though he be, yet in all that concerns his comfort, physical well-being, and contentment—in everything save the name, the condition of the slaves of the United States, as admitted even by the enemies of the institution, is far in advance of that of any similar number of labourers following similar occupations, in any other land under the sun.

Before proceeding to refer more in detail to facts concerning the existing condition of the African race in America—or before making a survey of some of the chief benefits which have resulted to mankind through the immediate instrumentality of African slavery in America, let it, for a moment, be assumed as granted that the abolition party has so far achieved its purpose as to convince even the slave-holder that slavery should cease to exist. What measures shall be instituted to accomplish the result?

It will be an approximation sufficiently near, to estimate the slave population at about four millions. The present money value of slaves in the prime of life would probably not fall short of eleven hundred dollars each. The average value may therefore be set down at about five hundred dollars each. This would make the grand total value of the entire slave population, *twenty hundred millions of dollars!*

It is not pretended that of this number five hundred have been placed in that position by the present owners, or I might say, by the present generation. They have been bought and paid for by the present possessors or their ancestors, under the operation and guarantee of the laws of the land. The slave-owner of to-day had no more instrumentality in the enactment of these laws than he had in the establishment of the institution of slavery. Both had their origin at a time when the country was under the exclusive dominion of Great Britain.

The slave-holder has thus become possessed of his property under all the solemn sanctions of the law. If a wrong has been done, it dates back to a period long anterior to his birth, and even before the existence of the Republic itself. He holds his slave by virtue of the same system of laws which entitles a citizen to the possession of any other description of property, and he cannot justly be deprived of its use without adequate compensation.

A single State in the vicinity of other slave-holding States may enact laws fixing upon a stated period after which slavery shall not exist. In this manner, slavery has been already abolished in the Northern or older latitudes of the American Union. But in every case the slave-holder has been able to protect himself against pecuniary loss by transferring his slaves into States where the institution still existed. Although by this means the *institution* of slavery has been abolished in many of the States, yet *the slaves themselves were transferred to a different locality, and they and their descendants are at this day in bondage.*

The abolition of slavery therefore in the present free States of the Confederacy, involved no pecuniary loss to the citizens who were their owners; nor did it change, in the smallest degree, the position of those who were then and there held in bondage. They only *changed their masters and their homes.* But in considering the question of the abolition of slavery throughout the entire Confederacy, with a view to the emancipation of the slaves, it assumes proportions of much graver magnitude. Not a single State of the American Union which has enacted laws prohibiting slavery within its limits, ever contemplated that the Act of Emancipation would cost its citizens a single dollar, or give freedom to a single slave. The object of the change which it was deemed desirable to accomplish, had reference solely to what was regarded as the interests of the dominant race. The rhetorical and poetical effusions which attended the discussion of the question, were of course signalised by the usual protestations of philanthropy, humanity, and benevolence; but the arguments of controlling potency were, that slavery had ceased to be profitable in a pecuniary way—that the climate was not adapted to that description of labour—that the change could be effected without cost—and that an Act of Emancipation was in reality but the recognition of an existing fact; for the reason that the laws of trade had already transferred the mass of the slaves to the warmer latitude of the South. By the provisions of the law, ample time was allowed to effect the transportation of the slaves, *as slaves*, to a more congenial soil.

It may be fairly assumed that this measure did

not have for its object any vindication of the 'inalienable rights of man,' or the eradication of the system of slave labour; else, instead of abolishing the institution in such manner as to afford time and opportunity to sell the slaves in a foreign market, steps would have been taken to secure their emancipation, even at the expense of a small tax upon the citizens. This could have been accomplished at a comparatively trifling cost, for the self-established laws of interest, more potent even in their moral influence than statutory enactments, had already, as before stated, caused the great body of the Africans to be transported from the colder latitudes of the North to the more genial temperature of a Southern sun. Thus only a comparatively small number of slaves remained to be affected by the Act of Emancipation. Cheaply as the Northern States might then have vindicated the doctrine of 'equal rights,' the cost, small as it would have been, was deemed too great. And happy as was the conjuncture for practically testing upon a small scale the capacity of the African for self-government, and the mingling together of the two races in a common brotherhood, the opportunity and the occasion passed away for ever.

Is it inopportune to ask from well-meaning and honourable citizens of the North, an answer to some questions which here naturally suggest themselves?

If you would not expend hundreds of dollars in giving freedom to your handful of slaves, how can you now ask that the South should expend hundreds of millions in giving freedom to her multitudes? If you dared not hazard the experiment of conferring equal political rights upon only thousands of Africans, how can you ask the Southern States to grant such privileges to four millions of slaves? If you could not fix upon any intermediate condition between absolute slavery and citizenship, for a number so small as scarcely to be estimated in the aggregate of your population, and thus allow of their remaining within your own States, how can you ask the South to place all her vital interests at hazard by the semi-enfranchisement of slaves, equal in number to one half of her free citizens? If by the operation of your laws the South became the purchasers of your slaves, how can you in honour seek to compass her destruction for the sin of slavery? But above all, if you found slavery 'a political evil and a sin,' and by the transportation of your slaves to the Southern States relieved yourself of that 'evil,' and abandoned the practice of that 'sin,' how can you now require that *slavery in the South shall be perpetuated by refusing to it any outlet?* How can you claim that the descendants of the slaves you sold in the Southern markets shall remain in perpetuity where you have thus placed them? How can you deny to those who have purchased them, the same privilege which was accorded to you of abolishing, or rather banishing the institution of slavery from their midst, whenever *the laws of self-interest* teach them that *it is not philanthropic* to hold their fellow-creatures in bondage?

How strangely perverse are the ways of man when governed and directed by fanaticism! The anti-slavery party would circumscribe the limits of slave territory in the United States, with the avowed intention of bettering the condition of the slave, while real philanthropy would indicate a policy precisely the reverse. The Abolitionist would crowd the slaves into as narrow a compass as possible, thus increasing their hardships, and at last endangering their own existence as well as that of their masters, while the granting of an outlet to their increasing numbers would perpetuate or even improve that mild system which now prevails throughout the Slave States. Man cannot force this great question to an issue, without involving one or both races in a common ruin. The Almighty above may wisely direct the great movement, which in the end will work out His purpose in reference to this people. Under the guidance of a superior race the Africans held in slavery in America have already made a movement towards civilisation, which has placed them far in advance of any of their race in their native land. How wicked, how cruel, to place in jeopardy all that has been gained, by adopting the violent changes which Abolitionists would inaugurate!

Conscientious Abolitionists should remember that foreigners and strangers cannot successfully accomplish the changes they propose. These can only be achieved by residents upon the soil, and familiarity with the question to be solved. Without the consent of the Southern people they cannot accomplish that which they propose, without sacrificing the white race, which will resist all interference to the point of extermination. It may occur that the destiny of the African may rise higher in the future than in the past—certainly his great progress while in the condition of slavery would seem to foreshadow such an end. But that end will come, if at all, without any violent changes. It will be reached day by day and week by week; and after it is achieved, none can tell the hour or the epoch which marked the change. Slavery has, without any violence and without external influences, and by giving to the laws of nature free scope, moved over a thousand miles of American territory leaving not a slave behind. Why should good men attempt to check it in its onward progress? If the laws of nature or of interest press slavery on farther and farther South, why not let it go, even though in process of time it should of itself, and by the operation of natural laws, pass away altogether from the territory where it now exists? How strange is that propensity, amounting to an absorbing passion in the minds of many men, which prompts them to overlook the evils which surround them at home, and direct their peculiar care and compassion to those whom they are told are the victims of wrong in distant lands. There is, however, a great difference in the aspect in which the evils in the one case and the other present themselves. They may behold those by which they are surrounded, but they likewise see the obstacles by which their removal is environed. Habit has made them familiar, long endurance has made them less offensive, and the wise amongst them know that social or political evils of long standing, engrafted in the mind of the public by custom, and penetrating every rank of society, can only be thoroughly eradicated by that community itself, and by a process often as slow and painful as that by which they were established. Violent changes in the long-established habits of a people are almost always productive of disaster, even when accomplished by their own volition ; but when brought about by the intervention of strangers, ruin to the cause which they seek to promote is one of the least of the evils which may be expected to follow. The Englishman may believe that his own government is founded upon principles more enduring and more just than any other, that its laws are founded in wisdom, and that its Constitution is a perfect guarantee of the liberties of the subject; but if they were suddenly forced upon the subjects of the Sultan, it can scarcely be supposed that they would appreciate its excellences, or profit by its provisions, or consent to live under its operation.

On the other hand, politicians discover what they conceive to be the evils which exist in other countries, as men perceive what seems to them the shortcomings of their neighbours; but they fail to see the obstacles which prevent their removal, or if they perceive, do not appreciate or understand them. A most impressive illustration of these truths may be found in the conduct of that large and respectable body of foreigners, who have been seized with the mania of eradicating slavery in the Southern States of the American Union. They seem utterly oblivious to the great fact, that neither history nor tradition record a single instance in which any race of men has made such rapid progress, in all that which the term 'civilisation' signifies, as the African slaves of these same Southern States, between the period of their enslavement and the present moment of time.

But to return from this digression. It is manifest that the abolition of slavery in the United States, under existing circumstances, would involve the entire loss of the total value of the slaves. How and by whom is this immense sum to be expended? No undue proportion thereof could, upon any principle of justice or morality, be charged upon those who may happen, at the moment of emancipation, to be in the legal possession of the slaves. It cannot therefore be compromised by permitting them to retain an estate for life, or for a limited term of years, in the services of the slaves or their descendants. The laws by virtue of which they hold them as property, guarantee the possession of them and their posterity for ever; and they might, with equal justice, be limited to the enjoyment of an estate for life in the land or the homestead purchased or inherited in fee-simple from their ancestors, as to be deprived of any part of their interest in the slave.

The question then still reverts: How is the cost value of the slave to be remunerated to the owner?

It would be unprofitable to occupy time in considering the means necessary to the accomplishment of that which a single glance suffices to show would be impossible. The loss could not be made up to the owner, nor any part thereof bearing any commensurate proportion to the entire value. It becomes necessary, therefore, in order to carry out our hypothesis, that the slave-owner, either by force or moral conviction, has agreed to surrender all his pecuniary interests, and submit to the ruin which would be entailed upon him by the destruction of all his property. Having consummated the Act of Emancipation by this enormous pecuniary sacrifice, we have but entered upon the threshold of the difficulties by which, to the eye of real philanthropy, the whole question is environed.

What must be done with these four millions of liberated African slaves?

Honest and well-meaning persons have said, without considering of the necessary means, 'Transport them to the land from whence their ancestors were wrested by Great Britain!' This, however, would be physically impossible. But even if it could be accomplished, it would be an act of inhumanity, involving a thousandfold more suffering than the worst form of slavery as now existing, to say nothing of the violence which it would be necessary to employ in order to force the freed man from the scenes of his former servitude.

This scheme failing, we are left without other alternative than to provide for their future abode in the land where their destiny has been cast. What, then, should be their political position in regard to their former masters? What privileges should be bestowed, and what withheld? Should they be admitted, either immediately or in the contemplation of the future, to a social or political equality with the European races?

As already declared, this could never be. The prejudices, the instincts of the latter, are all opposed to such an association. Nature itself revolts against the unnatural amalgamation, and education has rendered the antipathy ineradicable. Heaven itself has marked upon the brow of the African the seal of inferiority ; and no laws, however stringent—no physical power, however great, could enforce upon the whites the recognition of such an equality. To believe that they could do so, is first to suppose them already degraded.

None but an enemy to the dominant race, or an impracticable dreamer, could wish to witness such a consummation. The theory of the universal equality of all the races of mankind is most beautiful and attractive to the merely speculative mind; but when it is attempted to enforce it in the practical affairs of life, it is found to be a fallacy and a delusion.

Rejecting then this adjustment as unwise, unnatural, unjust, and, finally, impossible, there remains but one other alternative—and that is, while conferring upon them personal freedom from the restraints of servitude, and of a master legally authorised to control them and give direction to their labour, to withhold from them the political rights accorded to other citizens. We have already considered the manifest inconsistency and danger of recognising two sets of citizens, with unequal privileges, by a government which has for its corner-stone the principle of entire equality for all who have a right to be called citizens.

But would not such an enfranchisement, in its

practical results, prove to be a most cruel kindness? As a slave, he would have at least the protection of one master interested in his welfare; as a freedman, almost beyond the pale of governmental protection, with no one to take care of him, of a despised and inferior race, a stranger in a land of strangers, how miserable would be his fate! Even if every obstacle to the consummation of such a result were removed, philanthropy might well pause before conferring the boon of freedom at such a hazard.

As a slave, he would have *but* one master, whose duty and whose interest it would be to clothe, to feed, and to protect him in youth and in old age, in sickness, and in health. As a freed African, he would have many masters, but none who would feel any interest in his welfare. He would live miserably from the cradle to the grave, despised of all, and shunned by every one; and it is impossible for the practically benevolent mind to conceive how in any single respect his physical, moral, or social condition would be improved by this nominal change in his relations towards the more powerful race. On the contrary, the practical reasoner cannot resist the conclusion, that in all things his condition would be essentially worse.

It is thus discovered, by an investigation of the subject of slavery in America, and an analysis of its present condition, with a single eye to its abolition, that upon every hand we are met by obstacles beyond the power of man to obviate; and that no material change can be effected in the present *status* of the slave, without entailing far more deplorable evils than those which it would be proposed to remedy. Even after we have arrived at the point where all interests would acquiesce in any practicable scheme of emancipation, it is apparent that it would be impossible.

Whether for good or for evil, the institution of slavery exists, and will continue to exist, in some form or another, so long as the European and African races occupy together the same territory, or until some overruling power from without reduces both to a common subjection. Furthermore, whether or not it will be the fate of the white race, whose destiny has been cast with the transplanted Africans, to be held responsible for the existence of slavery, they will at least bear within them the consciousness, that for the offence, if it be one in reality, they are wholly free from a just responsibility.

But if slavery is a thing so detestable, why should not the friends of humanity utter their imprecations against those who entailed it upon mankind, rather than against the present generation of slave-owners, who have been obliged to adapt themselves to an existing reality, and who have only given direction to an institution which they had no agency in creating, and which they had not the power to eradicate? But, above all, how stupendous is the wrong of those who, from motives the most sordid, entailed slavery upon the Southern States of the American Union, now, from motives even less commendable, thrust themselves forward as the great champions of human liberty and universal emancipation!

I have only adopted this train of argument, and have for the moment acquiesced in the extreme views of the Abolitionist, in order that we might, without disagreement, follow out his schemes of emancipation in any direction which his inclination or his judgement might direct; and we have seen that whatever path he follows, he encounters evils of far greater magnitude than those which he seeks to eradicate. But I would be doing injustice to the Southern slave-holder — injustice to the benefits which the system of slave labour, instituted by others against his will, but by him developed to its present form, has conferred upon mankind — injustice to that overruling Providence which ordains all the institutions of man, were I to rest the defence of the Southern States of America upon any other foundation than that of having worthily employed the means which have been placed in their hands for the purpose of promoting the welfare and happiness of mankind.

LETTER III.

Classification of the Adversaries of Slavery in the Southern States—The London 'Times' on the causes of English Opposition to Slavery—What position would England occupy towards the Belligerents, if the Republican Party should attempt to carry its measures into effect—Would the South hesitate about defending herself to the last extremity?

Before instituting an enquiry into the advantages and disadvantages which have resulted to mankind from the judicious employment of slave labour in the Southern States of the American Union, it would be well to classify the different parties or interests which are at the present day banded together in hostile array against the States of the South, and which are now combined in support of the Republican party, each with the hope of accomplishing its own special purpose. To know who are the parties to a controversy often materially assists in directing the mind to correct conclusions in regard to the merits of the controversy itself. If a known adversary or rival urges me to perform an act, which he declares will result in great benefit to me, but which I perceive will be much more likely to yield advantages to him, I may be pardoned for at least postponing any action which would produce such result.

The anti-slavery party of Great Britain is conceded to be at the head of the hostile movement directed from abroad against the planting States of the South. Its partisans in America say that in this, their allies of England are influenced solely by considerations of philanthropy, benevolence, and an inborn love of freedom.

The plain outspoken matter-of-fact index of British public sentiment, the London 'Times,' furnishes in a late number, in brief but emphatic language, the key which affords an insight into the real motives that are thus slightly veiled under the assumed garb of benevolence and philanthropy. In discussing the importance of tropical productions as an auxiliary to British wealth and power, the 'Times' says:—

Now in England we say that the slave trade shall no longer be permitted to be carried on in any quarter of the globe, if by negotiation or by arms it can be repressed. In the case of the United States, indeed, we are compelled to content ourselves with the assurance that the American cruisers will do the work. *Will any one, however, say that it is not mainly owing to the ceaseless exertions, to the philanthropic energy, to the entreaties, to the persuasions of this country, that the Anti-slavery party in the States owes its strength? Blot out England, and English sympathies, and English power from the map of the world, and the battle between the North and the South would be fought on the other side of the Atlantic on very different terms.* Slavery shall not be in our own dominions, nor the slave trade anywhere if we can help it. Could we have gone a step farther and annihilated the peculiar institution in all other countries, as well as in our own, the problem would, in the main, have speedily received a satisfactory solution. This, however, was beyond our power, and consequently we find ourselves in this anomaly, that we, without a slave population, must compete in the markets of the world, with other countries which have slave populations, and that with respect to tropical productions.

This brief extract from the great London organ discloses the foundation upon which rests the hostility of the political Abolition party of England to slavery in America.

In considering the great issue involved in the present life-and-death struggle of the geographical sections in America—the one for political supremacy, the other to retain the control of its own domestic institutions — it is impossible for us to lose sight of the ever-present reality, that the adversaries of the South in America are fighting the battle in conjunction with the political Anti-slavery party of Great Britain. Although it is not to be supposed that the object of the great body of Americans who are enlisted in that conflict is primarily to achieve a triumph of their policy in the Republic, yet such would be the effect of a successful effort to impair by degrees, and finally to destroy, the institution of slavery in the Southern American States. But whatever may be the motives by which the great Anti-slavery party of England may be governed — however inconsistent may be their present attitude with that which Great Britain has in times past occupied — we are met face to face with the undeniable truth that this party is to-day the European leader of the anti-slavery movement against the Southern States. It is a fact, that its immense moral and social influence has been, and is still exercised with a view to create and to foster a public opinion throughout the civilised world adverse to the Slave States of the Confederacy. And it is also true that, partly through its instrumentality, and under its recognised leadership, a party has grown up hostile to the existing institution of American slavery and to the slave-holders, not only in Europe, but in the Northern States of the Confederacy, formidable in numbers, respectability, and influence. That this anti-slavery organisation in England should succeed in attracting to its views, and in infusing prejudices into the minds of others, where they, the unrelenting assailants, are always present, and where those who are assailed have no available means of defence, should not be a matter of surprise. But they even penetrate into the Confederacy itself, and there, as elsewhere, infuse their discordant principles into the hearts of native citizens of the Republic.*

* The following resolutions were adopted by the 'American Foreign Anti-Slavery Society,' thanking the people of Great Britain for the valuable aid received by them in furtherance of their war upon the South:—

'*Resolved*,—That we would express our deep gratitude to all those earnest men and women who find time and strength, amid their labours in behalf of British reform, to study, understand, and protest against American Slavery, to give us their sympathy and aid by munificent contributions, and by holding our Union up to the contempt of Europe, &c. &c.'

In order to account for the fact that the Abolitionists of Great Britain have been able to enlist in their interest so large a proportion of the literary men and women of New England, it must be borne in mind that, from the nature of their pursuits, they look with a sort of reverence upon England as the great fountain of English literature. They read English books, adopt English ideas and fashions, become imbued with English prejudices, and hence regard with partial vision all that emanates from that source. As the votaries of Fashion throughout the world cut their apparel, shape their hats, adjust their hair, and tie their cravats according to the dictum of the mantua-makers, milliners, and tailors of Paris, so does the class of literary men referred to, fashion its phrases and model its ideas according to the received standard of fashion in Great Britain.

It is under the intelligent direction of this class that the crude and fanatical ideas of the ultra schools of social reformers, which spring up through the immunity afforded by free government, are diverted from their impracticable general designs to the special

'*Resolved*,—That the discriminating sense of justice, the steadfast devotedness, the untiring zeal, the industry, skill, and genius with which British Abolitionists have cooperated with us for the termination of Slavery, demand our gratitude.

'From the Abolitionists of England, Scotland, and Ireland we have received renewed and increasing assurances and proofs of their constant and enlightened zeal in behalf of the American Slave. Liberal gifts from all of these countries, falling behind none of the most bounteous of former years, have helped to fill the scanty treasury of the Slave.'

purpose of swelling the power of the political adversaries of the domestic institutions of the Southern States.

These impracticable 'reformers' constitute the great body of those who desire, from perhaps honest and conscientious, though mistaken motives of philanthropy, to subvert the institution of Southern slavery, because its existence conflicts with the utopian principles upon which they think mankind should be governed. Their ostensible aim and real purpose are the same. However much it may be regretted that they will permit themselves to be the blinded instruments of gain-seeking men — however we may lament that obliquity of mental vision which would risk the hazard of so much evil for the doubtful prospect of achieving so little of good — still it would be unjust to deny or to doubt the sincerity of their convictions.

There is still another class in the Northern States of the Federal Union who engage in the clamour against what they denominate the 'slave power,' whose seeming opposition scarcely needs to be commented upon in enumerating the real antagonists of the institution of slavery, because their design is, not in reality to *destroy* slavery, but to *acquire a political supremacy* over the Slave States, and to *share with the planters the profits* of slave labour. I refer, of course, to the great manufacturing interests of

New England, and, I may add, of Pennsylvania. Wealthy beyond any other class, and employing their wealth in such manner as to give them great political consideration, they exercise a powerful and, I might say, a controlling influence in all local elections.

To a full understanding of the motives which impel this class of citizens to seem to seek what in reality they do not desire, a brief reference to the industrial pursuits of the different sections is necessary. The political power of the Confederacy may, in general terms, be said to be divided into two great classes, to wit, Manufacturers and Agriculturists. Upon any political question involving the interests of these, the other classes range themselves upon the one side or the other, as their interests, principles, or inclinations may suggest.

It has ever been the aim of the manufacturing interests to enforce, under various pretences, the payment of a portion of the earnings of the agriculturists into their coffers. Under the popular disguise of protection to home 'productions,' this system for a long time prevailed; and to this day our statute-books are disfigured by the relics of this most unjust system of forcing one class to contribute of their earnings to the wealth of another class. The doctrine of 'protection' became unpopular with the agriculturists in proportion as its true merits were discussed and understood. However the sacrifice they were called upon to make might be urged by appeals to their patriotism, an enlightened understanding could not fail to perceive that the real effect of such a system was to take away from the gainings of their labour, in order to add to the wealth of those who were already much richer than themselves. The numerical strength in this contest was in favour of the agriculturist, and in process of time the system fell into disfavour and into partial disuse.

For the manufacturers to wage a contest against such superior numbers, upon the direct issue, would be fruitless, because the combined South and West — both alike interested in protecting agriculture from such an unjust burden of taxes — would be able at all times to offer a successful resistance. The crusade against slavery, on the part of New England manufacturers, was designed, therefore, *to detach the great agricultural interests of the Free States in the West from their natural allies, the Southern States;* and thus, by dividing the adversaries of their favourite system, and creating between them an irreconcilable feud upon a collateral issue, conquer them in detail. Having wrought up the Western States to the proper pitch of enthusiasm against the existence of 'the great sin,' the manufacturers say, 'The best means of eradicating this evil is to build up the North at the expense of the South, by means of a protective tariff;' and they call upon the Western States to 'submit to a small pecuniary sacrifice,' for the attainment of so desirable a result. To the South they can say: 'See arrayed against you the moral power of Great Britain, exerting its ramified influence throughout the civilised world. Add to this the overwhelming, numerical, and political strength of the North and the West. It is not our wish to destroy you; therefore give us the protection we claim for our manufactures: that is, give us two bales of cotton of every ten you produce, and one-fifth of your annual products of wheat, and rice, and Indian corn, and we will find means to allay the storm which is ready to engulf you in irretrievable ruin.'

The scheme has been, unhappily for the interests of agriculture, but too successful. The protectionists have succeeded in attracting to their standard a large support in the Western Free States, where once the doctrine of free trade had complete ascendency; while the South, if she remains in the Union in the face of this overwhelmingly hostile array, which seems resolved to compass her destruction, is rapidly drifting to her only alternative of purchasing peace at the sacrifice demanded.

Considering the facts referred to, it would appear to be an error to suppose that the manufacturers, as a class, are in reality endeavouring to achieve the destruction of the institution of slavery. They only seek, through a protective tariff, to divide with the planters the earnings of slave labour; and they assail slavery with the view of making allies and instruments of the agricultural States of the West.*

Is there not danger that, in thus 'sowing the wind, they may reap the whirlwind?' It is easy to stimulate, but difficult to allay, the angry passions of mankind. A child may kindle a conflagration in mere wantonness, which a host may not afterwards be able to suppress. The voice of one gifted demagogue may incite a listening and attentive mob to deeds of violence and blood, which, once commenced, no eloquence could arrest. May it not be apprehended that, even in the hour of seeming success, they may reap a harvest of disappointment? Can the cautious calculating leaders of the Anglo-Republican alliance restrain the impetuosity and the zeal of the fanatical masses who have been attracted to their support by an appeal to passions which, in the flush of victory, are only to be gratified by the

* Since the foregoing was written there has occurred a striking verification of the opinion here expressed. Almost upon the instant of the withdrawal of a large number of Southern representatives and senators from the Congress, the Anti-slavery party, being thus left in a majority, adopted the 'Morrill Tariff Bill,' which, for its violation of every principle of free trade, and for its highly protective character, is unparalleled in the history of modern legislation anywhere in the civilised world. The controlling purpose of the political Anti-slavery party, which now holds possession of the General Government, appears to be, to deny to the South the privilege of commercial intercourse with any portion of the world beyond the limits of the Northern States, and thus to monopolise the lion's share of the profits of slave labour.

immediate enfranchisement of the slave and the destruction of the master?

Upon the occurrence of any event which would leave no room for doubt in the Southern mind that there existed a settled purpose, on the part of the powerful free North, to employ her political and numerical preponderance in destroying the institutions and the independence of the South, would the Southern States hesitate for a single instant longer in inaugurating prompt measures for their security and protection? Can it be expected that the South would delay until her enemies should have decided how and when the impending blow should fall?

Let not the peaceably disposed citizens of the North delude themselves with such a hope or expectation. Self-preservation is the strongest instinct of man's nature; and when the moment above indicated shall have arrived, if ever, it may fairly be assumed that the South will stand forth as a unit in defence of her rights, her interests, and her very existence as a political power in the State. All previously existing differences will disappear, and her united people will then and there demand that the battle shall be fought and decided. The issue of life or death will have been forced upon her, and the result will be the establishment of the independence of the South, or the immediate and unconditional liberation of the slaves. The conflict once inaugurated, what horrors may not fill up the interval to its bloody close!

Where, then, will stand the discordant parties and interests which have inaugurated this war upon the South? When the battle would be fiercest, and the issue the most doubtful, would England, in deference to the desires of her anti-slavery propagandists, stretch forth her arm to aid the North in the accomplishment of a victory, which would strike down at one blow that system of labour upon the products of which so many millions of her subjects are dependent for their daily bread? This interrogatory may not now be answered. She may hold herself in the position of an unfriendly neutrality towards both; but the England of to-day would not be the England of the past, if she permitted the sympathies or the sensibilities of her 'philanthropists' to mislead her at such a crisis.

As warmly as the political Abolition party of England has espoused the cause of the Republican party, it must not be supposed that they desire the immediate abolition of slavery in America, for such a consummation would find them unprepared to meet the crisis which would follow. Hence they have thrown their influence upon the side of the Republican party, under a tacit understanding among the leaders of each, that the process of abolitionising the South shall be sure but slow; thus affording what they believe will be ample time for Indian tropical productions to be augmented, as those in the Slave States of America diminish.

From this reference to the internal and external adversaries of the Slave States of America, it will be observed that they differ essentially in the immediate objects which they hope to accomplish when their victory shall have been achieved; and that there exists amongst them but a single element or class which may be fairly presumed to be actuated exclusively by conscientious and philanthropic convictions. This, however, is made up of the radicals, socialists, agrarians, and fanatics, both in religion and politics, to whose madness no response of reason would be available, but whose folly would of itself defeat their purposes but for the direction given to them by other, and cooler, and wiser heads.

But of all these opposing influences, it cannot be questioned that the London 'Times' is right in its rather boastful declaration, that if we were to 'blot out England, and English sympathies, and English power from the map of the world, the battle between the North and South would be fought on very different terms.' The indirect influence of the British Anti-slavery party in moulding public opinion without, and its direct influence within, in giving consistency, point, and unity to the efforts of those who, whether ignorantly or advisedly, perform for it the services of friends and allies, render it apparent that if the Southern States of the American Union can defeat the purposes of that party, the battle against their enemies is already half won.

I have thus hastily glanced at the different interests which are arrayed in hostile attitude against the Slave States, and I have referred impartially to what may be fairly presumed to be the moving cause of the opposition of each. In making these general classifications, however, I do not mean to say that there are not many individual exceptions, who are actuated by motives different from those which I have assigned as common to the party which seeks the overthrow of slavery in the South. But it is to be noted that all the enemies of the existing institution of slavery in the Southern States are from without. The assaults thereon emanate from those only who live under other governments—who are not themselves subject to the evils of which they complain, and who may perpetuate the exemption by remaining beyond the boundaries of its influence.

LETTER IV.

Opposition to abstract Slavery resolved into opposition to Slavery in America, without considering the circumstances of its existence—Slavery Romances have misled the Public Mind—The manifest injustice of crediting them as History—The attitude of the present adversaries of Slavery in times past—Achievements of African Slavery in America.

It is a truth not to be controverted, that the predominating sentiment of the civilised world at the present day is adverse to the existence of slavery. The instincts of an enlightened humanity are undeniably opposed to that condition of society which is supposed to exist as a necessary concomitant of slavery, and hence many are found to condemn its existence in America without duly considering that when two races so different and so unequal as those which inhabit the Southern American States are thrown together, there cannot be established between them the relations which may and should exist between different classes of the same race.

Under the lead and direction chiefly of the Anti-slavery party of Great Britain, this theoretical opposition to abstract slavery has been resolved most unjustly into a feeling of hostility to the institution known under that name, now existing in the United

States. This feeling has received from time to time fresh impulse from the slanderous publications of British tourists, who have more intellect than honesty, and a more ardent desire to reap a harvest of gold by pandering to the prejudices and vices of their readers, than the meagre rewards bestowed upon those who communicate unpalateable truths. Added to these are the productions which, with more or less of literary merit, have emanated from native Americans who desire by this means to ingratiate themselves into the favour of the British Anti-slavery party.

A discriminating mind, in estimating the value of these productions, should remember that they emanate *only from those who are wholly unacquainted by practical knowledge with the system they pretend to explain.* They are those whose whole lives have been spent in an atmosphere of hostility and hatred to the 'institution,' and who have visited for a brief period the locality where it existed, not to discover truth but from exaggerated and isolated facts to find material for the support of their theory out of which to fashion a 'selling book.'

Professedly illustrating the workings of the institution of slavery, all who are familiar with the subject know them to be slanders, and libels, and caricatures upon truth. Even as monstrous exceptions to the general condition of the slave and his master, every citizen of a Slave State knows that they have no existence except in the pernicious books referred to. Every unprejudiced, intelligent man who has had occasion to travel through the Southern States of America, has had reason to be astonished at the gross deception practised upon the public by these professional horror-mongers.

But even admitting for the moment that the fictitious characters so happily illustrated in these romances, whose imaginary wrongs have caused so many tears to flow from sentimental maidens and Abolition philanthropists, are the representatives of an existing reality; that they constitute exceptions to the general state of society, may be inferred from the fact that a knowledge of their existence remained unknown to the oldest inhabitants of the Slave States up to the moment when they were enlightened by these productions, the authors of which had probably never passed six months in a Slave State. How unjust to one's self, as well as to those who are thus wronged, to estimate the moral worth of the Southern States, or even the value of the institution of slavery, by these admittedly monstrous exceptions!

The gifted authoress of the most popular and most mischievous romance which has ever been published upon this subject, shortly after the public judgement pronounced her work a most brilliant success, visited England to receive in person the reward to which all acknowledged she was justly entitled at the hands of British Abolitionists. She was feasted and toasted in the aristocratic mansions of the great, and received the homage of the most distinguished British politicians. She returned after a season to her native land, and gave vent to her gratitude for the brilliant reception which had been accorded to her, by the publication of her 'Sunny Memories.' Suppose that she had entered England with the same feelings of hatred towards the aristocracy which she entertained towards the Southern citizens of her own country, and instead of taking up her abode in the palaces of the rich, she had entered the prisons where the vilest criminals were confined, and had promenaded the streets or penetrated into the dens of infamy and vice which, in certain localities, contaminate that great city; and out of the materials thus furnished, and with heroes and heroines thus discovered, she had published, after the prototype of Uncle Tom's Cabin, her 'Cloudy Memories' of London, as a true picture of English life, English habits, and English morals.

Unfortunately for the cause of justice, it is from materials even more meagre, and less illustrative of truth, that the diatribes against slavery are composed, upon which even many good men have allowed their opinions to be formed and their prejudices to be excited.

The Southern States of the American Confederacy rest under the serious disadvantage of being the subjects of assault emanating from those who entertain opinions upon the subject of Government the most widely variant; and unfortunately these extreme classes are those who act upon convictions of right without reference to any pecuniary interest which may be involved in the question.

The laws which recognise the existence of slavery, in their very nature and upon their very face deny the universal equality of the races of men. They assume that the African slave in America is not now, never has been, and never will be, a suitable companion or the equal of the white man, either socially or politically. Here then is a distinct issue, and an irreconcilable difference with, and an utter denial of, one of the most cherished doctrines of agrarian or radical Democracy. Hence the Southern States are assailed by all the 'isms' of the Old and New World. They are a target not only for those who advocate specifically the doctrines of Abolitionism, but for those also who, upon the baseless fabric of an impossible equality, have erected theoretical utopias in which the families of man of every clime, religion, and complexion may mingle together in a common brotherhood.

On the other hand, the Southern States and the institution of slavery are no less opposed by many of the leaders of that class in the Old World which claims to govern *the masses of their own race* by a right emanating directly from the Almighty!

In Great Britain, as well as in the more despotic governments of the Old World, the special advocates and defenders of the 'right divine' are leagued in a brotherhood of opposition to slavery in America, with all the fanatics of the New World, comprising the advocates of 'free love,' the 'Socialists,' the Infidels, the 'Red Republicans,' and 'Abolitionists,' whose crude notions of liberty and impracticable conceptions of government have contributed far more towards bringing discredit upon 'free institutions,' than in instilling into the minds of others the undeniable truths on which, to a certain extent, their pernicious theories are based. From those holding these extreme and apparently irreconcilable opinions in regard to the natural rights of man, have emanated the most virulent assaults upon the institution of American slavery.

A compilation of the creeds and platforms of the different anti-southern humanitarian societies of the North would present to unaccustomed eyes some very curious features, and would afford a wide field for reflection to their fellow-labourers of the Old World. For full accounts of the proceedings of these associations, the reader is referred to the Northern newspapers, they being too voluminous for insertion here. The distinctive characteristics of each, however, may be partially inferred from the titles they respectively assume.

The principles of the 'Agrarians,' by whatever particular title they may designate themselves, are the same as those of their European progenitors, except that in their American creeds they have added—'The exclusion of the South from the common territory, and the abolition of all political distinctions between the black and the white races.'

The 'Free Love' associations are the peculiar growth of Northern civilisation. In no other country have men and women been found ready to associate themselves together for the propagation in public of the peculiar tenets of this class of social reformers. Certainly in no other have they become an active power in the State, mustering their forces upon election day, for a demonstration against the barbarity of the marriage compact. As their name imports, they propose that such men and women as are 'attracted to each other by strong natural affinity shall live together as man and wife,' until time shall have developed a stronger affinity between one of the parties and another person of the opposite sex, upon the occurrence of which event the old connection is to be dissolved, and the new one created. They are opposed to the joint participation of the South in the territories of the Union, and in favour of the abolition of slavery in the Southern States.

The 'Woman's Rights' Associations are also spontaneous offshoots of Yankee civilisation, and flourish in their greatest vigour in New England. They embrace a very large proportion of the literary and 'strong-minded' women of the North, and many of the wives of distinguished politicians are the orators of their public meetings and anniversaries. They are formidable in numbers, intelligence, and zeal, and have exercised of late a powerful influence upon the manners, the opinions, and the principles of their countrywomen. They deny 'the right of man to have property in man,' as a general proposition, and are consequently opposed to the institution of domestic slavery in the South. They, upon the same principle, deny the right of 'men to have property in women,' and are in favour of conferring upon women the same political and social rights as are held and enjoyed by men. They propose that women shall have the exclusive control over their own property, and that the marriage relation shall confer mutual privileges, and be attended with mutual obligations between man and wife. They claim for women the right to vote in elections, and to be eligible to all offices under the Government. Although they have not been able thus far to accomplish the reforms they meditate, yet they have succeeded in arousing the public mind of the North to a serious contemplation of the radical changes they propose to inaugurate in regard to the previous relations of the sexes. Like all the other 'reforming societies' of their fellow-countrymen and country-women, they propose to strike their first and deadliest blows at the institution of domestic slavery in the South, under the impression that with the downfall of this great stumbling block in the way of 'equality and fraternity,' all minor obstacles will give way without a struggle, and that they will at once arrive at the fruition of all their hopes and aspirations. But the two bodies which may be regarded as the most formidable of all the enemies of the South, regarded as party associations, are the political clergy-men of New England, and the 'Free Germans.' The respect which is ever accorded to the authorised teachers of religion, added to the intelligence and learning of those referred to, give to their opinions a weight which is many fold greater than is enjoyed by any other class of citizens of equal number; while the latter are formidable on account of their great strength of numbers, and their consequent powerful influence in deciding the result of elections, in a country where the right of suffrage is accorded to all who have mouths to drink mean rum, rather than to those who have brains to vote understandingly. The impious claim made by these clergymen to speak in the name and by the express authority of, the Almighty, dele-gated to them on account of their holy calling, is scarcely less shocking to the sensibilities of good men and Christians, whose judgements have not been clouded by the sectional animosities which the struggle for political power has engendered, than is the openly avowed infidelity of the 'Free Germans.' The following protest, signed by three thousand and fifty clergymen of New England, which was presented to the Senate of the United States, on the 14th March 1854, in regard to an Act of Congress then recently passed, illustrate the spirit to which I have referred:—

To the Honourable the Senate and the House of Representatives in Congress assembled.

The undersigned clergymen, of different religious denominations, in New England, *hereby in the name of Almighty God, and in His presence, do solemnly protest* against the passage of what is known as the Nebraska Bill, or any repeal or modification of the existing legal prohibitions of slavery in that part of our national domain which it is proposed to organise into the territories of Kansas and Nebraska. We protest against it as a great moral wrong; as a measure full of danger to the peace and even the existence of our beloved Union, *and exposing us to the righteous judgement of the Almighty!* And your protestants, as in duty bound, will ever pray, &c.

Boston, Mass., March 1st, 1854.

A few days thereafter another protest of twenty-five clergymen was presented to the Senate of similar import, which says:—

The undersigned clergymen, of different religious denominations, in the North Western States, as citizens, *and as Ministers of the Gospel of Jesus Christ, hereby in the name of Almighty God, and in His presence, do solemnly protest* against the passage of what is known as the Nebraska Bill.

The protest further declares :—

> That *the ministry is the divinely appointed institution* for the declaration *and enforcement of God's will*, upon all points of moral and religious truth, and that as such it is their duty to reprove, rebuke, and exhort with all authority and doctrine.

Next in order come the Free Germans, co-labourers of the 'political parsons' of New England, in the cause of Southern Abolition, and general social reform. The organ of these (published in St. Louis), advocates the adoption and enforcement of 'the platform of the Free Germans of the Union,' in the following words :—

> The first and principal mark whereby we distinguish ourselves from religious people is, that in a belief on a God, and that which connects itself with this belief, we recognise a destructive cancer, which for thousands of years has been gnawing at humanity, and preventing it from attaining to its destiny. No individual can live as a human being—in no family can true happiness flourish—the whole human race is hastening on ways of error so long as the most abominable hobgoblins, 'God,' 'future existence,' 'eternal retribution,' are permitted to maintain their ghostly existence. It is, therefore, the greatest task of every genuine revolutionist to put forth his best powers for the destruction of the flagitious trio, viz., the hobgoblins, God, future existence, and future rewards and punishments. No revolution is more than half executed unless the *vi et nerve* of the great arch-monarch beyond the skies is cut asunder. Every attempted revolution is vain, if the ministers of this monarch are not exterminated, as we are wont to exterminate ruinous vermin.
>
> *Platform.*—The free Germans of the United States have found it necessary to organise themselves, for the purpose of being able to exercise a political activity proportionable to their number, and adapted to their principles. . . . They wish, after having

completed their organisation, to establish such a power of votes as to be able to decide the victory in favour of a party of true reformers.

Slavery Question.—Notwithstanding that we consider slavery to be a political and moral cancer, that will by and by undermine all Republicanism, we deem its sudden abolition neither possible nor advisable. . . . We demand that slavery be excluded from all new territories, indiscriminately, and for ever. We demand this the more, as a Republican constitution is guaranteed to every new State, and slavery cannot be considered a Republican element. . . . We demand that the Fugitive Slave Law shall be repealed. . . . We finally demand that in all national affairs the principle of liberty shall be strictly maintained, and even in the several States it be more and more realised by gradual extermination of slavery.

Religious Questions.—We consider the right of free expression of religious conscience untouchable; we therefore accord to the believer the same liberty to make known his convictions as we do to the non-believer, as long as the rights of others are not violated thereby. . . . Religion is a private matter; it has nothing to do with policy; hence it is despotism to compel citizens, by political means, to religious manifestations, or omissions contrary to their private persuasions. We therefore hold the Sabbath laws, thanksgiving days, prayers in Congress and Legislatures, the oaths upon the Bible, the introduction of the Bible into the schools, the exclusion of Atheists from legal acts, &c. &c., as an open violation of human rights, and demand their removal. . . .

Measures for the welfare of the People.—As the foremost of such measures, we consider the free cession of public lands to all settlers. To occupy nature, the soil, as exclusive property, this no individual has a right to do. . . . The welfare of a nation cannot be generally and permanently secured, unless the labouring classes be made independent of the oppression of the capitalist. In letting out state contracts, the preference should be given (if it can be done without running a risk) to associations of workmen, rather than to single contractors. In order that the attainment of justice may no longer remain a privilege for the possessors of money, justice must be dispensed without fees.

Constitutional Questions.—All elections, without any exception, should issue directly from the people.

Foreign Policy.—The policy of neutrality must cease to be an article of our creed. The rights of American citizens and emigrants, having declared their intention to become citizens, must be more energetically protected in foreign countries, since every American appears to monarchical and despotical governments as a representative of revolution against despotism; and the Republic ought to honour this point of view as the only one worthy and legitimate.

Rights of Women.—The Declaration of Independence says that 'all men are born equal and endowed with inalienable rights; and to these belong life, liberty, and the pursuit of happiness.' We adopt this principle, and are of the opinion that *women* too are included among 'all men.'

The '*platform*' of the 'Free Germans' in St. Louis, Richmond, Louisville, and elsewhere, are of nearly similar import. The Richmond platform is as follows, viz.:—

We demand—1. Universal suffrage. 2. The election of all officers by the people. 3. The abolition of the Presidency. 4. The abolition of senates, so that the legislatures shall consist of only one branch. . . . 7. All lawsuits to be conducted without expense.

Foreign Relations.—1. Abolition of all neutrality. 2. Intervention in favour of every people struggling for liberty.

Reform in what relates to Religions.—Abolition of laws for the observance of the Sabbath. Abolition of prayers in Congress. Abolition of oath upon the Bible. Repeal of laws exacting a religious test before taking an office.

Reform in the Social Condition.—Abolition of land monopoly.

Amelioration of the condition of the working classes. Establishing an asylum for superannuated mechanics. Granting a preference to mechanics before all other creditors. Taking possession of the railroads by the State. Supporting slave emancipation by Congressional laws. Abolition of the Christian system of punishment, and introduction of the humane amelioration system. Abolition of capital punishment.

I might furnish the 'platforms' of many other associations, each advocating its peculiar measure of 'reform,' yet all agreeing in opinion that to strike down what they are pleased to denominate 'the aristocratic oligarchy of the South,' must precede the full consummation of their schemes ; but those above referred to are sufficient to indicate the discordant and radical nature of the parties, which have agreed to adjourn all minor differences of opinion, in order to concentrate their united efforts against the domestic institutions of the South. When the Southern people consider that their fate in the Union depends entirely upon the votes of these men, all of whom are to them strangers and foreigners, who have no interest in their institutions, and whose passions have been stimulated against them, on account of their supposed aristocratic tendencies and habits, it will be manifest that the South must not hope much longer to evade or postpone a desperate struggle, in the issue of which all her vital interests will be involved.

This seemingly incongruous combination of discordant materials would, at a superficial glance, appear most unnatural; and such a unity of purpose between them might be accounted as accidental. A more thorough investigation of the subject of slavery in the United States, and of its practical bearing upon the social and political condition of the inhabitants, developes at once the natural causes which have produced this coincidence of feeling between those who are so widely asunder in their political principles. I may hereafter refer to these causes in detail. At present my purpose is simply to group together the elements and sources of that opposition against which the Southern States are called upon to defend themselves. While they have so many and such formidable adversaries, who have no practical knowledge in regard to the workings of the institution which they unite in condemning, who are in no manner responsible, morally or politically, for the sin — if it be one — of slavery, and whose motives even the most charitable will not ask us to admit proceed wholly from a principle of benevolence or philanthropy — it is a truth, which should not be without due influence, that in every State of the Confederacy where slavery exists there likewise exists a unity of opinion as remarkable for its undeviating and firm support of the existing relation between the two races as it is universal. The history of the world does not furnish an example of such unanimity upon any one subject, which has been so often and for so long a time a subject of active and thorough analysis and investigation. All conditions, all professions, all religions, agree that the institution of slavery in the Southern States, in consideration of all the circumstances under which it now exists, is right, morally and politically; and that the present relations of the two races, with such modifications as may in process of time flow naturally and imperceptibly therefrom, must be maintained at all hazards, so long as they occupy together the same territory.

When it is considered that of the European races resident in the Slave States but a comparatively small number are slave-owners, this unity of sentiment and opinion should have some weight with those who have themselves no practical knowledge on the subject, and who derive their information chiefly from the distorted descriptions of its avowed enemies, or from romances written by ingenious authors to make selling books.

Before an impartial tribunal, sitting in judgement to decide the question upon its merits, it would surely be regarded as a point worthy of consideration that those who testify against slavery, as at present existing in the Southern States, are ignorant from personal observation of its practical effects, because they do not live within the sphere of its influence; while, on the other hand, those who would testify in favour of the existing institution, and who will never consent that the relations at present subsisting between the African race and themselves shall be materially changed, are the citizens in mass, and, with scarcely an exception, who have passed their lives, and whose destinies have been cast, for good or for evil, where the institution has been established.

Such as I have described them are the adversaries and assailants — such are the defenders of slavery in the Southern States of the American Union. To the success of the former, it is necessary that they should establish — first, their right to decide what shall be the political and domestic policy of the States of the South; second, they must show that the institution of slavery has made the condition of the slaves worse than it would have been if they had never been placed in servitude; third, they must establish that more good than evil will result from its abolition; and lastly, it will be conceded, in consideration of the peculiar attitude occupied by the chief assailants, that they must show in what manner they can remunerate the owners for the sacrifices they will be required to make, should their slave property be set at liberty.

Even admitting that the responsibility for the existence of the institution of slavery does not rest with the present generation, it would still be asking too much to require the defenders of the Southern States to prove that their peculiar system of labour has attained to that point of excellence from whence there can be no improvement. All human institutions are imperfect: and it is not pretended that this forms an exception. That there are evils incident thereto is not to be questioned. It is sufficient, if it can be established, that more good than evil has resulted, and, in all human probability, will continue to flow from it; and that the results achieved through its instrumentality have tended materially to promote the general welfare of mankind, and that these same benefits cannot be obtained under any other system of labour which has been devised. That incidental evils may spring out of the system — that cruelties may be inflicted by the master upon the slave — that instances of inhumanity have occurred, and will occur, are necessarily incident to the relations which subsist between master and slave, as well as between father and child, husband and wife, master and apprentice, power and weakness; but if it can be established that such instances are only exceptional, and that the slaves, whose condition we are considering, are provided with more of the physical comforts of life — that they are less often overworked, and that, as a class, they are happier and more exempt from the ordinary ills of life than any like number of labourers in the world, of whatever race, colour, or nation, it would seem that those who are conscientiously opposed to slavery, upon the ground of its supposed inhumanity, should be satisfied to leave the matter where it stands.

Furthermore, although the public sentiment of the civilised world is averse to the existence of such a relation between man and man as master and slave, yet if, in addition to the manifold advantages to mankind which result from this institution, it can be established that the condition of the Africans, as slaves in America, is far better, in every essential particular, than that of any of their race ever has been, from the commencement of recorded or traditional history — that from barbarians and cannibals they have attained to a moderate degree of civilisation — that from heathen they have become Christians — that from a condition of wretchedness and misery they have become comparatively contented and happy — that having sprung from a race which has never achieved anything for the good of mankind — whose entire history furnishes not one single name which is associated with anything good — which has not in the past, in their native land, exhibited any qualities above the instincts of brutes—they have, nevertheless, through the instrumentality of the institution of slavery, been made to contribute, in an important degree, to the wants of the civilised world;—it is not demanding too much of an enlightened public sentiment to abate somewhat of the natural feeling of repugnance to the existence of this relation between man and man, in view of results so advantageous to the human race, and which are attended, incidentally, by so many blessings to those in whose cause so much unnecessary sympathy has been expended.

That the results enumerated have followed, and that they have been consequences of the existence of African slavery, is susceptible of easy demonstration. Nor will they be denied by those who have investigated the subject without prejudice, and with the single purpose of discovering the truth. But, unhappily, public opinion has been forestalled to a great extent, chiefly by those who have employed this instrument, not with a view to correct error and to propagate truth, but from the most sordid considerations on the part of some, and upon the part of others to gratify a feeling of unkindness and hatred towards those under whose auspices the products of slave labour have been made to contribute to the wants, the luxuries, and the comforts of the civilised world.

Instead of requiring the Southern States to prove

that their system of slave labour is without fault or blemish — instead of asking that it be tried by an ideal standard of abstract right, which will not allow the smallest evil with the greatest good — let us examine it simply as a human institution, with its good and its evil arrayed upon the one side and the other — 'nothing extenuate, nor set down aught in malice.' When we have looked into the leading features of its history, from its origin to the present day, and have marked out its achievements, for good and for evil, before we resolve upon its destruction, or even make up our minds to impair its strength and influence, let us compare it with all the other systems of labour which have been adopted by mankind, with a view to the achievement of the same results.

LETTER V.

Labour, the Foundation of the Wealth of Nations — Duties of Government — Declaration of Independence, and its correct Interpretation — Classification of Rulers, and the Governed — Names do not express the Qualities of Objects.

THE foundation of the wealth and prosperity of civilised nations consists in labour. It is of all the subjects which engage the attention of Governments the most important. The products of physical labour are essential to the greatness and power of any nation, whether it be the labour of her own subjects or citizens, or an appropriation of the labour of others for her aggrandisement.

Politically, there exist in every State two classes — those who govern, and those who are governed. When regarded in reference to all the relations which subsist between men towards each other, the latter class may be resolved into three, which are distinct and strongly defined in all the various relations of life.

There are in every civilised State — first the rulers those upon whom are conferred the right of establishing laws for the government of the great mass, who occupy the relation of subjects or citizens. In whatever manner this power is acquired, whether by inheritance, or the free choice of the governed, or by accidental circumstances, the duties of those who hold this important position are the same, however different in practice may be the performance. The foundation of these duties may, in general terms, be defined to be, so to govern as to confer the greatest sum of happiness upon those whose rights and interests are confided to them; that is, to confer the greatest amount of good to the greatest number, without infringing upon the natural or legally defined rights of any portion of those who may properly claim to be citizens. There are sacrifices to which the minority must submit in deference to the general good of the whole; but such sacrifices must, in all well-regulated governments, be founded upon recognised general principles, and can never be demanded, upon an emergency not fully provided for, unless in obedience to the universally recognised law of nature — self-preservation.

In the erection of a free government, as well as in the progress of its existence, the citizens have a right to admit or to deny to aliens or foreigners the full right of citizenship. Even though the government be founded upon the principle, that 'all men are by nature free and equal,' yet in its practical application it could only be intended to refer to those who were *specifically designated as citizens*. If such a principle in its broadest sense were accepted and adopted by a government, it would bear within itself the elements of a speedy dissolution. For the peace and well-being of society, there must be a degree of homogeneousness amongst its several members. Due regard must be had even to the prejudices of race, religion, and colour, to habits and to customs. It must be conceded, that however broad and comprehensive may be the principles upon which a government may be founded, its laws are *local* in their operation *as to territory*, and *specific* in their application as to *persons*. The Constitution of a free government, or the general principles on which by express or tacit consent a nation is to be governed, whether or not founded upon the principle of equality, is simply the article of agreement by which the parties to the contract or arrangement are to be governed, and is not designed to confer the privileges of the partnership upon any other persons.

The history of the establishment of the Government of the United States of America illustrates this general principle with perfect clearness. In the very inauguration of its independent existence, it is declared, that '*all men are created equal*, that they are endowed with certain *inalienable rights*,' that among these are '*life*, *liberty*, and the pursuit of happiness.'

It would be a most manifest injustice to the intelligence, frankness, and common sense of the distinguished patriots who, in the name of the people, incorporated these declarations in their first act of independence, to suppose that they intended them to be understood in a literal sense. In the first place, it cannot be said that any two men are 'created equal.' One is born the inheritor of riches, another of poverty; one strong, another weak; one intellectual, another stupid; and from the cradle to the grave these inequalities are perpetuated. But if we give to the expression a common-sense signification, namely: that all men who were then and there represented by them, and whose chosen agents they were, and in whose name they spoke, were desirous of establishing a Government *on the basis of a perfect equality of rights*, then it is the eloquent enunciation of a noble sentiment which the nations of the world might adopt with benefit to their subjects. Neither must we suppose that the authors of this famous declaration desired to express so absurd a sentiment, as that the rights of *life* and *liberty* conferred by the Creator were literally and truly *inalienable*. For in all civilised nations there must be a power, not only to *alienate* or to *deprive* a citizen of his *liberty*, but even of his *life*.

But the best commentary upon this sublime declaration of the general principles upon which the revolted colonies of Great Britain proposed to establish for *themselves* a new Government, and the surest means of arriving at a knowledge of the interpretation placed upon them by their authors, may be discovered in the specific laws and regulations which they founded in illustration of the principles thus announced.

Upon the establishment of the Constitution, those who were represented were the free citizens, of European blood, who had been the subjects of Great Britain, or who had participated in securing their independence. The preamble to that instrument declares that,

> We, the people of the United States, in order to form a more perfect Union, establish justice, insure domestic tranquillity, provide for the common defence, promote the general welfare, *and secure the blessings of liberty* TO OURSELVES AND OUR POSTERITY, *do ordain and establish this Constitution* for the United States of America.

It will thus be seen, that however general and comprehensive may have been the principles upon which the Government was based, yet in the very first act defining and applying these general principles, the *specific* purpose of the citizens in the formation of their Constitution is defined to be, *to secure the blessings of liberty*, not for mankind, *but for themselves and their posterity*.

So far from establishing, in a literal sense, the inalienable right of all men to liberty, Section 2, Article IV. declares:

A person charged in any State with treason, felony, or other crime, who shall flee from justice, and be found in another State, shall on demand of the Executive authority of the State from which he fled, be delivered up to be removed to the State having jurisdiction of the crime.

No person held to service or labour in one State, under the laws thereof, escaping into another, shall in consequence of any law or regulation therein, be discharged from such service or labour, but shall be delivered up on claim of the party to whom such service or labour may be due.

Section 9, Article I. declares, that,

The migration or importation of such persons, as any of the States now existing shall think proper to admit, shall not be prohibited by the Congress prior to the year 1808, *but a tax or duty may be imposed on such importation, not exceeding ten dollars for such person.*

The two last paragraphs refer to the Africans, who were or might be held as slaves. From these it will be observed, that the authors of the Declaration of Independence, and the framers of the Constitution, not only recognised the existence of the institution of slavery, but authorised its expansion by permitting the importation of more Africans with the view of reducing them to slavery, and gave to it a legally and constitutionally recognised existence by claiming the right to derive a direct revenue from the traffic.

There is scarcely an article of the Constitution which is not at variance with a perfectly literal construction of the mere words promulgated in the

Declaration of Independence. Not only was the servile condition of the African race fully recognised, but to Congress was reserved the right of declaring upon what terms foreigners, even of our own race, might be admitted to the rights of citizenship, with full authority to exclude them altogether from the exercise of those rights, or to dictate the terms upon which they might be permitted to reside in the country.

If Congress should to-morrow, in obedience to the will of the citizens, declare that no person born under a foreign government and not already a citizen, should be permitted thereafter to enjoy the rights of citizenship, who could say that the act would be in violation of any principle on which our Government is founded? The right to define the circumstances under which aliens may be made citizens, is an indispensable part of the sovereignty of a nation. This right of self-protection involves, as a necessary sequence, the privilege of total or partial exclusion, as the interests of the citizens may require.

Those who assume that *the words* of the Declaration of Independence should be construed literally; and in their application under the Constitution were intended to embrace all mankind, render a poor tribute to the sagacity or honesty of the fathers of the Republic, whose reason must have taught them that such a government would have been impossible;

and who in effect gave their sanction to laws which in all their parts, from the first clause of the Constitution to the last act of their illustrious lives, did violence to such an interpretation of their meaning and intention!

But, say the more reasonable advocates of a literal construction, 'There must of course be understood to be exceptions to the general application of these principles. In announcing that all mankind were born free and equal, it was not meant thereby, that the rights secured to our own citizens were necessarily incident to foreigners or aliens who might come amongst us. Nor was it meant, that the rights of all men to "life" and "liberty" were, as therein declared, literally inalienable, because it is essential to the good of society, that there should exist a power in the State to take away the life or the liberty of a citizen who commits certain crimes.'

This is certainly true, but if reason compels us, in justice to the authors of that work, and in obedience to the dictates of common sense, to admit that there are some exceptions to the universal application in practice of the general principles therein enunciated, by what rule of interpretation is it declared, that the exceptions enumerated above are all that can be permitted? In effect we discover by investigation, that not only do the laws and customs of every government admit of other exceptions than those referred to, but the constitutions and laws of every State of the Confederacy equally do violence to a literal construction of the rights of man as set forth in the instrument referred to—as an example, the universally recognised right of a parent to the services of his offspring up to the age of twenty-one years, and the similar right of the husband to the services of the wife during her entire life. Thus we find, that probably two-thirds of the citizens of America are, by the universally recognised laws of the land, and without the pretence of crime, held as 'chattels' bound to service and labour, without any fixed compensation. Others virtually occupy towards them in the estimation of the law the relation of master.

But there are still other cases in which the Constitution and laws of the United States, as well as the laws of all other organised governments, deny even to free-born citizens of mature age, unstained by any imputation of crime, the 'inalienable right' to the enjoyment of life and liberty! The farmer may be taken from his plough, the mechanic from his tools, the merchant from his desk, and all be forced to leave family and friends, and march at a moment's notice to face death upon the battle-field, even though his judgement and inclinations may oppose the war in which his country may be engaged. Against his will, and in violation of his personal interests, and without having done a crime, his inalienable rights, according to the literal phraseology of the Declaration of Independence, are violated ! Yet what sane man would not admit that this constitutes another proper occasion for the refusal to recognise the existence of the 'inalienable right' to either 'liberty' or 'life?' But as if in very mockery of their own interpretation—or to show to the world how utterly they in practice set at nought and deride the rule which they would apply to the South, a portion of the Northern Free States, by constitutional provisions or by prohibitory laws, deny to all persons of African blood the right even to cross their borders. If any negro should rashly violate this law, he is heavily fined and sent beyond the limits of the State. If he is unable to pay the fine, he is sold at public auction to whosoever will pay the amount assessed for the shortest term of service. In the greater number of the Free States the African is allowed to reside, but is perpetually debarred the enjoyment of any of the rights of a citizen ; while in all he is regarded, by the manners of the people, if not by the laws, as an outcast, an alien, and almost an outlaw.

Let us then do justice to common reason, to the signers of the Declaration of Independence, and to the framers of the Constitution. Let us consider that acting in the *name* and as *the representatives* of the revolted provinces of Great Britain, become free by their glorious deeds, the general principles which they enunciated were designed, in their practical application, *for those only whose agents they were, and in whose name they spoke*, namely: *the free white inhabitants* of the sovereign States they represented, *for* THEM *and for their* POSTERITY! Then there is found to be a sublime harmony in the principles they declared, and in the practical application of those principles, worthy, in all time to come, of the admiration of that posterity for whom were thus secured and consolidated the blessings of liberty.

But to resume the subject from which I have for a brief space digressed. The subjects or citizens of the State may be divided in general terms into three strongly defined classes.

First—Those who neither labour nor give direction to labour; who are possessed of the means of support without being obliged to resort to the drudgeries of labour or trade, and who have come into the possession thereof by inheritance—by superior intellectual endowments, or by accidental circumstances.

Second—Those who give direction to labour; who do not actually produce by their own hands, but who make available the results of the labour of others. These occupy the station of intermediaries between the consumers and the producers—between those who labour and those who purchase the products of labour.

Thirdly—The great mass of mankind who, from necessity or choice, give sustenance to the world by the labour of their hands; who cause the earth to bring forth its fruits to feed the hungry; who produce the material to clothe the naked; who fashion the ships to transport the products of one country to another, and who, in fine, produce all that which is employed in ministering to the physical comforts, the convenience, and the luxuries of the human race. Upon this last class depend not only the greatness and wealth of empires, but the very existence of all the other classes which go to make up the aggregate of a nation. Production is necessary to the wealth of a nation. Wealth is an essential element of power, and power is indispensable to the protection of independence and liberty from external violence. Every dollar of value added to the productive industry of the State, adds to the wealth and security of its citizens. The cotton bales produced upon the Southern plantations by slave labour, as well as the barrels of flour which repay the toil of the free labourers of the West, alike contribute to the wealth of New England. They are soldiers, fully armed for the defence of the Republic, but powerless for harm to its citizens.

That Government is therefore best, without reference to its form or name, which confers the greatest amount of happiness upon all its citizens, and which at the same time encourages and induces the greatest amount of production. The history of the world has exhibited that the benefits conferred by governments upon mankind are not always indicated by the name or the political form by which they have been known or designated.

The free republics of Southern America, regarded as a whole, have proven to be unworthy and incapable of fulfilling the legitimate ends of government. Anarchy, imbecility, and at times the most odious tyranny, have marked their downward progress from the date of their independent existence even up to the present moment of time, when some of them have almost ceased to be regarded as among the family of nations.

The labouring classes of France, under some of her most despotic rulers, have been left in the enjoyment of the greatest amount of real liberty and prosperity; while perhaps the most cruel despotism under which that beautiful country has ever groaned, was during the brief period of the first republic, when the very name of liberty was made odious by its excesses—when the blood and tears of millions of her citizens deluged the land; and when the civilised world stood aghast and horror-stricken at the contemplation of scenes enacted in the name of freedom, as fiercely cruel and despotic as had ever in times past distinguished an epoch in the career of any other civilised nation.

In the United States of America, upon the other hand, there exists a confederated republic where, according to theory and practice, up to the present period in its history, human liberty is happily blended with human progress, and where the two have marched hand in hand together. In all its acquisitions it has conferred upon the conquered the boon of its own political institutions, and has made them equal participants in the benefits thereof, and in the advantages of its growing power.

How can the anti-slavery American who contemplates the achievements of the infancy of the republic, attempt to destroy one of the chief elements of its greatness, for the doubtful prospect of accomplishing even all the good they hope for? Alas! that the thirst for present gain, or the madness of sectional hatred, should close the eyes of so many worthy and patriotic citizens, to the danger of taking even one more step in the direction which their avarice or their passions — not their reason — are leading them.

The brief reference made to well-known facts of history illustrates simply that neither the name nor the form of a government indicates, with positive distinctness, the degree of real liberty or prosperity enjoyed by its subjects. A despot even might confer upon his subjects all the liberty they desire, while the citizens of a republic, by a perversion of the principles of such a government, or an unwarrantable exercise of power on the part of a majority, or by the still more available despotism of a dominant section, may be made to endure the most odious tyranny.

While this is true in affairs of State, it is equally so in many of the affairs of life. Theorists are too apt to draw conclusions from the *names* of things, rather than *from the things themselves*—from the shadow rather than the substance. Even moralists are but too prone to direct their anathemas against theoretical, rather than real vices; against the garments which might seem to indicate the presence of vice, rather than against vice, which may clothe itself in the habiliments of virtue.

He who seeks to find truth, who aspires to arrive at just conclusions, without giving undue influence to his own mere prejudices or those of others, should remember that the names of things are not always even shadows of the objects they profess to describe; that the mere characters which designate a particular object, have nothing to do in making up the qualities of the object itself; and that theories, beautiful in themselves, and seemingly susceptible of the clearest demonstration, are often wofully at fault when applied to the practical affairs of life.

LETTER VI.

Different Systems of Labour considered — Free Labour more or less dependent upon Capital — Southey on English Labour System — Products of Slave and Free Labour compared.

SINCE on the productions of labour rest the foundations of the wealth and power of nations, it is a question of controlling interest for governments to decide how, and under what form, the greatest amount of production can be obtained, consistently with the well-being and happiness of those who labour, and the general prosperity of all. Although each nation has a more direct interest in its own productions than in those of others, there is a community of reciprocal interests as well as obligations among the family of nations, which make the proceeds of the labour of each important to the others. A State therefore should encourage and foster any particular branch of production in which it possesses natural advantages, not only for its own sake, but also for the promotion of the interests of mankind.

In general terms there may be said to be two classes or systems of labour, namely: that which is more or less voluntary, according to circumstances, and which is denominated 'free labour,' and that which is involuntary or forced, which is called 'slave labour.' That these titles or names afford no clear indication of the relative happiness, comfort, or even freedom of those who are ranked respectively under one or the other of the above designations, is susceptible of easy demonstration by reference to past and now existing facts.

Strictly speaking, there can scarcely be said to be such a thing as free labour, when applied to the great mass of mankind who are obliged to bestow their physical services for an employer in order to procure the bread necessary to sustain life. Take as an example the great body of operatives throughout the civilised world. *They must work or starve!* They must perform certain tasks which are placed before them, or must submit to a deprivation of the common necessaries of life. Not only must they accomplish these tasks at the bidding of another, but having received the scanty wages which are said to be their due, and having purchased therewith the coarse fare which is necessary to appease the pangs of hunger, they have nothing left for the morrow; and so day by day the same alternative is presented to them — *to do the task assigned them or to starve. The labourer has the physical power* to stay away from the workshop, but *the alternative* is ever present to him. Nature asserts its dominion, and again and again, until life's end, he voluntarily returns to his daily and never-ending toil. This is denominated free labour! The illustration will not be said to be an exaggeration. It does not even convey to the mind a picture so sad as the reality, in the case of more than a majority of the day-labourers of Europe. I have referred only to strong men, not helpless women and children, whose necessities are all the greater for their weakness, and whose weakness makes them still more dependent and still oftener the subjects of injustice and wrong. All who have investigated the subject know that these are the alternatives and conditions upon which free labour is performed by a body of human beings, even in free and enlightened England, more numerous than the entire number of slaves in America.

I only refer to this state of things as a fact which none will deny. Not by way of complaint; for it may be an unavoidable evil attendant upon an over-crowded population. But it serves as a definition of what is meant by 'free' in contradistinction to 'slave labour.'

It is not my purpose in these letters to adduce specific proofs in regard to all the facts which I assume to be true. I intend to deal with the subjects frankly, and in reference chiefly to general principles. In illustration of these principles I will adduce only such truths as will be readily admitted by the intelligent reader. To mis-state, or even to exaggerate these facts would be only to weaken the cause which I defend; and to illustrate the operations of a general system of labour by its exceptions, would be to imitate the injustice which has been so much practised by the writers as well as the readers of anti-slavery romances. I neither mean to deny the evils which are incident to the institution of slavery upon the one hand, nor the great benefits which have resulted to mankind from free labour upon the other. But I do mean to say and to prove that both systems, as mere human institutions, are attended in their practical developments by both good and evil. That neither one is adapted to all the wants of man, nor to all the productions of the earth. And that the institution of slavery in America has produced, under the intelligent guardianship of the present generation, more of good to mankind with less of evil to the African or of injustice to any, than either one of all the various systems of free labour which have been adopted as substitutes therefor, since the termination of the American war of Independence.

Southey thus describes the condition of the free labourers of England:—

> In no country can such riches be acquired by commerce, but it is the *one* who grows rich by the labour of the hundred. The hundred human beings like himself, as wonderfully fashioned by nature, gifted with the like capacities, and equally made for immortality, are sacrificed *body* and *soul*. Horrible as it must needs

appear, the assertion is true to the very letter. They are deprived in childhood of all instruction and all enjoyment of the sports in which childhood instinctively indulges — of fresh air by day and of natural sleep by night. Their health, physical and moral, is alike destroyed; they die of diseases induced by unremitting task-work, by confinement in the impure air of crowded rooms, by the particles of metallic or vegetable dust which they are continually inhaling; or they live to grow up without decency, without comfort, and without hope — without morals, without religion, and without shame, *and bring forth slaves like themselves to tread in the same path of misery.* . . .

The English boast of their liberty, but there is no liberty in England for the poor. . . . When the poor are incapable of contributing any longer to their own support, they are removed to the workhouse. I cannot express the feelings of hopelessness and dread with which all decent people look on to this wretched termination of a life of labour. . . . To this society of wretchedness the labouring poor of England look as their last resting-place on this side of the grave; and rather than enter abodes so miserable, they endure the severest privations as long as it is possible to exist.

These are the words of an Englishman, who understood the subject about which he wrote. But still it would be an error to suppose that there is no liberty, even for the poor in England. On the contrary, in many of the essential elements of freedom, our own Constitution and laws are founded upon the Constitution and laws of Great Britain. The evils to which reference is made grow naturally out of that system of free labour which is a consequence of the present systems of civilised governments throughout the world; and though they exist to a greater extent in England, with its over-crowded population, than in America, still they follow, as an unavoidable sequence to laws which recognise the rights of property.

I have before me the voluminous reports of the Parliamentary Committee, which, a few years ago, investigated the condition of the labouring poor of England. Large as are the volumes which contain the result of this investigation, covering thousands of pages, each page is a record of misery, destitution, hardships, and crime, which can scarcely be contemplated without a shudder of horror. Is there any remedy for the evils thus detailed? Can laws be enacted by which they may be eradicated? Practical philanthropy must answer, that while they may be ameliorated, yet so long as one man is very rich, and five hundred are very poor, they cannot be eradicated. So long as the laws permit all men to accumulate wealth, there will be five hundred who are poor to one who is rich. What interest has *the one man* in the fate of the *five hundred*? First, to avail himself of their labour at the lowest possible remuneration; second, to obtain, in the shortest possible space of time, the greatest possible amount of labour. When the work is finished, or when the labourer is physically unable to work any more, the interest of the employer ceases. The estate of the rich man in the sinews of the poor terminates, and then the workhouse claims its prey!

But away with statistics and printed testimony. I appeal to the judgement and common sense of every intelligent reasoner. I appeal to the indelible record, written in ineffaceable characters upon the heart of every observant traveller in Europe and the more civilised portions of Asia, for the exact truth of what I am going to say.

One half of the free labourers of the so-called free States of the world, at this very moment of time, men, women, and children, are in a state of moral and physical destitution. One half of these earn a most scanty subsistence by performing the tasks which are set before them by a nominal employer, but a real master! The other half of this unhappy class, unable to work, or to obtain work, *are driven to the practice of the most loathsome vices*, not from choice, but from an inexorable necessity! One half of the free labourers, who are in a condition something better than these, are nevertheless obliged, by the greatest of all tyrants, necessity, to labour and toil at the bidding of a superior for their daily sustenance, with the ever-present consciousness weighing upon their minds and spirits, that if sickness, for a single day, intervenes, their scanty wages will be stopped. If their disability is of long continuance, starvation, or the workhouse, are ever before them as alternatives.

This classification of the free labourers of the world assumes that one-fourth are in a position of independence, in which they may, to a greater or less extent, discuss with their employers the terms upon which they will bestow the labour of their hands. Is there an intelligent candid observer who will say that I have made too low an estimate of these, or that I have exaggerated the number of the dependent and destitute?

To the ignorant it is sometimes not well to tell the whole truth. A good cause is often weakened by endeavours to force too much knowledge upon those who are incapable of understanding. The mind naturally rejects all the testimony in favour of any proposition, if a portion thereof seems to be an exaggeration, a misapplication, or a misstatement.

But, just as surely as water becomes hard like stone in a certain temperature, do the inequalities recognised by the laws of all civilised nations of the present day, in the relative wealth of the different classes, produce that virtual slavery which, however disguised under attractive names, is *still the subjection of one man to the will of another.* It flows naturally and of necessity out of that condition and organisation of society which we call civilisation; and in order to realise in practice the theory of perfect equality and fraternity upon which 'abolitionism' rests for its foundation, mankind must be reduced to a common condition of barbarism. The laws of nature, however, are all against such a consummation. Heaven has bestowed upon members of the same race widely different capacities, which each is ready to acknowledge in some form; while the distinctions in different races are even more strongly marked. These differences and distinctions cannot in practice be obliterated, or even essentially modified, unless the Almighty first changes what has been hitherto an invariable law of nature. Nor can the African slave in America ever occupy permanently a position of equality with the superior race by which he is surrounded, because the superior race could, and in process of time would, reassert the supremacy with which it is endowed by nature. If it be admitted that the African cannot, and should not, be made the equal of the Anglo-Saxon socially and politically—a proposition which no sane man of European blood would controvert if his destiny were cast in that land where the two races have been brought together—the only question which remains to be decided, in fixing upon the *status* of the African, is one of mere detail, involving no principle which would justify the interference of foreigners. Instead of making themselves unhappy about the fate of the Africans in the far away wilds of the American continent, our philanthropic kinsmen of England, at least, should rejoice, and be proud, that under the benignant and humane control of a portion of their race and kin, these slaves have been made happy and contented with their lot, and that, through the instrumentality of this agency alone, they stand at the head of their race in the march towards civilisation.

Great Britain, in many respects, stands foremost among the great Powers of the world. Of all the governments of the Old World, her Constitution and her laws embody the noblest principles. The press is free, and the complaints of any class of citizens may be spread before mankind without hindrance from any quarter. She stands foremost in the rapid march of improvement, which has signalised the present generation. Her governing classes, and her subjects, taken collectively or individually, are, in many respects, worthy of the highest respect of mankind. It is, therefore, fair to consider that the condition of her free labourers is at least equal to the average of the free labourers of the world. Now, when I declare that in the estimate I have made, if I have exaggerated at all, it has been in assuming the class of labourers which enjoys a partial freedom as larger than the facts would warrant, I know that I am sustained by the documentary testimony published by Parliament; and I am sure that every enlightened and candid Englishman, who has made himself acquainted with the subject, will not hesitate to admit the truth of what I have said.

So far, then, as regards one half of the labourers of the world, free labour may be defined to be the inalienable right of the subject to starve, rather than perform the tasks which are commanded by a master. It is certainly a glorious privilege; but alas for the weakness of poor human nature, few are found willing, by accepting voluntarily of the alternative, to prove themselves martyrs in the glorious cause of freedom! We may pity them for their weakness, we may weep over their sad fate, but we cannot blame them for preferring to obey the instincts of nature rather than the promptings of manhood.

Far be it from me to say that it would be proper to take away fron the free labourer this glorious birthright of liberty, poor as it is, at a moment when infirmities and want are pressing upon him. Nor do I mean to express the opinion that the introduction of a more humane system would under existing circumstances, be practicable. But I do mean to say, that all the different systems of labour which are in operation throughout the world are attended with evils. If each nation would therefore endeavour, with an honest purpose, to modify or remove these from their midst, instead of seeking tò reform their neighbours, true philanthropy and benevolence would be much the gainers.

Although it may be assumed that in certain latitudes and under certain circumstances (both of which conditions are fulfilled in the Southern part of the continent of America), African slave labour is the best, the mildest, and the most humane of all other systems, yet it is not pretended that the interests of mankind require that it should be universal. Common reason teaches that the same rule or system of labour cannot be applied to the over-crowded continent of Europe and to the sparsely populated wilds of tropical America. Neither can the human race be generalised in such manner as to apply the same fixed rules of government to all. There must be an adaptation between them; laws sufficiently stringent to answer all the purposes of society, when applied to certain communities, would prove wholly insufficient under a different state of circumstances, for the protection of the weak, the peaceable, and the well-disposed, against the encroachments of the wicked and the strong.

Free labour in Europe may accomplish all that could be desired in regard to material developement, because not to labour is to starve. But in tropical countries such an inducement to work is wanting, because a bountiful nature almost spontaneously produces all that is necessary to the absolute physical wants of man. Therefore when the alternative is presented to a freeman to labour or not to labour, he chooses the latter, for the very sufficient reason that he can subsist without it. There is no fact more clearly established by actual experiment, than that neither the European nor any race of freemen can or will labour successfully in tropical climates. Even in the more temperate latitudes of the Southern States of the American Union, the articles of tobacco, cotton, rice, and sugar have only been successfully produced in large quantities through the instrumentality of slave labour.

Should, therefore, slave labour be abolished, and real free labour be substituted therefor, tropical productions must, to a great extent, cease to contribute to the necessities or to the luxuries of mankind; or they would at least, from their limited production, be attainable only by the wealthy classes.

The philanthropist should bear in mind that the greater part of that soothing beverage prepared from the coffee bean, which is alike the cheap luxury of the rich and the solace of the humble and the poor of every land, *is the product of slave labour.* The cane sugar and the syrups, which from their cheapness have become accessible to the poor, and which may be found in every labourer's cottage in America, and to a great extent throughout the world, are alone made accessible to them through the instrumentality of slave labour. To these may be added the articles of rice and tobacco, the use of which has become almost universal among the great body of labourers throughout the world. Cotton, by means of which mankind is clothed, is the product of slave labour.

From the single Slave State of Brazil alone there is an annual importation of coffee into the United States of about *one million of bags*, valued at fifteen millions of dollars. It is consumed by every family, and by almost every inhabitant of the Republic.

Of the cane sugar which is exported from the countries where it is produced, for foreign consumption, about seven hundred thousand tons are the result of slave labour! Less than five hundred thousand tons are the product of Asiatic and African races, subjected to the European Powers, while the entire product of free labourers of the European races, sold in foreign markets, would not supply the necessities of the city of Boston alone!

Of cotton, the product of the world offered for sale in the European and American markets is now about four and a half millions of bales; nearly four millions of which are produced by the Southern States of the American Confederacy, something more than half a million by subjugated Asiatics and Africans; while that produced and sold by free labourers of the European races would not supply a manufacturing township of Massachusetts!

He whose heart throbs with a single generous or benevolent sentiment towards the labouring toiling millions of poor, may well for an instant pause, and ask himself if it is the part of true philanthropy to strike off, at one blow, so many of the few comforts which their limited means permit them to enjoy? I know that it is difficult for him who has at command the ready means to purchase all that his appetite craves, without regard to cost, to imagine that the deprivation of one or two simple articles can amount to any great sacrifice. But such should remember, that while they may procure substitutes, the poor have no such resource. While they, by means of their wealth, may still supply themselves with the articles referred to, even at their enhanced value, they have only been made accessible to the poor by means of their cheapness, and their use must be abandoned when they become dear.

Upon a memorable occasion, a number of the inhabitants of Boston, in defiance of British power and British interests, heroically entered the English ships which lay in their harbour, and cast into the sea the tea of which their cargo consisted. The patriotic citizens refused to enjoy an article of luxury, which they conceived could only be procured by a submission to an unlawful act of tyranny on the part of their rulers. This noble sacrifice of their appetites to their patriotism was noised abroad in every land. It has been the fruitful theme of the poets' songs, and is the bright spot in the pages of her annals over which the historian loves to linger. To this day, the

Bostonian refers to the act of sacrifice, as the most brilliant and enduring testimony of the patriotic devotion of his ancestors to the cause of freedom. Although the deprivation was only to exist during a brief season, the world has not for this cause abated its admiration for the heroic achievement over their appetites.

The anti-slavery party of to-day demands that the toiling millions of mankind shall strike off for ever, from the list of their comforts and their necessaries, the products of slave labour. How vast the difference in the sacrifice made by the Bostonians and that which is thus required from the poor of the world!

Compare the products of slave labour, and the uses to which they are applied, with some of the more important achievements of so-called free labour, in the same field.

England developes the sublime system of free labour, by forcing a poisonous drug upon millions of the human race. The slave labour of the Southern States of the American Confederacy sends forth its four millions of cotton bales to every quarter of the globe, to clothe the naked.

New England distributes, among other of the great productions of her free labour, throughout the world, that liquid fire which burns out the honour, the morals, the health, the lives of all who come under its pernicious influence; spreading crime, and misery, and degradation in every land. Slave labour offers, in lieu of this hellish draught, that mild, and soothing, and healthy beverage, which is alike the solace of the palace and the cottage.

Far be it from me even to desire to depreciate the magnificent results of free labour, both in England and America. In the developement and expansion of the mechanic arts, and in their application to the wants of man ; in the vast improvements which have been introduced into almost every employment of civilised nations, *both* are in advance of any other and of every age, of which history affords us a knowledge. As an American and an Anglo-Saxon, I am proud of these great achievements ; but as a Southerner, born in a land to which slavery has been transmitted as an inheritance, for good or for evil, I am prouder still that the products of this slave labour have supplied raiment, and food, and other comforts for the rich and the poor of every land; *while no single commodity* which has been sent forth to the world *has contributed, in the smallest degree, to increase the vices or miseries of mankind.*

We have been taught in the holy Book to judge of the tree by its fruits—of men by their acts—and may we not be allowed to judge of systems by their results? Shall mankind be for ever fettered in its judgement by a reverence for mere names, or by respect for mere theories? Shall we reserve all our anathemas against vice for the garments in which our fancy may clothe it? Or shall the wolf in sheep's clothing be suffered to enter among the flocks and herds, because we do not choose to look beneath the garb of innocence which guilt assumes to hide its criminal intent?

LETTER VII.

Unfavourable results of Emancipation by England — Beneficial results of Slave Labour in the United States — Comparison of the condition of the Slave and Free States of the American Continent — Great importance attached by England to tropical productions — The interests of England and the Planting States identical.

I HAVE assumed as facts — that slave labour has supplied for the use of mankind the necessary articles of cotton, sugar, tobacco, rice and coffee — that free labour never has succeeded in producing them — and I have inferred that if slave labour should be abolished, the great mass of those for whom the consumption thereof has become almost a necessity, would be obliged to abandon their use altogether.

If any practical proofs are desired to establish the want of adaptation of the European races, or of free labour, to the purposes of production in the tropics, it has been amply demonstrated by the results which have followed the abolition of slavery in the Colonies of England and France, and in the present condition of the Governments of the New World.

In all South America, the only Government which has attained to any great political importance is Brazil.

It is the only nation which has kept pace in its improvements with the advancement of the world, and it is the only independent Government on the American Continent, except that of the United States, where slavery has not been abolished.

The institution of domestic slavery has existed in the United States of America from a period long anterior to its independent existence as a nation, up to the present moment of time. Never in recorded history is there evidence that any other country or any other people have made such rapid advances to greatness, wealth, and power. While it is not contended that this result has been wholly achieved through the instrumentality of the institution of slavery, none will deny that the productions of slave labour have contributed powerfully and materially to its accomplishment.

This fact is fully established by the exports of domestic produce to foreign countries. Although the population of the free States is as about two to one over that of the slave States, yet the exports from the slave States during the last year (1859) amounted in value to nearly two hundred millions of dollars, while the entire exports of the free States fell short of eighty millions. The value of the cotton alone exceeded one hundred and sixty millions. Although these aggregate amounts will be doubtless increased in the present year (1860), yet these exhibit the relative exports of the two sections. This immense sum goes to the enrichment of the entire nation, and, in some shape or other, finds its way into almost every county in every State in the Confederacy. Politicians may talk flippantly of sacrificing this great interest 'upon the altar of freedom,' and fanatics and vain theorists may be really ready for the sacrifice; but unless common sense be entirely banished from the land, or lost in the mad passions excited by sectional hatred, it is still to be hoped that enough of true Americanism is left to prevent even one more serious movement in that direction.

These productions of the Southern States have not only entered largely into the consumption of the inhabitants of the earth, but they have given employment to millions of labourers, whose daily bread is dependent upon the supply of cotton. These products of slave labour are necessary to the happiness, the prosperity, almost the very existence of society itself, as at present organised throughout the civilised world.

On the other hand, look at the picture of desolation, anarchy, and thriftless imbecility which have marked the history of the Governments of Mexico and Central America. A fairer or a more productive clime is scarcely to be found upon the earth. There, Nature has lavished her choicest, richest bounties.

With a soil as productive as any in the world—a climate, which, with such a soil, produces almost spontaneously the best fruits of the earth—from one extremity of this favoured land to the other, the eye wanders in vain in search of a single spot which has been made to yield of its abundant capacities to the wants or the luxuries of civilised man.

These results cannot properly be attributed to their political institutions; for upon the one hand, we have the example of the Republic of the United States, with a form of government similar, in all essential particulars, to those of Central America and Mexico; and upon the other hand, we have the example of the Monarchy of Brazil, where, as previously stated, a comparatively rapid progress and developement have been made. Neither can the result be ascribed to the alleged degeneracy of the Spanish-American race, for there is no evidence that they are inferior to the Portuguese inhabitants of Brazil. Moreover, such an assumption is proved to be unfounded by the present condition of the inhabitants of the Island of Cuba. These are of the same race and of the same religion, and they inhabit a country similar in climate, soil, and productions to that favoured land occupied with such fruitless results by the inhabitants of Central America and Mexico. Under all the disadvantages of her political condition—governed as she is and has been for the benefit of a foreign master, with no special evidences of paternal fondness, the Island of Cuba has still contributed materially to the supply of mankind with those tropical productions, which, from being at one time luxuries attainable only by the rich, have become necessaries all over the civilised world, for all classes of society.

This brief reference to the relative condition of the governments of America, and the comparative prosperity of the inhabitants, exhibits the fact that in every portion of that great continent where African slavery exists, without reference to the form of the government, prosperity prevails, and the lavish bounties of nature have been made available to the wants of man. While, upon the other hand, wherever the institution of slavery does not exist, in all that region where sugar, coffee, cotton, and rice form the staple productions, or where slavery has been violently abolished, ruin, decay, and desolation have been the result. The fruits which a bountiful Nature has placed within their grasp remain ungarnered—ungathered! So far as the rest of mankind are concerned, the very land itself might be blotted from existence without material loss or regret, except for the hope that something may be hereafter done to elevate it to that rank among the nations of the earth which Nature seems to have designed that it should occupy.

But it is not alone among the independent governments of the New World that the existence of slave labour has been proven to be necessary in the developement of tropical productions. England herself having abolished slavery in her provinces, with all her recreative power, and with all the stimulants of pride and interest to urge her to its accomplishment, has been unable to restore life or animation to her stricken palsied provinces! Desolation abounds where verdant fields once bloomed. Decay has followed where were once rife the evidences of prosperity; and ignorance, indolence, misery, and vice now reign supreme amongst that unhappy class, whom the cruel philanthropy of England has enfranchised.

These truths are scraps from history. They exist at present as undeniable facts, which all who choose may verify. They are spread before our eyes in characters which cannot be misunderstood, if the purpose be to judge fairly and frankly by results, in lieu of theories. Where African slave labour exists in the southern latitudes of America, prosperity abounds, and the world is furnished with the richness of the products of that favoured clime. Where it does not exist, there has been comparatively no progress—no production—no prosperity! Where it has existed, but has been abolished, ruin, decay, and imbecility have followed!

It being then an undeniable truth, that hitherto the world has only been supplied with the productions of tropical climates through the instrumentality of slave labour, and that all attempts to secure this result by free labour have been unsuccessful, even supported by the mighty influence and power of Great Britain, should the institution of slavery in the Southern States be stricken down in deference to the real or affected philanthropy of those who created it? Of those who kidnapped and transported from Africa, or of those who, at a later period, sold for money in hand, all of these very slaves, or their ancestors, whom they would now emancipate; and whose tender sensibilities were never aroused in favour of the victims of their own cupidity until they had received the full 'wages of their sin,' and had transported the 'human chattels' to their possessors, to be held in bondage, they and their descendants, by them and their posterity, for ever? In view of these facts, is it not fair to presume that there is some moving motive of self-interest, which has a deeper hold upon their hearts than the philanthropic considerations by which they profess to be governed? Whatever may be the sentiments and feelings of that portion of the civilised world which is not actively engaged in this crusade against the South upon the abstract question of slavery, should they not hesitate long and ponder deeply before they say 'God speed' to the enemies of the planting States of the Confederacy in their present struggle? Having satisfied themselves that the existing relations between the African and

European races, living upon the same soil, cannot be changed without bringing ruin upon one or both, let them consider the probable consequences to mankind, if unhappily this selfish assault should terminate in the success of the assailants.

I have a right to suggest these considerations, also, to those Americans who are labouring with so much energy and zeal, in conjunction with others from without, to stimulate the hatred of mankind against the Southern States, with the avowed or concealed purpose of reducing those States to the condition of the British tropical possessions. There is all the greater propriety in making this appeal to Americans, because it is not claimed that the consummation they desire would add to the material interests of any other nation or people than those whose interests are believed to be adverse to theirs.

Let me not be misunderstood. I know that it is the theory of many of the politicians of England, as indicated by the London 'Times' in the article from which I have made a brief extract, that the British possessions in India can only be successfully developed by a gradual but sure process of emancipation in America, to be followed by the entire extinction of slavery. This may or may not be true, but if I might venture to avow a difference of opinion from those who ought to be more capable of deciding upon the true policy and interests of that country, I would say that the hopes which may be founded upon such a contingency would, in practice, prove to be a delusion. England is already great in herself, and powerful and rich in comparison with the other leading Powers of the world. Now, the prosperity of the slave States is the prosperity of England. A combination of circumstances, wisely directed by the indomitable energies and gallantry of her citizens, have made her one of the ruling nations of the world, in a military sense, as well as in commerce and manufactures. In regard to the latter, she stands almost without a rival—certainly without an equal. On the other hand, the Southern planting States, owing to the causes before referred to, are the greatest producers of that commodity which is manufactured at such an enormous profit by Great Britain. Would it not be better that each should go on in the career which they are now following, and, acting upon that fundamental principle of political economy which commands nations to develope their own resources at home, to sell where they can realise the greatest profit, and to buy where they can buy the cheapest, content themselves with their present prosperity, rather than seek a doubtful advantage from the destruction of the prosperity of others? It may be an error of judgement, but I cannot resist the conclusion that England is greater and more powerful to-day than she would be if slavery should be abolished in the planting States of America, by even the slow process which the leaders of the political anti-slavery party propose to inaugurate. And in this matter, let me add that about which I may speak with the confidence of one who is familiar with the subject by a lifetime experience and observation. The relations subsisting in America between the Africans and the inhabitants of European blood can never be materially changed by the consent of the latter: which consent would be essential to '*a gradual*' enfranchisement of the slaves. Slavery, under the circumstances there existing, can only be eradicated by violence, sudden and overwhelming! The first step taken by her enemies looking to emancipation, would arouse the entire South to an energetic and a bloody resistance, such as the world to this day has never witnessed! Let no one be deceived in regard to the results which would follow swiftly upon the heels of such a movement! The four millions of Africans, who are now inhabitants of the South, can only be emancipated and left upon the soil by the extermination or the entire subjection of eight millions of whites!

Many of the anti-slavery advocates profess to be governed only by a desire to eradicate what they are pleased to denominate 'a great sin.' Others insist that they only 'follow the promptings of humanity,' in seeking 'to restore the African to his native freedom.' Others again ignore the rights of the black man, but look with compassion upon the white race, who have been 'born under the influence of the demoralising institution.' And these are all the more intent upon accomplishing their mission of mercy, because those for whom their sympathies are so much excited persistently refuse to see the horrors of their situation. Others, we are bound to believe, are stimulated only by their hatred of the Southern people. But by none of the hostile elements which go to make up the aggregate of that party which in Europe and America seeks, either covertly or openly, to destroy the institution of slavery in the Southern States of the Confederacy, is it pretended that any human being beyond the limits of those States will derive any—the smallest benefit therefrom, except that class of politicians just referred to.

That they do not over-estimate the augmentation of wealth and power which might come into the possession of Great Britain, if their schemes should be realised, may not be questioned against the judgement of such distinguished statesmen; but it is equally true that they underrate the obstacles to their accomplishment. Even though the entire Northern section of the Confederacy should unite with them heartily in compassing their objects—even though they should secure the reins of power in the general government of the Confederacy, still the South would not consent to the self-sacrifice, and her opposition would be fatal. The States of the Confederacy are, in every essential respect sovereign, and the small State of Delaware alone, with her five hundred slaves, could not under the Constitution be coerced to emancipate them, even although the Federal Government, and every other State in the Union, should unite in demanding it.

In illustration of the important influence which these productions exercise over the destinies of the civilised world, I will extract a few paragraphs from a late publication in which Mr. McQueen announces the policy of his country. The fearful struggle of Great Britain in the long series of wars to which Mr. McQueen refers, is worthy of a passing notice. Never before did any other nation meet and overcome so many and such powerful enemies. All Europe, as it were, was combined in solid phalanx against her. Some stimulated by a hereditary hatred; others by jealousy and envy of her power; others by fear, and others by the necessities of their position. All entered upon the struggle with the single purpose of destroying the power of that nation whose navy was in every sea; whose flag floated over vast possessions in every quarter of the globe; whose armies were unsurpassed in bravery or skill; and whose purse seemed almost inexhaustible. The world in arms was arrayed against her, under the leadership of the greatest military chieftain of ancient or modern times. Napoleon the Great headed the hostile array! The result is before the world. The

Government of Great Britain still stands amongst the foremost Powers of the earth, illustrating still the same heroic determination, the same energy, the same skill in maintaining her supremacy, which has ever excited the admiration and respect even of her enemies, with the same absorbing selfishness which has ever repelled the undoubting confidence or the love of mankind.

During that fearful struggle [said the author referred to] of a quarter of a century, for the existence of a nation against the power and resources of Europe, directed against her by the most intelligent but remorseless military ambition, *the command of the productions of the torrid zone*, and the advantageous commerce which that afforded, *gave to Great Britain the power and the resources which enabled her to meet, to combat, and to overcome her numerous and reckless enemies on every battle-field, whether by sea or by land, throughout the world.* In her the world saw realised the fabled giant of antiquity. With her hundred hands she grasped her foes in every region under heaven, and crushed them with resistless energy. . . . The increased cultivation and prosperity of Foreign tropical possessions, is become so great, and *is advancing so rapidly the power and resources of other nations, that these are embarrassing [England] in all her commercial relations, in her pecuniary resources, and in all her political relations* and negotiations. . . . If *the cultivation of the tropical territories of other Powers be not opposed and checked* by British tropical cultivation, then the INTERESTS and the POWER *of such States will rise into a preponderance over those of Great Britain*, and the power and the influence of the latter will cease to be felt, feared, and respected amongst the civilised and powerful nations of the world.

When we consider that mankind generally, but

more especially the governments which are instituted by men, in the very nature of things, seek their own aggrandisement, even at the expense of doing an incidental injustice to others, the citizens of the Republic should make due allowance for the zeal of British political abolitionism in its attempt to destroy an institution which in its operations they conceive to be inimical to their interests. When England defended and upheld and propagated slavery in America, it must be remembered that the territory and the slaves were hers; now that the ownership of that territory and those slaves has passed into other hands, it could scarcely be expected that her policy in reference to the industrial pursuits of that country would not undergo a radical change. That the Anti-slavery party of Great Britain in assuming the leadership of the emancipationists of New England, and in the announcement of its intentions, should be profuse in its protestations of a merely benevolent and philanthropic purpose, should not be a matter of surprise; but in deciding upon the weight to which their counsels are entitled, we should, as men, consider the magnitude of the interest involved, and as Americans, we should not suffer ourselves to be deceived in regard to their real sentiments and purposes, in our admiration of the outer garments with which they have enveloped them.

In order that I may not be misunderstood, I will

here again state my own belief that the policy of this party in assuming a hostile attitude towards the developement and the power of the planting States of America, is neither conducive to their own interests nor those of mankind. England should shape her policy in accordance with the promptings of a more enlarged statesmanship. No other two nations of the world have so many inducements to cultivate a sincere and enduring friendship. Every additional bale of cotton which may be produced in the planting States, adds just in that proportion to the material power and wealth of Great Britain. Nay, more than this, there are political considerations and heart sympathies, which when left to their own free action, impel them towards each other, and which it were wise that England should consider and respect. It is a short-sighted policy on the part of any government or people, however powerful, to repel by injustice or even unnecessary harshness, the sympathies of those with whom from natural causes they might be supposed to entertain sentiments of kindness. None know better than those who are familiar with English history, upon whom rests the responsibility for the establishment of slavery in the Southern States of the American Union. None know better than intelligent Englishmen how wisely and how humanely the Southern States have given direction in the interests of mankind, to that institution which they had no agency in erecting and which they had not the power to subvert. None know better than the great English statesmen, that the adoption of the policy urged upon the South by the anti-slavery propagandists, could end in nothing but misery for the slave, and utter irremediable ruin for the white race. And none know better than they upon which side of the line dividing the South from the North they might expect with confidence to find a magnanimous foe, or a generous friend, upon a contingency which might develope the one or the other of these relations. But even though the British anti-slavery leaders give no heed to such considerations, they should remember, that the friendships they cultivate in the United States, having their foundations in a common sentiment of hatred, are not to be relied upon in the hour of trial and danger; while the animosities thus engendered live to bear fruits long after the causes which produced them have disappeared.

LETTER VIII.

Causes of disaster to Republics—Tendency of Slavery to produce equality in the dominant race—Morals of Slave and Free States—Capital and Labour united in Slave States.

THE unsuccessful efforts which have been made in Europe to construct free governments upon the ruins of despotisms, have had their origin in the ignorance of the masses of the populations. This ignorance has been made use of by more enlightened demagogues to subvert the very Governments which they professedly sought to establish. The ignorant people were led to believe that liberty and license were synonymous, and that freedom consisted in the absence of the restraints of law. The calamities which have generally followed upon the heels of every successful effort to overthrow Despotisms, have been brought about by the excesses induced by such violations of the principle upon which free governments should be founded. Moreover, these same ignorant classes were in turn equally the instruments by which Despots have been able to resume their lost power.

In the formation of the different Governments of the American Confederacy, if the negroes had been made citizens, they would have constituted the material out of which demagogues would soon have produced a state of affairs that would have caused a radical change in the form of the Government. Happily, such a policy was not adopted, and hence the Slave States entered upon their career as Republics without being subjected to those dangers which originate in the ignorance and incompetency of its citizens. The material which has been successfully employed in the Old World to make Republics impossible did not exist. That class of the community, which elsewhere led by wicked counsels produces revolution, was unknown in the Slave States. The humblest white man felt that there were below him, socially and politically, a considerable portion of the population. He had all the incentives of pride to fulfill properly the duties which, as a free citizen, he was called upon to perform. No matter how humble his position, he never occupied that station in regard to the wealthier portion of the population which would impress upon him a feeling of inferiority. He performed none of those menial services for others which would degrade him in his own estimation, or which, from the nature of his relations to his employer, would make him but an instrument in the hands of his superior. All these services were rendered by slaves.

The existence of slavery thus rendered facile the

establishment of free government by the dominant race. There was no hazard in conferring equal political privileges upon the whites, and the natural influence of slavery has been to create a feeling of pride and personal independence among the superior race, which makes them more capable of performing the duties of free citizens.* These States have by this means been exempted, in a great measure, from those popular tumults which have been the graves of the Republics of the Old World. In effect, while the free States of New England have been overrun by fanatics who display their absurd and pernicious principles under the forms of 'Fourierism,' 'abolitionism,' 'atheism,' 'free love-ism,' 'woman's rights-ism,' and many other 'isms' equally detestable, they are absolutely unknown in the Slave States, because the populations from which proselytes to such doctrines are usually obtained, do not there exist, and there are no materials out of which the intelligent, but vicious or fanatical leaders can construct a party.

* Mr. Burke, one of the greatest statesmen whose name is recorded in the annals of British History, thus speaks of the influence of slavery upon the dominant races, in an address delivered in Parliament upon the subject of the American rebellion.

'Where this is the case, those who are free are by far the most proud and jealous of their freedom. I cannot alter the nature of man. The fact is so, and these people of the southern colonies are much more strongly, and with a higher and more stubborn spirit, attached to liberty than those to the northward. Such were all the ancient commonwealths. Such were our Gothic ancestors, and such in our day were the Poles. Such will be all masters of slaves who are not slaves themselves. In such a people the haughtiness of domination combines itself with the spirit of freedom, fortifies it, and renders it invincible.'

The abolitionists of England, as well as of the Northern States of the Union, without designing to do so, confirm the facts above stated. It is often with these a subject of mortification and complaint that the Southern States, as they aver, generally select their Representatives in the Congress from among their most intelligent citizens, and retain them for a long period in the management of their public affairs; while in the abolition districts, scarcely have they elected a man of ability, ere he is thrust aside by another, who, in his turn, is superseded almost before he has made himself familiar with the routine of his duties, by one more radical and more skilled in the subtle arts of demagoguy. This is the testimony furnished by the enemies of slavery. In truth, however, it may be readily inferred that, from the causes which exist, such results would naturally follow. The effect of slavery has, therefore, been to establish free institutions for the dominant race, and upon a solid and durable foundation.

To one who is familiar with the workings of the institution of slavery as at present organised in the Southern States of America, the extreme, almost fanatical, unreasonable and blind hostility manifested thereto by many really philanthropic men, who are sane upon all other subjects, is entirely inexplicable according to any ordinary rules for interpreting the conduct of men. They seem to forget all the lessons of history. They seem not to know that even the long-recognised relations subsisting between different classes of the same race cannot be suddenly eradicated without involving disaster to all, even though the distinctions may be purely artificial. The offspring of the European peasant might be clandestinely placed in the cradle of the monarch, and become an anointed king, while none could detect the transformation. But the African, whether as a slave or a freedman, bears ever upon his black and marked visage, and transmits to his posterity, the indelible record of his former condition of servitude. As a slave he may be treated with kindness, humanity, and even affection, but as a freedman mingled with the race of his former master, he always has been, and unless man's nature changes, always will be, treated with contumely, harshness, and cruelty, whenever he attempts to assume an equality of rank with those who have been his superiors, and who will never consent that he shall be an equal. This may be abstractly wrong; but you must uproot the foundations of our nature, and make men anew, before you can eradicate the principle which calls it into action. It cannot be then, that they oppose the slavery of the Southern States, because it conflicts with the doctrine of the universal equality of the races of men, for this belief can only be entertained by impracticable theorists, and is opposed to all government upon any principle hitherto successfully practised. Neither in the case considered, can it be on the score of humanity, pure and simple; for I presume it will scarcely be denied by the intelligent common sense class whom I am now addressing, that the system of slavery, as now existing in the American planting States is not only the mildest system of labour which exists, but, by the admission of even the most persistent and uncompromising enemies of the Slave States, the slaves are more kindly dealt with, are better fed and clothed, and more rarely overworked, than any similar number of free labourers in the world. It cannot be because of the demoralising tendencies, or vices incident to slavery; for if they have eyes they must see that there is more vice and immorality, more human degradation, more unpitied misery, illustrated by the history of any one single day of the year in the city of London, or Paris, or Vienna, or even New York and Boston, than a whole year would bring forth amongst all the slaves of America. It is true that among the slaves there is vice, for they are human; but they are never forced to the alternative of *vice* or *starvation*. They may yield to the temptations of a naturally wicked heart, but never are they induced by necessity to the commission of crime. The wicked imaginations of obscene men and women picture among the families of the Southern States scenes of immorality and debauchery. Who does not know, that in any one of the cities I have named, as well as in hundreds of others which might be enumerated, the vices referred to are practised to a larger extent between master and servant, or 'help' of the same race, in one month, than during half a generation in the Slave States, between master and slave? In the one case there exists a natural repulsion, as well as the stimulant of pride. Even these barriers, however, are powerless to prevent altogether this species of vice. But let any one compare in his mind, the relative inducements, incentives, and opportunities for the commission of the vices referred to, between black slaves and their owners, and white hired servants and their masters, and he may decide the question for himself, without desiring further testimony than the existing relations of the two would furnish.

Let me refer, for an instant, to the revolting spectacle which meets the eye in all large cities, under the operation of what is denominated the system of free labour. Look, for example, any evening of the year, upon the crowded streets and avenues of the great cities of England or even of New York. There you behold—not hundreds—not thousands—but tens of thousands of human beings, fashioned after the model of the fairest of God's creatures, offering themselves in the highways and by-ways, body and soul, to any purchaser who will give them money to buy bread. They would even work for the pittance of ten cents or twenty cents a day—the scanty wages allowed to a free labourer of their class—but there are none to give them employment. There is no fire in the miserable apartment to give warmth to its inmates. There is no morsel of food to appease the pangs of hunger. The tempter is present pointing to the manner of obtaining both: the purchaser is without. Are the victims young and well-favoured? they offer *themselves* in exchange for that which will support life. Are they old and without charms? they beg of those who may fall in their way, in the name of humanity, for something wherewithal to sustain a little longer their miserable existence. Perhaps the first person they encounter is a clergyman of the Abolition school. He turns coldly away from the blandishments of the one and the tears of the other, and entering his study, sits down to compose an appeal to mankind in behalf of the suffering slaves of America! No sentiment of pity for the misery which exists around him; no horror of the crimes or vices which he cannot fail to see; no earnest effort to amend that system which is the fruitful parent of so much misery and vice, can move him to employ his great intellect, or exert his great influence where it might be availing. For him and for his class there is but one great sin, and that is the sin of American slavery in a distant land. There is but one object of compassion, but one which calls for the exercise of benevolence, and that is 'the little negro baby.'

This clergyman is unfortunately but the type of a class, which for the sake of humanity it were to be wished were less numerous. Unhappily, *Old* England is not the only land in which they are to be found. The example has not been without influence across the Atlantic, where it has assumed a form even more revolting.

We may make due allowance for the injustice done by the political abolitionists of Great Britain to the planting States of America, because they believe that they have a great interest in embarrassing first, and in overthrowing afterwards, the institution of American slavery. We may respect the convictions of the dreamer, who hopes to witness, with the disappearance of slavery, the realisation of what is regarded by practical men an impossible equality. We may pardon the politician who takes advantage of the popular excitement to secure his way to place and power. But for the professed teacher of God's Holy Word; for the man who claims to be a disciple of Christ, and a follower of His holy counsels, but who prostitutes the pulpit to the purpose of inciting hatred instead of love; who preaches for blood and war instead of peace; who from the holy desk distributes 'Sharp's rifles,' and other instruments of murder, with instructions to go forth and slay; who, in effect, teaches his congregation that all the other sins of the world are as nothing compared to the sin of slavery — who can regard him in any other aspect than as the enemy — whether innocently or otherwise it is not my province to judge — of that meek and lowly Jesus whom he professes to serve?

But to resume the consideration of the objections to American slavery. It cannot be because of the degradation it imposes upon the African, for no informed man will be found to assert that any of his race have ever, in any time past, occupied a position so elevated in the scale of humanity as those who are now held as slaves within the Slave States of America. Upon this point there exists no contrariety of opinion. The ultra abolitionist, and the extreme slavery propagandist, are, in regard to this fact, in perfect accord. Neither can it be that this opposition arises from any promptings of Christianity, because, though heathens in their native land, slavery has christianised them. Many of these philanthropists say that none can be saved who die without a knowledge of Christ, yet, but for the existence of African slavery, who can believe that fifty of these four millions of slaves would ever, according to this view, have 'fallen into the way of salvation'? Would they have consigned these people to the horrors of eternal punishment? If the doctrine to which I refer be true, such would have been their terrible fate but for their enslavement. The philanthropic and benevolent, both of England and America, send forth their Christian missionaries to every benighted land, into which these self-exiled teachers of our sublime faith can procure ingress. They endure patiently hardships, dangers, and death, in their zeal to promote the cause in which they are engaged. Yet all the labours of all the missionaries who have been despatched to heathen lands from England and America since the revolution, have not converted to Christianity one-tenth of the number which slavery has brought into the fold of our Saviour.

If the advocates of the universal equality of man are really desirous to witness the establishment and perpetuation of free institutions, as now existing in the United States of America, partial though they admittedly are, and confined to the European races, why should they wish to place them at so much hazard, to subject them to so fearful an ordeal, as to insist upon the recognition of an equality between races so far removed from each other by education and habit, so dissimilar in all things? If they consider that the failure or success of the 'experiment' of free government, now being made in the New World, will have an important bearing upon the fate of free institutions for centuries yet to come, why should they desire to stake all upon the cast of a single die? Why should they wish to deprive the 'experiment,' now in the morning of its success, of its surest bulwark—why should they desire to hazard the interests of millions of the white race, for the purpose of conferring a doubtful benefit upon but comparatively a handful of Africans?—and all for no probable good, except to test in practice the proof of a theory which the vast majority of mankind believe to be founded in error?

There exists still another class, both large and formidable, who oppose slavery upon grounds altogether antagonistic to those we have been considering. They profess no sentimental philanthropy, no belief in the natural equality of the African, no sympathy for sufferings which they say do not exist, no disposition to elevate him for his own sake to political independence. Their opposition is founded upon the belief that slavery is inimical to free labour.*

A practical acquaintance with the facts would satisfy any one who investigates the subject that

* Mr. Seward, who probably represents more faithfully than any other Northern politician the sentiments of the great body of the Anti-southern party, has repeatedly warned the South by unmistakeable acts if not by words, that the intention of the North was to overthrow its institutions, and to build up in their stead a system more in accordance with the interests of his own countrymen, who might choose to emigrate into the Southern States. In a speech delivered by him in the United States Senate, he uses the following emphatic language:—

'The white man needs this continent to labour upon. His head is clear, his arm is strong, and his necessities are fixed! He must and will have it.'

Mr. Seward would seem from the above to believe that if slavery should be abolished, the poor Africans would soon be exterminated when brought into contact with the race of white men who he says 'must and will have this continent for their own exclusive use.'

this assumption is wholly groundless. In free States there is a perpetual conflict between *capital* and *labour*. There may be a truce from necessity, but the war is renewed when that necessity ceases to exist. Capital is ever seeking to procure labour at the minimum amount for which it may be purchased. Labour seeks to obtain from capital the highest reward for its services. This contest must be perpetual until all men become labourers or all capitalists.

The terms on which this perpetually recurring battle is fought are most unequal. The decision is almost always in favour of capital. The issue may be held in abeyance for a season; a momentary success may even give heart and courage to the labourer; but in the end the crowning victory has always been secured to capital. Why? because capital may exist indefinitely as to time, *without eating*. The labourer *must have his daily bread*! *Bread* may only be had for *money*, and *capital* will only bestow that money for labour. Labour may fight bravely and hopefully for a day, but it goes to bed on an empty stomach. It may arise in the morning refreshed by its slumbers and courageously renew the battle, but it retires at night oppressed with the pangs of hunger! On the third day it may struggle against its sleepless, cautious, passionless, heartless foe with the desperation of despair. On the fourth day it yields itself as vanquished, or perishes. In either event capital is the victor.

In Slave States, or at least to the extent to which slaves are held and the general influence which it naturally exercises, capital and labour form but a single interest—there cannot be a conflict, because capital is labour and labour is capital. The interests of capital and labour are one, because the two are identical. The capitalist seeks by every means in his power to enhance the value of labour, because labour is his only capital. If labour recedes his capital declines. If labour advances his capital is augmented.

In Slave States, therefore, labour is always comparatively high, and free labour, as well as capital, is the gainer thereby. There is not a country upon earth where free labour commands so high a price, estimated by the cost of subsistence, as in the Slave States of the American Union. And I may add, that in no other country is there as much true contentment, happiness, and comfort, or as little destitution or want, as exists among the labouring population of the Slave States of the American Union, of whatever colour, race, occupation, or condition.

Beyond the sea-board cities, pauperism may scarcely be said to exist in the Slave States, and mendicants, except from abroad, are utterly unknown. Of professional robbers and pick-pockets there are none, but such as are attracted from the Free States by that prevailing feeling of security among the inhabitants which makes them careless in protecting their property. Even the courtesans who walk the streets of Southern cities are for the most part contributions from the civilisation of Free States. The reports furnished by the daily press, as well as the records of the courts, establish the fact that there is less crime among the population of the South than in any other civilised country of like numbers. In corroboration of the facts here referred to, it is only necessary to state another fact, the existence of which is without a parallel in any other country, or in any other age; namely — that with the exception of a few dozen straggling men in uniform, upon the sea-board fortifications, there is not to be seen within the jurisdiction and limits of the Slave States, with its eight millions of freemen and four millions of slaves, *one single soldier nor an armed policeman*! To the mind of the statesman and the philanthropist, this truth is pregnant with the refutation of the allegations made in ignorance by the enemies of the South.

These are my sincere convictions, founded upon experience and observation. They may be tinctured by my never disavowed love for the land of my birth; but I am thus far sustained by the unanimous testimony of all, who, like myself, have had a life-experience on the subject about which I have thus presumed to differ from so many hundreds who have never placed foot upon the territory where slavery exists.

While the Southerner and his family sleep in perfect security, with unbarred doors, surrounded by his contented and happy slaves, the foreign abolitionist is racking his brain and torturing his imagination to devise measures to break up this harmony, and to set the one against the other in bloody strife. The loyalty of the slaves to their masters, and the feeling almost akin to affection which subsists between the two, is without a precedent or a parallel in the intercourse and relations which subsist between masters and servants in any free state of the world ; and in any time of danger the Southerners would rely with far more confidence upon the fidelity of the great body of the slaves, than could the higher classes upon those who, in free states, occupy the position of menials or dependents.

But it is objected that the slaves are not educated. While many wise men doubt whether it would add to the happiness of the slave, or the good of society to bestow upon him an education above the necessities of his position, yet if it is an evil, we have only to thank the Abolitionists for its existence. All of us who have reached the age of forty years can remember when the teaching the negroes to read was not only not interdicted, but was encouraged by the slave-holders. We can also remember the period of time when necessity compelled the Southern States in self-defence, in view of the character of the literature which was spread before them by the Abolitionists, to deny to the slave-owners the privilege of educating their slaves. Notwithstanding this general prohibition, many are still taught to read and write. The civilised African of the South is proverbially yielding and impressible in his nature. Above all, he is an undoubting believer in the Christian religion, and entertains the highest respect for those who are its recognised expounders. When he is taught by the publication of fanatical clergymen of the North that it is his right and his duty to take away the lives of those who are interposed between himself and liberty, it is not wonderful that it should make an impression upon his susceptible nature, and that the necessity of self-protection should at once indicate to the master the importance of neutralising, as far as possible, the influence of such counsels.

There is another objection which it may be admitted is well taken, but even in regard to this, great progress has already been made. I refer to the marriage relation. In respect to this, however, it may be truly said, that there are fewer births out of wedlock among the slaves of the planting States, than in many of the most refined and enlightened communities of civilised Europe. Admitting, moreover, the fact that in many respects the Africans have not been brought to the high standard which has been attained by those of European blood, yet when we contrast their condition now with what it was when they became slaves to the white men, our only wonder is, that they have been made to advance so rapidly from the depths of barbarism to a comparative state of civilisation. It must be borne in mind that the Africans in their native land have neither the same habits nor the same tastes as the Europeans. Seventy millions of them are said to be to-day the slaves of cruel and savage masters of their own race. They have no marriage ties which assimilate to that which is common in Christian nations, nor is chastity a quality which is held in high esteem. In short, they are now, and have been during the period of their entire history, the most brutal barbarians. It could scarcely be hoped that their descendants in the New World would have emerged wholly from the condition of their ancestors, and have adopted all the customs of Christian communities. Nor is it fair under the circumstances that they should be held to practise the virtues of fidelity and chastity, by the same rigid laws which are enforced by the highly civilised and Christian populations of New York, London, Paris, or Vienna.

But there is still another important consideration, which is opposed to the enfranchisement of the slave, even if it were possible; that is, a due regard to the interests of the millions of the white race who now reside, and whose destiny has been cast in the Slave States. What would be the condition of the free white labourers in the midst of these millions of freed Africans who from being capital would be converted into competitors for the stinted pittance which capital would bestow for labour? The free-born mechanic and farm labourer would be reduced to the alternative of competing with the African upon equal terms. Suppose that which it is impossible to believe, that the free whites would submit tranquilly to the galling and revolting association, is there a philanthropic friend to the free labourers of his own race who would wish to reduce them to a condition so humiliating? The standard value of labour would be that which unscrupulous capital would stipulate with the ignorant and indolent African. Free white labour would be powerless to defend itself against injustice, because there would be an ever-ready substitute of African labour, which capital could employ during the rare intervals in which intelligent labour might vainly seek to secure a proper reward and acknowledgement for its toil.

The rich man could fly from the contaminating association. The poor from necessity would be bound to the soil. Upon the rich would fall the present pecuniary sacrifice, but upon the poor would rest the perpetual record and presence of the wrong.

I have here assumed what I know to be an impossible contingency. An overwhelming military force may liberate the slaves—armed invaders from the North may destroy the value of the slave to his owner and to mankind—John Browns may kindle the torch of servile insurrections; and the Southerner may live to see his dwelling in flames and his hearthstone made desolate; but all the power of their enemies cannot induce the freemen of the South, of any rank, condition, or occupation, to adopt the freed Africans as their fellow-citizens, nor to tolerate any change in their relative conditions that would remove the barriers, social or political, which now separate the races.

But why should not good men consider the subject of slavery as it exists in the Southern States without allowing themselves to be influenced by unfounded prejudices or sectional animosities, and look only to the results which it has achieved? Though they may be opposed to slavery in the abstract, is it more than just that the Slave States should have the benefit of that inexorable necessity which, without any agency on their part, left them no alternative consistent with their safety but to adopt and perpetuate the institution of slavery? This conceded, examine and decide if the Southern States have not properly employed it in the interest of mankind, and with a due regard to the comfort and happiness of those who were thus placed under their charge and direction. If still there exist doubts, compare that system of labour with the systems of so-called free labour, which civilised nations have adopted in order to achieve similar results. No friend of the Slave States would fear the decision of any impartial, just, and intelligent tribunal.

LETTER IX.

Influence of Public Opinion—Origin of the Anti-Slavery Sentiment in England—Failure of schemes to destroy the value of Slave Labour in America—Revolting Inhumanity of the systems instituted to supersede Slave Labour—Comparison of the Slavery System with those proposed as Substitutes—Subjugation of India by England—A trial by the Moral Law.

THERE has been no period in the past when the policies of governments have been so much moulded by the general public sentiment of mankind as at the present epoch. Electricity and steam have brought countries once remote from each other into almost immediate contact; and the commerce which has been thus stimulated between the nations of the earth has brought about a mutual dependence which renders the productions of each important to the others. The facilities offered by rapid and constant communication are alike mediums for the transmission of truth and falsehood. Unfortunately, the latter travels with a celerity to which the former rarely attains. Upon the establishment of the Republic of America in the last century, with its boundless and inexhaustible resources, certain timid adherents of the monarchical school imagined that they saw danger to all existing governments which were based on 'the right divine,' if the experiment should prove a success. How was this success to be averted? The great field for the production of the most important staples, with the labour which could alone develope them, were in the possession of the new Government. The British politician, whose mind was stimulated by a natural resentment growing out of the war which had but just terminated, did not require a Delilah to tell him in what consisted the strength of the young Samson. It was true that there were still some island slave provinces remaining to Great Britain; but the dominion of the great continent wherein had been cherished and nurtured into giant manhood the institution of domestic slavery, was henceforth to be the possession of a rival, and mayhap an enemy. To wage a moral war against the Americans on account of the institution of slavery, required, first, the sacrifice of her West India colonies. This could only be accomplished at a heavy expense, and by an act of great injustice to her dependent colonists; but greater were the results which it was hoped would be achieved, and she started out upon her new career with an energy and a zeal, and a disregard to cost, which no other nation than England knows how to put in practice. Slavery was abolished in all the provinces remaining in her possession, and the world, from that day to this, has resounded with the denunciations of her army of philanthropists against the Americans, for the toleration of that very slavery which she herself established and enforced by her laws and by her sword up to the very hour of her severance from her northern colonists!

Well does Britain deserve the title of 'Great.' She enforces the respect even of those whom she assails, while repelling their esteem. She is great in all things! Great in her virtues and in her vices — great in her physical power and in its application, when necessity demands its exercise — great in her adversity as in her prosperity — great in the sacrifices she is ever ready to suffer for the accomplishment of her policy — great in the facility with which she can change her code of morals in complaisant obedience to the exigencies of her pecuniary or her political interests — great in the unrelenting sternness with which she grasps the vast domain of India, with its subjected hundreds of millions of light-skinned Asiatics, as when, under the promptings of her soft and gentle nature, she stretches forth her strong right arm to shield the black-skinned African from the perpetuation of a wrong which she herself, in the pride of her civilisation, had inaugurated upon the territory of a distant continent! But having decided, after a thousand years of dalliance in the primrose paths of sin, that the institution of slavery 'was not fit to exist in England, for reasons peculiar to her own condition,' never did she appear greater than at that epoch of her illustrious career when, with the tinge of honest indignation mantling her weather-beaten cheek—the tears of sympathy for suffering humanity streaming from her ever-watchful wary eye — her heaving bosom convulsed with emotions in which pity for the slave and indignation against the enslaver struggled for supremacy—with the confidence of an honest purpose and the pride of conscious merit, and in the interest of injured innocence — she suddenly threw down the gage of battle before a startled world, as the foremost champion of universal emancipation!

We must admire thee, old England, for thy greatness, though we may not love thee for the evil thou wouldst bring upon us! And yet the day may come when thou wouldst perhaps desire to recall the harsh words thou hast uttered and the harsh deeds thou hast done to us; and mayest regret, that in giving aid and comfort to the enemies of the South, thou hast repelled those who are not the least noble, chivalrous, or generous amongst the descendants of English ancestry in the New World.

Fortunately, as well for the slave as his master — fortunately for mankind — but especially fortunate for the humble and the poor throughout the civilised world—the clamour against the Slave States has been thus far unavailing. With but a limited accession to the population from abroad, the descendants of European ancestors have increased to 8,000,000 of souls, while the Africans, without any importation since 1808, have increased to 4,000,000. There does not exist at the present day any population of similar numbers in any other land under the sun, where there is more real prosperity and contentment than in the Slave States of the Union.

The world seemed ready to adopt any alternative, however wicked or inhuman or cruel, if it could only dispense with the form of slavery existing in the planting States of America; but failure has attended every effort. The British politicians who instituted the moral war against slavery, hoped that in abolishing 'the institution,' and leaving the slaves as freedmen in the provinces in which they had been held in bondage, there would continue to result the same amount of production. This they expected to increase by the introduction of other Africans or Asiatics, who, instead of being slaves for life, should serve their masters for only a limited period—say eight years—at a small stipulated rate of wages. The amount to be paid to this class of labourers would, of course, be established by the employer—the savage, or semi-savage, as the case might be, being too ignorant to understand anything of the value of his labour. The system was supposed to possess a great advantage over that of absolute slavery, as it did not involve the expense to the employer of giving support to those who were too old or too young, or too infirm for active labour.

If the substitute had been successful in achieving their purpose, slavery in America might possibly have abolished itself, because of its unprofitableness. The new system would have destroyed the value of the slave; and inasmuch as the Southern States, from the peculiar nature of their institutions, and for other causes, could not permit the freed African to occupy their territory in common with the white race, they would themselves have been amongst the foremost in supplying the British colonies with labourers from their slave population. The great struggle of the Slave States would have been directed towards opening a way for the exodus of the servile race.

This scheme offered to its originators a double advantage; for while it would have been, if successful, a source of unbounded wealth to European nations with foreign tropical possessions, its entire want of adaptation to the peculiar circumstances of the Republics of the New World, would have driven the United States of America from the field of competition for the great prize of tropical products. I have already explained that it would be an act of political suicide, if nothing worse, for these States to introduce or tolerate in their midst a barbarous or a semi-savage population of a different race and complexion, who would occupy any other relation to the European masters than that of perpetual servitude.

Nations having provincial tropical possessions do not rest under any such restriction. The difference in this respect between the relative positions of Great Britain and the American planting States of the Confederacy, may be more readily conceived by supposing that the British Government were to introduce into the United Kingdom ten millions of Africans, who, after having served an apprenticeship of eight years, should be turned loose upon society as equal participants in the benefits and blessings of the English Constitution. Although under such circumstances, even Mr. Bright might abate somewhat in his demand for universal suffrage, yet, though no other champions of the equality of races should spring up to claim for these the 'rights of manhood,' it will be readily admitted that the political, moral, and social evils which would result would be a thousand-fold in excess of any benefits which might be expected from their presence. If Englishmen, who are sincerely desirous of witnessing the abolition of slavery in the American planting States, from pure and unselfish motives, will bring the matter home to themselves, they will readily admit that the total or even partial enfranchisement of four millions of black African slaves, amongst a population of eight millions of white Europeans, living under a Constitution which guarantees equality of right to its citizens, would be an act of madness!

But to return from this digression. While mankind should rejoice that this scheme, which would have produced so much misery to the instruments whom it was intended to employ in its prosecution, has utterly failed in accomplishing the practical results hoped for, yet none can withhold from Great Britain the tribute of their admiration, for the boldness and grandeur of the conception, and the more than imperial profusion with which she has lavished of her immense resources the amount necessary to fairly test the feasibility of nurturing into life and giant manhood this offspring of the American revolution.

But the sacrifice was unavailing. Too late it was discovered that the African would not work without a master! No stimulants of pride or ambition could move his soul to rise above the level which it would seem that the God of nature has assigned to him. While the productions of the Slave States of America have increased in a ratio never before equalled in any country, the possessions of Great Britain, where this experiment was inaugurated, have been receding in the amount of their productions, until they now bear no comparison even to their former products. All present to the eye of the observer a picture of comparative desolation.

The failure of this scheme, which involved the impossible employment of nominally free African labour, led to the inauguration of another, far more revolting to every sentiment of humanity than the most cruel form of slavery, even in the days when all the Christian Powers of Europe were the patrons of, or participators in, all slavery enterprises. This new scheme is known under the general designation of the 'Cooly system,' because the greater number of those who have been subjected to the horrors of this atrocity of the nineteenth century have been Chinese. All the barbarous and semi-civilised nations of the world, however, have been subjected, in a greater or less degree, to the terrors of this revolting system. No other records of its enormities are necessary to convince the intelligent mind of its true character, than a simple detail of the plan and manner of its execution.

The Cooly broker, by means of his agents, seizes upon his unsuspecting victims wherever they can be found. These, when brought into the port for shipment, are confined in the most loathsome prisons, and are not allowed to hold any communication with their countrymen without. Upon the arrival of a purchaser, a paper writing is produced in the French, the English, or the Spanish language, as the case may be, by which these poor wretches are bound to work for their owner for the space of eight or ten years, at a promised rate of compensation varying from two to four dollars per months. The 'free and unbiassed assent' of the Cooly having been thus obtained, he is bound as a malefactor and conveyed aboard the ship which is to convey him to his destination. The ship obtains clearance, and sets sail with her living cargo of 'free labourers,' crowded to a degree of suffocation which, before the end of the voyage, reduces their number from deaths to about three-fourths of their original number. In many instances this great mortality is frightfully increased. On board of one American ship which put into Manilla, in 1855, out of a cargo of four hundred and fifty souls, three hundred were smothered to death in one night from the closeness of the quarters in which they were confined! The end of their voyage at last arrives. Thrice happy those whose sufferings have already ended in death, and whose bodies have been cast into the sea. These 'free labourers' are disposed of to the highest bidder, and are placed upon the plantations of the purchasers. The owner has only by contract an estate for eight years in the sinews of the freeman. His only interest, therefore, is to concentrate all the physical capacity of the man within that compass of time; and rarely indeed is it that there is any substance left in him at the expiration of his period of enslavement. If there is, what means has he to return to his native land? The miserable pittance allowed to him has in all probability been paid in such manner as to be exhausted before the period of his freedom commences, and he must sell himself for another term of eight years, for the doubtful prospect of again revisiting his far-off home. Mr. Abbott, who has written a valuable work upon this subject, says in reference to the details of this inhuman system in Cuba:—

> It seems to me, that human misery could sink to no lower depth. The doom of the Coolies is vastly worse than that of the slaves. Those wretched Chinese are lured to leave their homes upon the promise of being fed and clothed, and receive four dollars per month. Thus, at the end of eight years, they would possess $384. This seems like an immense sum to a poor Chinaman, to whom a cent a day is a very reasonable competence. *But none return!* They are sold upon their arrival for about $400. If their owner can wear them out in eight years, *so that they die, he of course has nothing to pay* [for their wages, during their term of servitude]. If he cannot, he sends them to some distant plantation, or *sells them again for another eight years.*

This system has been attended with a partial success. So far as present gains are concerned, it has the great advantage over slavery of cheapness. It is impossible to obtain accurate statistics in regard to the numbers of human beings who have been thus sacrificed, to find a substitute for the slave system of America. It would probably be safe to say that the whole number, thus immolated during the last fifteen years, does not fall short of two millions of souls. With the stimulant of success, it cannot be long before the aggregate amount of those thus employed will exceed the entire number of slaves in the United States!

Where slumbers the philanthropy of the abolitionist of England, while this crime against humanity, more horrible far than the worst form which slavery has ever assumed, is thus lawfully prosecuted in the open face of day? Where sleeps the piety of Sharp's rifle clergymen of New England, while this enormous sin is robbing millions of semi-civilised human beings of liberty, of hope, of life? Alas, the fountains of their sympathies have been exhausted and absorbed by their devotion to the 'little nigger baby robbed from his mother's arms.' They believe that to hate anything but the slave-holder of America would be but an idle waste of the fire of their holy passions!

In instituting a comparison between these two rival systems, statistics are wholly unnecessary in arriving at just conclusions in regard to their respective merits. We may refer to practical effects to test the truth or soundness of our judgement upon doubtful points, but for arriving at just conclusions upon the question here at issue, nothing more is necessary than to examine the circumstances and terms under which they exist.

Under the slavery system in the United States, the slave is held as such from the cradle to the grave. At full maturity he is worth to the owner from ten to twelve hundred dollars. The latter has every stimulant of gain and self-interest to bring up the infant to manhood in the full possession of all his natural strength and health. He can only do this by sufficient food and clothing and rest from toil. When the slave has attained to man's estate the owner has an equal interest in preserving his health and physical strength to as late a period of his life as possible. This can be done by exacting only in a moderate degree the exercise of his physical strength. He must be sufficiently supplied with healthy nourishment—he must be warmly clad in winter; but above all, he must be made contented and happy in order to retain him at his full value. Any violation of these rules can only result in diminishing the value of the slave and the wealth of his owner. He may change masters, but always the same rules and regulations must be observed by the new proprietors; and this is the routine of slavery. If the slave is in full health and strength, he makes up twelve hundred dollars of the capital of his owner. If he is disabled by tyranny, or by improper or scanty nourishment, or by overwork, he is not only valueless, but an encumbrance and an expense; for the law compels the master to support his own slave under all circumstances, or in case of failure he is taken away and transferred to another. Does a man set fire to his own house for the purpose of looking upon the conflagration? Would he destroy the value of his property for the gratification of his spleen? *

* M. de Tocqueville, as well as many other respectable writers upon

Such are the circumstances under which the slaves transmitted to the Southern States by Great Britain

the relations subsisting between the white and black races, concur in the statement that the Southerners are far more tolerant and humane towards the blacks than are the people of the North. It would seem, in truth, that the Yankee, with all his experience, is utterly incapable of understanding the nature of the African. He either treats him with a disgusting familiarity, coupled with an ostentatious deference, or, on the other hand, with a supercilious arrogance, and a cruelty where he has the power to do so, utterly at variance with that which he receives at the hands of the Southerner. This difference of treatment will account for one of the causes which induce so many Africans to prefer being slaves to Southerners rather than to be freedmen among Northerners. Not only is this difference observable in the individual intercourse of the two, but what may seem stranger still, the legislation of the South is, in many respects, far more favourable to the blacks than that of the North, except where Northern legislators are enacting laws for the evident purpose of displaying their hostility to the South. From a mass of matter bearing upon this subject, I select an article of the Constitution of the State of Texas, similar in its provisions to the Constitutions of all the Slave States, and also extracts from the Constitutions and laws of the Free States.

From the Constitution of Texas (a Slave State).

Article VIII.—1. They (the Legislature) shall have full power to pass laws, which will oblige the owners of slaves to treat them with humanity; to provide for their necessary food and clothing; to abstain from all injuries to them, extending to life or limb; and in case of their neglect or refusal to comply with the directions of such laws, to have such slave or slaves taken from their owner, and sold for the benefit of such owner or owners. They may pass laws to prevent slaves from being brought into this State as merchandise only.

2. In the prosecution of slaves for the crimes of a higher grade than petit larceny, the Legislature shall have no power to deprive them of an impartial trial by jury.

3. Any person who shall maliciously dismember or deprive a slave of life, shall suffer such punishment as would be inflicted, in case the like offence had been committed upon a free white person, and on the like proof, except in case of insurrection of such slave.

Law of Illinois (a Free State), enacted in 1853.

If any negro or mulatto, bond or free, shall hereafter come into this State, are now held. Englishmen should remember that there is as great a difference between the condition of the American slave of the present day and that of his ancestors when first kidnapped and sent a savage into their provinces, as between the mild government of their model Queen Victoria and that of the tyrant Henry VIII. Then he was a savage and a cannibal, while now he is civilised and a Christian. I say nothing here of the actual condition of the slaves of the South, because I think the candid and unprejudiced mind can arrive at just conclusions without the aid of such testimony. Would that

with the intention of residing in the same, every such negro or mulatto shall be deemed guilty of a high misdemeanour, and for the first offence shall be fined the sum of fifty dollars, to be recovered before any justice of the peace in the county where the said negro or mulatto may be found. . . . If the said negro or mulatto shall be found guilty, and the fine assessed be not forthwith paid, it shall be the duty of the said justice to commit the said negro or mulatto to the custody of the sheriff of the said county, or otherwise keep him, her, or them in custody. . . . . The said justice *shall, at public auction, proceed to sell the said negro or mulatto to any person* who will pay the said fine and costs, for the shortest time; and the said purchaser shall have a right to compel the said negro or mulatto to work for and serve out the said time, &c.

From the Constitution of Indiana (a Free State), adopted in 1851.

Article XIII.—1. No negro or mulatto shall come into or settle in the State after the adoption of this constitution.

2. All contracts made with any negro or mulatto coming into the State, contrary to the provision of the foregoing section, shall be void; and any person who shall employ such negro or mulatto, or otherwise encourage him to remain in the State, shall be fined in any sum not less than ten dollars, nor more than five hundred dollars. . . .

4. The General Assembly shall pass laws to carry out the provisions of this article.

honest enemies of slavery could visit the Slave States in person and see for themselves the workings of that system against which cupidity, malice, prejudice, and ignorance have erected such a mountain of calumny and hatred !

Let us consider further and compare the morals of the anti-slavery, or so-called free labour system, which model Christian Powers have inaugurated or tolerated as a substitute for slavery.

In the commencement, the horrors of the kidnapping and transfer of the Coolies or Africans, as the case may be, to the place of their destination, are the same in both ; with this difference, however, that comparatively few slaves are now introduced into America, and none into the Southern States of the Confederacy. However, I propose to consider that both are in active operation. Once arrived in the country where his services are to be rendered, the Cooly's condition and that of the captured African sent into slavery diverges. For eight years the Cooly is sold ! for eight years he must, as a slave, obey the commands of a master ! Suppose that the same master is the proprietor of a plantation worked by slaves in the planting States of the Union, and of another worked by the eight-year apprentices in Cuba. We have seen what would be his incentives to good and ill-treatment in the former,—how different would be his interests in regard to the latter !

Eight years constitute a long period for ceaseless toil under a master who has no interest left in the victim after the expiration of that period. If he can only be worked to death there will be nothing to pay! Upon a reasonable calculation, how much of life and vitality would remain after this terrible drain of eight years, in a tropical climate, upon his powers of physical endurance? Could it be hoped that he would ever reach the end of a second term, though he had passed the first and lived?

Every truly philanthropic mind is forced to adopt the conclusion that this 'substitute' is, upon the ground of humanity, not only more objectionable than the slave labour which it was intended to subvert, but that it is, and in its very nature must for ever be, under any and all circumstances, more cruel, more atrocious, more detestable, and more productive of human misery than the most revolting form in which slavery has ever been exhibited to mankind, even though we trace its history back to the period when English cupidity and Spanish cruelty first inaugurated the system.

If this species of traffic in human flesh is continued, as it has been prosecuted by the open sanction or secret connivance of the Great Powers, in less than half a century its victims will, in all probability, be greater in number than all the slaves in the Southern

States. Already they may be counted by millions, and yet no 'tracts' nor 'songs' have been sent over from England to America to be read and sung by the congregations, to stimulate fanaticism against 'the foul wrong.' No pulpit, desecrated by political parsons, has rung with maledictions against the nations which permit the crime. No Sharp's rifles have been subscribed by New England clergymen, to assist with powder and ball in the extermination of the 'pirates' who pursue this 'nefarious traffic in blood and sinews.' The skin of the Chinaman is not quite black enough to win their sympathies.

The Anti-slavery party, however, has perceived that if the judgement of mankind is averse to the mild system of slavery which exists in the Southern States of America, it is scarcely to be hoped that, when the peculiar excitement of the day shall have passed away, the 'Cooly system' will meet with even as much favour. It has, therefore, been unremitting in its efforts to induce the nominal freemen in the despotic governments of Asia to assist in supplying the looms with cotton. But the return of material has scarcely surpassed in amount the weight of the seed which she has distributed. They have penetrated every province and island embraced within the dominions of the Sultan of Turkey; but the Bedouin and the Druse, the Maronite, the Greek and the

Armenian, the Christian and the Turk, alike refuse their tempting inducements.*

* This may possibly be attributed in part to the misdirected efforts of those engaged in this enterprise. The writer seized the occasion of a recent tour through portions of Asia Minor and Egypt to make a superficial examination of the capacity of the soil, and climate, and labour of those countries for the production of cotton. It is almost needless to say that he found the quality of the staple in Asia Minor very inferior, and the quantity per acre unremunerative to the labourers. This may in part only be attributed to the unskillful manner in which the work of production is done, yet for this evil I could discover no remedy. The same soil which would produce cotton will likewise bring forth, in fully a like proportion, the grains and grasses necessary to give sustenance to man and beast, and with less than half the labour. If the inhabitants will not produce the latter, how can it be hoped that they will be induced to cultivate the former?

It may be said that the Government of that country may adopt a more enlightened policy than hitherto, and, by proper encouragement, stimulate its subjects to a more enlarged production. But if this course should ever be adopted, it must be borne in mind that the same enlightenment which would bring about this change would not confine its operations to the single article of cotton, but would cover every other agricultural production of which the soil and climate are capable.

With every disposition to witness the successful culture of the cotton plant in the dominions of the Sultan, I could suggest but one course by which such a result might, to a limited extent, be reasonably hoped for, namely, to induce the inhabitants to cultivate that staple only in small quantities, *per căpita* of those employed in agriculture. Let the proportion of cotton produced upon each plantation be small, compared to other agricultural products, so that the labour of the naturally indolent inhabitants would not be overtaxed by the heavy drafts thereon which is requisite to the growth and production of cotton. Endeavour to obtain a large supply by multiplying the numbers of those engaged, rather than by exacting an equal amount from a smaller number.

In Egypt the cotton produced is of far superior quality, and the yield to the acre much greater. In truth I saw fields of cotton, not far distant from Cairo, apparently equal in every respect to that produced in America. This may be attributed as well to the superiority of the soil and the facilities for irrigation as to the fact that here there *are larger proprietors, who may command an adequate supply, and a better class of labourers.* Still I could not but reflect that every bale of cotton produced in Egypt diminishes, to at least an equal extent, the supply of

The planting States of the South would cheerfully and gladly aid them in promoting the growth of cotton in other lands, because it would relieve them from their present isolation, and would build up a cotton interest, which would not be without its advantages to them as well as to the consumers. No observant man can doubt, that the demand for cotton will keep pace with the supply, even although every field adapted to its cultivation, which is accessible to European markets, were called into successful requisition.

There are many benefits which would result to

grains and other productions necessary for the sustenance of man; and that any great diversion of Egyptian soil to the culture of cotton would be neither desirable nor probable, since it would supersede, not only a more useful, but a more profitable crop. However this may be, it is not to be doubted that Egypt is susceptible of a very large production of cotton of a good quality.

One fact, however, seemed to me inexplicable. It is well known that the present limited supply of cotton from Egypt was only obtained after a great effort to induce the landed proprietors to engage in its cultivation, and under the stimulant of a constant demand at yearly increasing prices. Yet it is safe to say that the amount paid by the Egyptian proprietor for the services of ten 'fellahs,' or farm-labourers, is scarcely equal to the amount which the labour of one 'negro fellow' costs the American planter. The amount expended by the Southern planter in feeding and clothing one of his African slaves would feed and clothe five times the number of Egyptian labourers with a bountiful provision, to which in their wildest flights of fancy they can scarcely be supposed to hope for; while the amount of service required from the former is certainly not greater than is exacted from the latter, in proportion to their relative capacities for physical exertion. I could not understand, therefore, why the production of cotton in Egypt was not vastly more profitable than in America, unless there are other advantages possessed by the latter over the former which are not readily apparent.

the Southern States by the expansion of cotton cultivation in other countries. The hostilities which have grown up among foreign Governments against the Government of the United States, which may be attributed almost as much to the flippant arrogance of the Northern press as to our rapid growth in wealth and power, finds the occasion to vent itself upon the institution of domestic slavery which exists in many of the States under the sanction of the Constitution of the Union. The Northern press, therefore, in order to be considered the leading champions of progress in the path of 'universal equality and fraternity,' and to take the wind out of the sails of their adversaries, out-Herod Herod in their denunciations of the institution of slavery, and, by their proverbially reckless misstatements, furnish the material to foreigners for still stronger and more authentic evidences of the wrongs perpetrated by the Southern States against the African. The Northern States are all the more ready to engage in this warfare against the institutions of the Southern States, because in thus isolating the latter from the sympathies of the world, it places them more completely in the power of those who desire to rule them for political or pecuniary advantages. Moreover, the fact that the world is almost entirely dependent upon the Southern Slave States for its supply of the great staple completes their isolation; and hence, in the very natural efforts of Europe to find other cotton fields which may relieve them in some measure from their dependence upon the South, they endeavour to bring into disrepute the peculiar system of labour which is employed in the production of that essential commodity. That I am not mistaken in the causes which have produced this clamour against the Slave States and their institution of domestic slavery, is clearly established by this—that even the most enlightened, unrelenting, and fanatical abolitionists of England seem to be utterly oblivious to the fact that the institution of African slavery now exists, under circumstances precisely similar to those in the Southern States of America, throughout the great and growing empire of Brazil.

It is thus made manifest that, if other cotton fields could be found, the clamour against the South would subside and finally disappear. Run-mad philanthropy would find other occasions for developement; and we might hope, in the interests of humanity, that it would find objects more in need of their tender solicitude, and nearer to the scene of their operations, than the happy and contented Africans who grow cotton on the other side of the great Atlantic.

In the interests of the Southern States alone, and without reference to any collateral disadvantages, it may well be doubted whether the employment of so great an amount of her labour and wealth in the production of one single article of commerce, is in accordance with her true policy. As a part only of a great confederacy this might be true, if the animosities of those with whom they are associated did not indicate the possibility of a catastrophe in which the South would be thrown upon her own internal resources; in which case it would be absolutely essential that she should be capable of producing all that is necessary to self-maintenance.

But hitherto all efforts to induce free labour voluntarily to engage in this branch of agriculture have been unavailing. Whence this failure? A superficial class of politicians in England believe that it is wholly in consequence of the existence of slavery in the country best adapted to the culture of cotton. This is only true to a limited extent. The real reason is, that free labour will not, to any great extent, cultivate this troublesome and uncertain crop, even under the most favourable auspices. It is true, that upon the occurrence of any disaster to the institution of slavery, an enormous augmentation in the price might induce an evanescent fever of production; but nature's laws would sooner or later assert their dominion, and the tide of labour would again flow back into the channel from whence it had been unnaturally, and only for a season, diverted.

Whence this repugnance of free labour to expend itself in the production of this article? We who have spent our lives in the South are familiar with the causes; but how difficult it is to impress truths upon mere theorists, without experience or practical knowledge, who, on account of adverse interests or prejudices, are predisposed to deny their existence!

In the first place, cotton is only produced in warm latitudes, where all men, especially Europeans, are naturally disinclined to constant labour. Secondly, the soil which will produce cotton is equally adapted to the production of that which may be eaten as soon as produced, without involving the necessity of sale or exchange. The culture of cotton requires almost ceaseless labour from the commencement to the close of the year. There are times and seasons, altogether irregular in their recurrence, and which may affect only a portion of the crop, when the labour must be multiplied tenfold, or the greater portion thereof will be lost. The isolated free labourer cannot command this additional force; nor could any cultivator rely upon being served by free labour in the case considered, for he would be completely in the power of his employers. Even in the Slave States, upon the occurrence of a contingency like that referred to, the proprietor of a cotton plantation is often obliged to accept the services of labourers not engaged in this culture, by giving to them one-half of all the cotton they may 'pick' from the bowls. On the other hand, the free labourer may, by working three or four months in the year, produce upon the same soil all that which is necessary to his sustenance or to his comfort. Thirdly, the cultivation of cotton by an intelligent free labourer is less profitable than other branches of agriculture in which he may with equal facility engage, while the occasional uncertainty of the yield renders it too precarious to be relied upon as an exclusive means of subsistence. The culture of cotton is only profitable where many labourers are directed by the same head: and it is a fact well established by practice, that the proprietor of a small number of slaves finds more profit in other branches of agriculture and in 'stock raising' than in the culture of cotton.

Without considering the abstract rights or wrongs of African slavery, the establishment of that system of labour introduced cotton as a great element of commerce to the civilised world. The expansion of the cause has developed the effect, until cotton has been made to occupy a more important place in commerce, and has been more closely interwoven with the domestic industry of civilised nations, than all the other products of labour which are not essential to the sustenance of life.* The philosophical mind can

* Estimating the weight of the bale at four hundred pounds, the quantity of cotton exported from the Southern States was in 1821

arrive at no other conclusion than that the effect would, to a great extent, disappear with the removal

312,233 bales; in 1829, 662,093 bales; in 1839, 1,034,060 bales; in 1849, 2,566,505 bales; and in 1859, 3,466,170.

I might go back a few years to the point of time when the first bale of cotton was produced in the planting States of America; but the above figures indicate the rapid developement of the production, under the system of slave labour, since it first became an important object in commerce. India existed, and cotton was cultivated there long before the continent of America was discovered. There was ample time to develope the culture of this staple in that vast region before an African was ever transplanted to America. I cannot discover from the past the slightest reasons for believing that the production would be suddenly or proximately augmented to sufficient proportions for the increasing wants of mankind, either in India or in any part of the world, even although slavery should be abolished, and the cultivation thereof be discontinued throughout the planting States of America. The energy and skill of the Southern planters, favoured by a soil and climate peculiarly suited to its production, and possessed of that description of labour by which alone it has been developed, has nurtured from infancy to giant manhood this colossal trade. He must be sanguine indeed who believes that the destruction of this labour, and the consequent necessity which would compel the Southern States to cultivate other crops upon their cotton plantations, would tempt the free labour of the world, or even the nominally free labour of Asia and Africa, to supply the deficiency which would thus be created. To expect such a result is but the dream of the enthusiast, and is so contrary to natural laws, which are as severe as they are unalterable and universal, that our wonder is that intelligent men can be so blinded by their passions or their interests as to induce them to seek such a vain chimera.

The cultivation of cotton in other quarters of the globe may, and it is to be hoped will, be developed by natural causes, and under the influence of natural laws. And the day may arrive when the institution of slavery in America may, under the operation of the same causes, fall into disuse, and be finally extinguished. But a violent interference, with a view to change these laws, must result in disaster to every interest involved. If each nation would therefore seek to develope its own resources, by the employment of legitimate means, instead of endeavouring, under the flimsy garb of a spurious philanthropy, to destroy the prosperity of others, mankind would be the gainer — each nation individually would be the gainer — but above all, the slave himself would be the gainer, of the cause. Heaven alone can change the invariable laws of nature.

The political Abolitionist of Great Britain, however, will not credit the facts here stated, and he believes that with the downfall of slavery the uncounted millions of India would at once supply all deficiencies in the product of tropical commodities. It is a well-known historical fact that the zeal of British philanthropists, who instituted and prosecuted to a successful close the war against slavery in the British dominions, was stimulated to increased energy and efficiency by the active support of the East India Company. What were a few millions of pounds sterling, in the beginning, to the grand results they hoped to achieve? The attainment of these would have indeed been worthy of a great sacrifice, and great was the sacrifice that was made to reach the promised, but ever-receding goal. Admitting, however, that the British Abolitionist, who seeks to employ this substitute for American slavery labour, is only actuated by a benevolent purpose, does it never occur to him that other 'friends of the human race' might, upon the principle he himself has laid down, call in question the right of England to the

who although now in that condition which men call slavery, occupies a position higher than any others of his race, whether it be those who have never left their native jungles, or those still more unhappy, who after a period of enslavement, have been turned loose to fight the battle of life with their former masters as their rivals.

dominion of India? In estimating the sum of real philanthropy and regard for the rights of man, which may be accorded to them for their efforts to eradicate the sin of slavery from America, and to implant prejudices in the minds of others against the Slave States, the unbiassed mind naturally institutes a comparison between their *practice* in regard to India and their precepts in regard to America. The Southerner, at least, when brought to trial before the civilised world by the British Abolitionist, for the crime of holding, by comparison, only a handful of Africans in bondage, may be justified in demanding by what right England holds India in subjection. Under what code of morals can England lay claim to that extensive territory on a far distant sea, and in another quarter of the globe, if she agrees to be governed by the same law of morals which her philanthropists seek to enforce upon the South? Has India ever menaced the integrity of the British Islands, or injured a hair of the head of any Englishman who had not first entered its territory as a master and a conqueror? There do not exist to-day as many human beings held as slaves in the Southern States of the American Union as have been sacrificed in establishing and perpetuating the dominion of Great Britain over the soil of India. Was the conquest made from any feeling of benevolence towards the human race, or to improve the condition of the inhabitants? The events of one day, if we are to credit British historians, would furnish a record of more misery, more destitution, more utter, hopeless, unpitied wretchedness than would the history of an entire generation of all the African slaves now held in bondage upon the soil of America. There, again, the 'tracts' and 'pious songs,' sent over the water for the use of American congregations, are silent—no moving story or pitying verse recounts the sad fate of the poor Asiatic.

This may not be 'slavery' according to a literal definition of that term; yet what is it but a much more cruel form of 'servitude' than exists in the American planting States?—for the master does not bestow even a crust of bread upon his more than slave. In fine, I would put this last interrogatory to the real philanthropist of Great Britain, who passes weary days and sleepless nights in devising schemes for the amelioration of the condition of the American slave, while holding up his master to the gaze of mankind as an enemy to the human race: If the enslavement of a comparative handfull of Africans in America is a crime of such enormous magnitude, where can we find words to express the enormity of England's wrong to India?

I do not wish to constitute myself an arbiter or judge between England and India. It is not my province even to decide whether more benefits than evils have resulted to mankind from the subjection of

India by England. Whatever may be the abstract rights or wrongs involved in the issue, it is a practical fact, that to-day, as well as in all times past, powerful nations and superior races subject and hold in dependence weaker nations and races; and it may be fairly assumed that such will be the case in all time to come. It is, and always will remain, an unsettled question, how far civilised nations may properly go, in compelling indolent or wicked barbarians to change their idle or brutal habits of life, and forcing them to contribute their due proportion to the necessities or the luxuries of the civilised world. But British emancipationists may not justly complain if they are held amenable to the requirements of the MORAL LAW, by which they profess to be governed, and which they seek to enforce upon others. They may be justly brought to trial under the rules which they have instituted in their assaults upon the planting States of America; and by these they stand condemned; for no enlightened and impartial tribunal would decide that there exists a solitary reason founded in philanthropy, justice, abstract right, benevolence, or generosity, which should induce the Slave States of America to emancipate the Africans, over whom they exercise dominion, that does not appeal to Great Britain, with far more force, to abandon the soil of India, and restore to its inhabitants their long-lost liberties. It may be said that the term which is employed to express the condition of the African in America, is not applicable to, and does not define, the relation which subsists between the Indiaman and his conqueror. This may be true; but the principle is abstractly the same in both, though the wrong done may be different in degree; so may the circumstances under which the wrong was done, and is perpetuated, modify the judgement of mankind against the wrongdoer. Still the injury and the injustice are identical in kind. It is probable, however, that neither will voluntarily consent to the sacrifice of the great interest involved. It is quite certain that any advice volunteered by foreign nations, urging upon England the adoption of a policy, however just and humane, would be regarded by all Englishmen as a most officious intermeddling in affairs in regard to which they were alone responsible, and in the decision of which they would listen to no umpire. Does it never enter into the minds of foreign Abolitionists that their ceaseless attempts to excite the prejudices of mankind against the Southern States and their institutions, and their efforts to subvert their domestic institutions, are also very properly regarded as an officious intermeddling in affairs that do not concern them? And if they are really governed by philanthropic motives, can they not perceive that such interference is calculated to retard, if not wholly to prevent, the accomplishment of the purpose they seek?

It may be asked what I have done for the defence of the South, by establishing the fact that other nations of the world perpetrate wrongs of a like character against their fellow-men? I answer, much, very much. When I establish that the world has been unable, after the most strenuous efforts, to stimulate any system of productive labour in the tropics which is not more objectionable to the eye of real philanthropy than the slavery system of America, there exists only one question which the friend of mankind is called upon to decide. Namely,—would it not be better in the interest of the human race that the slave-labour system of America should be left to work out its own destiny and its own remedy, rather than by its violent overthrow to deprive mankind of the fruits of its labour? Nay, more than this. If we have indeed sinned in the sight of heaven, which we do not believe, we may, in mitigation of the judgement against us before that high tribunal, point to the evil example of those who are our accusers; we might ask with confidence for a suspension of the execution until England shall have surrendered India, until France shall have withdrawn from Algeria, until Russia shall have abandoned Circassia, and until the Sultan shall have restored to the Greek his long-lost inheritance; for they are, at least, much *older* sinners than we.

LETTER X.

Summary of the relative advantages of different systems of Labour—Results of the comparison—Characteristics of Great Britain—An Anti-Slavery Poem—Does not fairly illustrate John Bull—Reflections of a Philanthropist upon subjects suggested by the Poem—Europe has only recently abandoned the African Slave-trade—The Southern States have always opposed it—The institution of Slavery more Humane now than formerly.

I HAVE briefly glanced at some of the various systems of labour which have been proposed as substitutes for the institution of African slavery in America. Each in its turn has resulted in failure; or those which have been attended with a partial success, have been pronounced by the judgement of the most enlightened philanthropists to be, in every respect, more objectionable than the worst form of now-existing slavery. So far as practical results are concerned, we stand now precisely where we did when Wilberforce and his followers preached their first crusade against the slave-trade. The confident predictions of that day, that free African labour and the cultivation of the rich soil of India, by the subjugated natives, would entirely supersede and render valueless the institution of slavery in America, have been proved to be idle dreams. American slavery has gone on increasing in value and importance until the present moment of time, when, if we could imagine such a calamity, its sudden suppression would produce disaster and misery throughout the civilised world. England, which is the great purchaser of cotton, admits that no other system can successfully compete in its production with slave labour. But many of her leading statesmen, as before said, also insist that if the institution of slavery should disappear, the free labour of India, and of other tropical countries, would promptly engage in the cultivation of those articles which are now obtained almost exclusively from slave labour. They believe that the large number of labourers who would under such circumstances be added to the productive force, would be able to approximate to nearly the same results as are now achieved under the slavery system.

I can discover no reason for believing that these hopes would be realised. Still less can I see any interest which mankind has in making the experiment, even with a probable prospect of success. But above all, I can discover no advantages in the proposed change which ought to induce America to strike so fatal a blow at her own power and influence; and unless our own folly or madness drives us to this act of self-immolation, no earthly power, having the will, possesses the ability to deprive us of our control over that monarch of commerce which to-day exercises its peaceful dominion over the kingdoms of the earth.

In considering this subject, I have instituted a fair comparison in regard to the morality and productiveness of 'slave and free labour' in what are denominated tropical products—and, as my brief references have shown, to the advantage of the former; while upon the question of *humanity*, we have tested American slavery by a comparison with those systems which have been employed to supersede it. I am well aware that the vast majority of those whose minds have been warped by long-cultivated prejudices, will not see the advantages which have resulted to mankind through the instrumentality of the institution of slavery, nor the enormities of any other system which holds out the hope of gratifying their feelings of animosity. They will continue to shut their eyes to evils upon the one hand, and benefits upon the other, if these conflict with their theories; but the prejudices, the passions, the injustice of mankind, cannot make truth fiction, nor change right into wrong. Laudations of the system of free labour, as illustrated by its practical workings, throughout the greater part of the world, cannot put bread into the mouth of the starving, nor of itself bestow a real independence upon those who labour for their daily sustenance. On the other hand, the most moving picture of the horrors of slavery cannot destroy the existing fact, that no other labourers in the same field have as many of the comforts of life, with as few of its troubles and trials, as have the slaves of the Southern States of the American Union. Neither can any amount of calumny which ignorance, or malevolence, or both combined, may heap upon the slaveholder of the Southern States, deprive him of that inward consciousness that he has worthily employed the power which the Almighty has placed in his hands—that he has been instrumental in diffusing amongst the mass of mankind comforts and necessaries which have contributed in an eminent degree to their happiness, and that he has sent forth nothing which has ever added to the unhappiness, or increased the vices of his fellow-men! With all this, he feels that in diffusing these blessings, and in adding to the wealth, influence, and importance of his native land, he has gone on improving the condition of those who have been his instruments for accomplishing so much good, until he can safely challenge a comparison in this respect with that of any similar number of labourers in the world!

In my comments upon the policy of the anti-slavery party of England, I have done nothing more than to test it by the rules which it has laid down as binding upon America. If these laws have condemned them, it is not my fault. There may be much that may be said in extenuation of England's faults, if it be admitted or claimed that the exigencies of a nation do not at all times permit it to follow that straight line which the rigid rules of abstract right require; but many of her statesmen do not admit that the Slave States of America shall be entitled to the benefit of such a plea, and impartial minds will decide that she has no right to an exemption which she is not willing to concede to others. The Abolitionists of England have endeavoured, by every means at their command, to stimulate the prejudices of the world against the planting States of America on account of negro slavery. If both were put upon their trial before a just and intelligent tribunal, which would be condemned as the criminal most deserving of punishment? which the most worthy of the approbation of mankind?

In my references to the English emancipationists, who will say that I have unwittingly been guilty of an injustice in the conclusions at which I have arrived? Suppose that an intelligent historian were called upon to describe the general characteristics of the British Government and people; he would say with truth, they stand preeminent for practical good sense, clear-sighted sagacity, self-will, self-confidence, obstinacy, contempt for the feelings, the opinions, and the interests of others, where they have an interest to subserve, selfishness, pride, a love of independence and of conquest, indomitable courage and boldness, and, above all, a readiness at all times to make any sacrifice for the indulgence of these propensities. But, upon the other hand, who would not smile if the historian were to add, that they are peculiarly characterised by the possession of qualities which come under the designation of tenderness, or sensibility, or sentiment, or an unselfish regard for the feelings or interests of others, or, in fine, that they are distinguished as a people for the display of what may be denominated the finer and gentler feelings of the human heart? It is fair to conclude that the smile even of an Englishman would degenerate into a more boisterous expression of merriment, if the said historian were to adduce testimony in support of their claim to the possession of these heart-sympathies, by quoting lines from the 'tracts' or 'pious songs' composed and sent from England into America, for the use of anti-slavery pastors, and their congregations; as for example:

'I was a helpless negro boy,
That wandered on the shore;
* Thieves stole me from my parents' arms:
I never saw them more!'

* When the touching appeal from which these lines are extracted was first republished in America, the Tract Society, not duly regarding the sensibilities of the anti-slavery public, substituted for the two first words of the third line, the words '*men took*.' The convulsion which followed this sacrilegious transformation of the text, shook the Christian abolition world of the North to its very foundation. The New York press groaned under the weight of the ponderous articles which related the events of the great internal struggle. The unfortunate society which had perpetrated the outrage was denounced as an emissary of the devil, and what was still worse, a tool of the 'slave-ocracy.' The great contest among the Lilliputians, between the 'big-endians' and the 'little-

I have said that the Englishman might laugh, but to the philanthropist, impressed by their pictures of the horrors of slavery, these touching lines might induce a train of reflections, which would awaken emotions far different from those which produce merriment. The mind might very naturally wander over the pages of English history which record the tears, and blood, and desolation of India. The peculiar friend of *sombre colours* might behold, through the mists of the past, the embarkation of Africans doomed to hopeless and eternal servitude in Spanish mines, or upon the North American plantations of Great Britain. From the mast-head of the

endians' was mere child's play compared to the terrible energy of those who arrayed themselves under the banner of 'Thieves stole' against those who defended themselves under the flag of 'Men took.' The 'Thieves stole' party were of the opinion that the Tract Society had sold itself to the emissaries of the slave Powers, and that one of the least evils which might be apprehended therefrom would be the encouragement it would afford to the re-opening of the African slave trade, with all the horrors of the 'middle passage.' The 'Men took' advocates defended themselves with a vigour which showed clearly that they were not going to succumb without dragging their adversaries down with them. They insisted that, as the Southerners never had been engaged in the business of taking 'wandering negro babies from their mothers' arms, on the coast of Africa — in fact, never had been engaged in the slave trade — and as it was likewise true that all the Africans, babies included, who had ever been transported to the Slave States had been sent thither by the British and the Yankees, it ought to be clear to the dullest comprehension that their object in altering the text was to smooth over the sins of the latter, and not to conciliate the present slave-owners of the South, who could not feel any personal interest whatever in the settlement of a question which involved only the acts of their avowed enemies. For full details of this exciting controversy, the reader is referred to files of the leading New York daily papers.

slave-ship floated the flag of that Britannia which 'ruled the waves.' Commingled with the wild shrieks of husband and wife, father and daughter, and of that 'helpless negro boy, torn from its parents' arms,' were heard alone the words of that tongue which has been immortalised by the writings of a Shakspeare and a Milton. Incredulous philanthropy might refuse to credit even the evidence of its senses, and exclaim, 'It is a pirate ship and a pirate crew, who have stolen the livery of heaven to serve the devil in!' Show your authority, commander; leave not the incredulous to doubt about the lawfulness of your honourable calling. The Royal Charter is unfolded, which recites that after a long and bloody struggle among the Christian nations, Great Britain being of the victors, claimed and received, as her portion of the spoils, an exclusive right to deal in slaves, and to transport the same from the coast of Africa.

Those are curious pages in history which record that the *madness* of the eighteenth century throughout the civilised world, embracing all the Christian Powers of Europe without distinction, was the establishment upon the American Continent, by the most cruel and inhuman acts of barbarity, of that same African slavery which it has been the *mania* of the first half of the nineteenth century to eradicate, and that too, after the atrocious features of the slavery which they created had been supplanted by the mild and almost patriarchal system which now prevails, at least throughout the planting States of the Federal Union.

The solution of this apparent anomaly may be readily discovered in the great revolutions that occurred between the two epochs referred to, which robbed Europe of the greater portion of its North American possessions, and which threatened, at some time or other, to free the entire continent of America from European domination. The slaves, with the territory they inhabited, thus changed masters; and the new possessors, from the condition of vassals, became the equals and the rivals of their former masters.

The enthusiasts who choose to imagine and to declare that this public sentiment of the nineteenth century in Europe, had its origin in a new revelation of the Divine will, or in some hitherto misunderstood or undiscovered law of Divine justice, and in a consequent loftier conception of public morality than was possessed by their ancestors, may gratify the vanity of the age by such a solution, but the intelligent reader of contemporaneous history will find no difficulty in arriving at the conclusion, that this revolution in public sentiment owed its origin and its developement, not to *moral* but to *political* causes.

I do not doubt the sincerity of the great body of Europeans at the present day, who express the belief that the institution of African slavery upon the American continent is a 'great evil,' and perhaps 'a sin;' nor, on the other hand, do I doubt the sincerity of their ancestors, who believed that in kidnapping Africans and transporting them as slaves to their plantations, they were adopting the only means by which those savages and heathen could be civilised and christianised. But I have as little doubt, that the public sentiment of Europe during each of the periods referred to, was moulded in accordance with the circumstances by which each was surrounded. The fact exists, that as long as the American continent was held as European provinces, slavery was approved and practised by all the European nations having American possessions; and when the American continent became, to a great extent, independent of foreign dominion, Europe for the first time beheld the enormity of the institution of slavery which it had created.

It is also a curious fact, that while the nations of the Old World, which established slavery upon the American continent, are at the present day its uncompromising foes, the most prominent defenders of the institution are found in the only country which opposed its propagation, with all the feeble powers they were able to exercise—namely, the Southern States of the American Union.*

For many years previous to the American revolution, the colonists of Great Britain in vain sought to prevent the importation of African slaves; but the mother-country turned a deaf ear to their petitions and remonstrances. Queen Elizabeth chartered the first company of which there is any record for the supply of slaves to the Spanish provinces, of which she was herself a shareholder. King Charles II., in 1662, created a monopoly in favour of a company which was authorised to convey to the British colonies three thousand slaves per annum. The King also offered by proclamation to such of his subjects as would emigrate to America, one hundred acres of land for each four slaves they would purchase. There was throughout England a universal outcry against this monopoly, not on account of its supposed sinfulness or inhumanity, but because the desire was universal to engage in this attractive and lucrative commerce. At length, in 1708, the House of Commons, in response to the universal desire of the merchants who had not been hitherto permitted to

* Lord Brougham, in the appendix to his able work on the British Constitution, says:—

'It is only fair towards the Americans to consider, *first*, that they had originally desired to have no slave trade, and that the mother-country had most wickedly, as well as most foolishly, refused to free them from this guilt; *secondly*, that they abolished the traffic the instant their Constitution allowed them.'

participate in the profits, resolved, — 'That the trade was *important*, and ought to be *free* and *open to all the Queen's subjects* trading from Great Britain.' It was not, however, till the year 1749 that the Government threw open the trade to all British subjects. The Act referred to recites that,—'The slave trade is very advantageous to Great Britain, and necessary for supplying the plantations and colonies thereunto belonging with a sufficient number of negroes at a reasonable rate.' During a large portion of this time, as before said, the poor colonists were in vain protesting against the continuance of this traffic, or endeavouring by legislation to throw around it such restrictions as would at least diminish the number of slaves. The State of South Carolina, in the year 1760, enacted a law prohibiting entirely their further importation; but for this act of temerity the Governor was severely reprimanded by the British Government. The Act was rejected by the Crown, and the Governors of all the other colonies were *warned against permitting such legislation in future*. In the island of Jamaica a similar effort was made to suppress the traffic, and a Bill actually passed the Assembly to that effect in 1774. In response thereto, the Earl of Dartmouth, then Secretary of State, addressed Sir Basil Keith, the Governor of the province, saying—'*The measure has created great alarm to the merchants of Great Britain engaged in that branch of commerce,*' and prohibiting him, '*on pain of removal from his Government,* to assent to such laws.'

The last remonstrance addressed by the American colonists to the Imperial Government was in 1775, after the commencement of the war which ended in their severance from the mother-country. In reply to the representations made by the agent of the colonies, the Earl of Dartmouth, Secretary of State, responded in the following emphatic language:— 'We cannot allow the colonies *to check or discourage, in any degree, a traffic so beneficial to the nation.*'

Previous to the formation of the Constitution of the United States, the slave trade was prohibited in many of the States. In South Carolina, there was, by enactments of the Legislature, a total suppression of the traffic from 1787 to 1804, when it was reluctantly reopened, until 1808, and from that time to the present it has never been revived.* During this

* The legislation of the American Slave States during more than a hundred and sixty-five years, whether as colonies or afterwards as independent States, commencing certainly as far back as 1698, has been illustrated by constant efforts either to embarrass or entirely to prohibit the slave trade. Solitary and alone, among the nations of Christendom, though fruitlessly against the unanimous policy of the European Governments, they struggled to prevent the increase of slaves from Africa upon the American continent; and never from that day to this have they swerved from that line of policy. It may be interesting to the reader to glance over the Acts of the legislatures of South Carolina, Virginia, Georgia, or other Slave States, to see with what earnestness they laboured to accomplish this end.

The Act of Assembly of South Carolina of 1698 recites that,

period of about four years, there arrived in the harbour of Charleston 202 vessels with the aggregate

'Whereas the great number of negroes which have of late been imported into this colony may endanger the safety thereof, if speedy measures be not taken, and encouragement given for the importation of white servants,'—requires each planter for every six negroes to take one white servant.

The Act of 1714 imposes an additional duty of 2*l.* upon every slave over twelve years imported from any part of Africa. The following is the preamble to this Act:—

'And whereas the number of negroes do extremely increase in this province, and through the afflicting Providence of God the white persons do not proportionably multiply, by reason whereof the safety of the said province is greatly endangered: for the prevention of which, for the future, &c. &c.'

Act of 1716, 'to encourage the importation of white servants into this province.' 'Whereas sad experience has taught us, that the small number of white inhabitants of this province is not sufficient to defend the same even against our Indian enemies; and whereas the number of slaves is daily increasing in this province, which may likewise endanger the safety thereof, if speedy care be not taken to encourage the importation of white servants.'

The Act of 1717, after the preamble, 'And whereas the great importation of negroes into this province, in proportion to the white inhabitants of the same, whereby the future safety of this province will be greatly endangered, for the prevention thereof, &c. &c.,' imposes an additional duty of 40*l.* upon every negro slave, 'of any age or condition whatsoever, and from any part of the world.'

It will be readily seen that this Act was designed to prohibit altogether the importation of Africans, without violating the orders of the British Government, which denied to the colonists the privilege of excluding them by direct legislation. In the next Act, however, the preceding law is regarded as a prohibition.

The Act of 1744, 'for the further preventing the spreading of malignant and contagious disorders,' has the following preamble: 'Whereas it hath been found by experience, that since the importation of negroes and slaves from the coast of Africa into this province hath been prohibited, this province in general, and Charleston in particular, hath been much more healthy than heretofore it hath been, &c. &c.'

The Act of 1750 and the Act of 1751 impose a tax upon the importation of slaves, to be devoted to the encouragement of white servants.

number of 39,075 slaves. Of these there were belonging to,

It would appear from the following Act that the laws hitherto enacted had failed to accomplish their purpose.

The Act of 1764, after the preamble, 'Whereas the importation of negroes, equal in number to what have been imported of late years, may prove of the most dangerous consequence, in many respects, to this province, and the best way to obviate such dangers will be by imposing such additional duty upon them, as may totally prevent the evils,' imposes an additional duty of 100*l*.

Let us now pass from this period of colonial vassalage, and see what was done by the independent sovereignty of the State of South Carolina.

In 1787 the Legislature enacted that no negro or other slave shall be imported from Africa, and no slave shall be imported from any other State, unless accompanied by his master.

A subsequent Act of the same year declares, 'that any person importing or bringing into this State a negro slave, contrary to the Act to regulate the recovery of debts, and prohibiting the importation of negroes, shall, besides the forfeiture of such negro or slave, be liable to a penalty of 100*l*., in addition to the forfeiture in and by said Act prescribed.'

The Act of 1788 prohibits the importation of negroes or other slaves, unless at that time the property of citizens of the United States, and within the limits of the United States, under pain of forfeiture and 100*l*.

The Act of 1792 after the preamble, 'Whereas it is deemed inexpedient to increase the number of slaves within the State, in our present circumstances and condition,' prohibits the importation of slaves from Africa, the West Indies, or other places beyond seas, for two years.

The Act of 1794 extended the prohibition to 1797.

The Act of 1796, after the preamble, 'Whereas it appears to be highly impolitic to import negroes from Africa, or other place beyond seas,' prohibits such importation till 1799, under pain of forfeiture, and a fine upon the captains.

The Act of 1798 extended the prohibition to 1801.

And by Act of 1800, extended the prohibition to 1803.

In 1803 the prohibitions were virtually violated by the introduction of Africans through the ports of the Northern States and the interior. The legislature, to prevent this clandestine trade, permitted the ports to be opened until 1808; after which there was a final Act, prohibiting the trade, the policy of which was concurred in by all the Slave States.

How many amongst the thousands of dupes who, under the influence

Natives of Great Britain	91	ships
„ „ France . .	10	„
Northern Free States .	88	„
Southern Slave States .	13	„

of highly-wrought wood-cuts, portraying the horrors of the African slave ships, attend the anti-slavery meetings in Exeter Hall and elsewhere, are aware of *the fact that during a period of considerably more than half a century not one hundred Africans have been imported into the planting States of the American Union?* Certainly the leaders of these meetings are fully acquainted with this fact; but what are we to think of the morality of those who, in order to stimulate the hostility of the ignorant against the American planting States, thus deliberately propagate a belief in the minds of others which they themselves know to be false? They cannot excuse themselves by denying that they in words give expression to the falsehood, for they put forth these pictorial illustrations of an era in the African slave trade when that branch of commerce was conducted under the exclusive patronage of the European Powers, while they mean that the public shall understand that it is illustrative of a custom which now prevails in the Southern States of the Union. This they do in the face of the fact that not three slave ships have landed upon those shores, nor have, either directly or indirectly, introduced slaves upon their territory, since they refused, in 1808, any longer to permit the English or Yankee ships to continue this traffic.

But this is not the only illegitimate means by which the promoters of this 'philanthropic crusade' against the South succeed in instilling prejudices into the minds of the people of Europe. None know better than the intelligent Englishman, except it be the people of the United States, how little reliance may be placed in the Northern sensation press about the period of an election. Horrible stories are concocted and put afloat, with a view to stimulate the passions of the ignorant voters. In some cases they descant upon the blood-thirsty ferocity of the Southerner. As an example:—A newspaper correspondent tells a story of a Southern gentleman who—I believe about the year 1856—upon a wager of a pair of boots, actually visited a Yankee town, killed the first man he met, took off his scalp, and, with the bloody trophy borne high above his head upon a pole, returned to claim the prize, amid the plaudits of his admiring fellow-countrymen! My unsophisticated fellow-countrymen, if they gave a moment's thought to such a story, would never imagine that in enlightened England such self-evident fabrications would even be laughed at, as clever electioneering devices. Yet, on the contrary, the most enlightened men in that land, overflowing with intelligence, and

The number of slaves imported was —

By foreigners . . .	21,027	35,632
,, Northern States .	14,605	
,, Slave States		3,443

These facts show, that from the very first ship which landed the first cargo of slaves upon the soil of the South during the period of its colonial vassalage up to the very last which the people of the South, having acquired their independence, would allow to be imported into their territory, the traffic was carried on, and the human chattels were almost literally forced upon the reluctant South, by the very people who are now denouncing her before the civilised world, and calling down upon her the maledictions of God and man, for the enormous crime of holding these same Africans and their descendants in bondage.

It must be remembered that it was not alone for a season of short duration that these were the cham-

boasting of its superior civilisation, catch up the story, and send it broadcast over the civilised world, as a 'striking illustration of the demoralising influence of the institution of slavery.' You hear it from the stand of the lecturer — you see it posted in placards, with pictorial illustrations, upon the corners of the streets of their cities — you read it in their newspapers — but, stranger than all, you find it in their ponderous volumes, printed in the highest style of the 'art preservative of all arts,' where it is laid away in their libraries — a record, *as they* would say, of the criminality of the Southerners, but, as the sober judgement of posterity will decide, a confession of the inherent weakness of the cause of their adversaries, and of the grossly unjust means by which they have sought to mislead that public whom it was their duty to correctly inform.

pions of slavery and the slave trade in its most hideous form; but it was for centuries the policy of the nation, sanctioned and practised by the people, made lawful by the Parliament, made religious by the ministers of Christ, made fashionable by the Court, and made honourable by the approval and patronage of the Crown. This traffic in human flesh did not have its origin and exodus during the dark ages of the world, but it flourished as well in the days of the glorious Queen Elizabeth, and during the reign of the Stuarts, as under the Protectorate of the Puritan Cromwell, and of 'honest old George the Third;' and its practice was never abandoned, until the *present Slave States of America*, having become free from European dominion, *closed their ports peremptorily and for ever* against the further introduction of slaves from the coast of Africa!

Then, and not till then, did the slave merchants of England, standing upon the decks of their rotting slave ships, awaken to the horrible nature of the traffic in which they had been so long engaged. Then did the clergymen receive the new revelation, and announce from the holy desk that slavery was a 'sin in the sight of God,' and that he who thereafter practised it would be 'a fit subject for divine wrath.' The Parliament, with the approval of the Crown, at once declared it piracy, to be punishable with death under the gallows, for their subjects to engage any longer in that nefarious traffic, which they had but the moment before, and during hundreds of years, sanctioned by their laws and enforced by their bayonets upon unwilling subjects!

There are no facts of history which call to mind more forcibly the true saying that 'truth is stranger than fiction,' than those here stated. The transposition of the parties to this struggle was as sudden as it was complete. There are those now living who were born at an epoch when the only enemies of the slave trade—the only civilised people who struggled earnestly, however fruitlessly, against its continuance, were the slave colonies, now the Slave States, of the American Union. While those who forced the slaves upon them against their will, and who officially declared that the 'colonists could not be permitted to check or discourage, in any degree, a traffic so beneficial to the nation,' embraced not only the people of Great Britain, but those of nearly all Christendom!

If the proposition were seriously made to-day to reopen the African slave trade, the number of citizens of the Slave States who would favour it would no doubt be as small as in any population of like numbers in the civilised world. Not from any feeling of mock-philanthropy—not because they believe that the condition of the Africans would not be improved thereby, but they would exclude them in their own interest. For the same reason, amongst others, that they would not consent to the removal of the social and political barriers which divide them from the civilised African slave, they would not consent to mingle up with their American-born slaves the barbarians from Africa. Such an infusion of native Africans would have the worst possible influence upon the now contented slaves, and might possibly render necessary in self-defence a return to that odious system which in former days degraded the institution of slavery.

In closing this reference to the parties who are responsible for the institution of slavery in America, I will only add, that if indeed the Slave States of the American Union are guilty as charged, they have the authority of heaven's holy Book for believing that it is not these, their accusers, who are the divinely appointed agents of the King of kings to cast the stone which is to deprive them of life.

Is it wonderful that the Southerner should turn with bitter scorn from the admonitions and maledictions of these, and, appealing to God and the sober judgement of upright men, find recorded upon his own conscience his vindication against such charges, preferred by such accusers, even though his fellow-men should refuse to do him justice?

I have said that the institution of slavery, now in the United States of America, is so much more humane than that which existed under the rule of those who first inaugurated the system, as scarcely to bear any resemblance thereto. In order not to tax the reader with the necessity of crediting the mere statement of a fact without proof, I beg to refer to some of the causes which have produced this change.

Formerly the slaves were savages, and of course it was necessary to guard them with more vigilance. They did not speak the languages of the countries to which they were transported, and they were for the most part, in fact altogether, distributed by the European Powers throughout their colonies. The proprietors of the plantations often resided in the mother-country, and governed their slaves by the employment of agents. Moreover, there was but a comparatively trifling value attached to slaves, and the loss of one or a dozen by bad treatment was of but small pecuniary importance.

Now, the slaves are civilised and speak the language of their masters. They may be left in the enjoyment of almost as much freedom of action, when unemployed, as they desire. They reside with their masters and form a part of the household, and their masters are themselves the political sovereigns of the country, in conjunction with their fellow-citizens of the same race. Each slave has a large money value, so great indeed, that the interest upon the capital employed, with other incidental expenses, makes it the most expensive labour in the world. If free labour could be induced to cultivate the sugar and cotton fields, slavery might possibly abolish itself on account of its greater cost. The two races having existed together for so long a time, it is natural that both should now understand and adapt themselves to their respective positions. All these causes have produced such a modification in the practical effects of the system by the improvement of the condition of the slaves, as to divest it of almost all those features which at one time shocked the sensibilities of the world. It would readily be conjectured that such a result would attend the causes enumerated, without appealing to existing facts in corroboration thereof.

But if any additional proofs were required to establish the truth of the facts here stated in regard to the radical amelioration of the system of slavery, as known to Europe by the history of that institution in the past, they are furnished by the statistics of slavery at the different epochs referred to. The whole number of Africans imported into the British West Indies during a period of less than two hundred years, is estimated at 1,700,000 to 2,100,000; while those who remained to be registered for emancipation, were but 780,000. In the Island of St. Domingo, the number of negroes imported during ninety years, ending in 1776, is estimated at 800,000, while at that date there remained but 290,800. The decrease in other islands has been in like proportion.

In the Slave States of the American Union, the whole number of Africans imported falls short of 400,000, while the present slave population of the fifteen Southern States is estimated at about 4,000,000. The natural increase during more than three quarters of a century is thus about twenty-eight per cent. for every decade, without the importation of a single slave, for nearly sixty years.

It is not surprising that the sensibilities of mankind were shocked, in presence of the deplorable results of slavery as existing in the West Indies. Thousands have arrayed themselves against the institutions of the American Slave States, without considering that the form of slavery which was under European auspices so odious and detestable, had long since ceased to exist upon the American Continent. As well might the Frenchman of to-day find fault with the Government of the Emperor Napoleon, because of the tyranny of Louis XIV.; or the subject of Her Majesty the Queen of England desire to overthrow the monarchy, on account of the atrocities of Richard III.

In considering the probabilities, or rather the possibilities, of effecting the abolition of slavery in the planting States, and the substitution of another class of labourers, it is necessary to observe that there are difficulties in the way which have never attended any other scheme of emancipation in any other country. In the Northern States of the American Confederacy, when slavery became unprofitable, it was, in common parlance, abolished. This is not, however, literally true. As I have before said, no slave was necessarily made free by these acts. The dominant race rid itself of a population which had ceased to be necessary or profitable, by selling them, before the day of emancipation had arrived, to the neighbouring Slave States. With England, so far as the great body of the nation was concerned, emancipation in her colonies was only a question of pounds sterling! The Africans were not inhabitants of the British Isles, and by consequence thereof, the difficulty of greatest magnitude was not encountered—namely, the getting rid of the degraded population. Now, the Slave States of the South cannot, as the Northern States did, make a profit out of emancipation, by removing them to a country where they would be more valuable; nor can they, as England did, get rid of the population by the mere sacrifice of their estimated money value. The slaves liberated in the South, in a body, must, of course, remain upon the soil. Supposing that, in a pecuniary point of view, the time should arrive when this course would be deemed most profitable, there arises the political difficulty that the institutions of the country are Republican in form, and all whom the laws recognise as citizens should have equal rights. This fact also precludes the Southern States from adopting the 'Cooly system,' or any other which involves the employment of Asiatics or Africans, to supply the place of slave labour.

Inasmuch, therefore, as the European races will not, to any considerable extent, labour in the production of cotton, rice, and sugar, it follows that with the abolition of slavery the production of these articles in the United States would, to a great extent, cease. With the Governments of Europe the case would be different. They could transport any number of Asiatics or Africans to their colonies without any danger to their institutions, because the mother-country would not be affected thereby. They could with impunity cover their islands and distant possessions with the most barbarous tribes and protect their property against any threatened conversion to the use of these savages by a few cannon. But to introduce such a population into the United States, in the midst of the families of the inhabitants, except under the system of absolute slavery, would be an act of suicide. It is not difficult to perceive that if the abolition of slavery in America can be accomplished, the United States, having no distant colonies, would cease from that moment to be formidable competitors in supplying the world with tropical productions.

My object in these letters has been rather to state admitted facts than to make arguments in favour of or against any particular systems. That I have stated them frankly and without any colouring which could pervert their true meaning or significance, will not, I think, be questioned. Whether these facts will produce upon the minds of others the same convictions as upon mine, will of course be dependent upon circumstances. I am well aware that I have added no new light to the subjects about which I have written — the particular truths I have stated are known to all. My purpose, however, has been to present these isolated facts in a body, so that they could be considered together. In the investigation of a subject, in order to understand it, it is necessary to consider all the facts which bear upon it. Partisans often select a number of admitted facts, and, by omitting another, establish a falsehood without having stated an untruth. Oftener still they start out by the assertion of a proposition which none will deny, and, leaping over a hundred truths, arrive at false conclusions.

Never has any subject been treated so unfairly as that of the institution of slavery in America. Its enemies start out with the declaration that one human being should not be held in slavery by another, and the abstract fact being generally conceded, they find no difficulty in concluding that the slaves should be set free and their masters consigned to eternal perdition! The Slave States of the South have been required to submit the trial of their cause upon that single issue of abstract right. Every system of government that has been invented by man would be overthrown under the application of the same rule. Human institutions will not stand the test of a trial against abstract right. I have, therefore, chosen to examine the peculiar circumstances in which slavery had its origin — its progress, and its present condition. Admitting its imperfections, I have compared it with the good and evil of other systems which have been devised to supersede it.

It is to be regretted that the systematic and ceaseless assaults of the Anti-slavery party of Great Britain upon the Southern States, should render it necessary for them, in self-defence, to turn upon their assailants and defend themselves by an enumeration of their own faults, vices, and crimes. It would be much more in accordance with the fraternal feelings which ought to animate the two great nations of Anglo-Saxon origin to institute comparisons in regard to the benefits rather than the evils which each have conferred or inflicted upon mankind. Nor do I doubt that there are very many Englishmen among all classes of society who deprecate these constant, and irritating, and unfriendly assaults upon a community of States which England has thus far known only by the benefits which she has derived from her intercourse with them.

Would that the great body of the English people could break the chains of prejudice in which they have been bound by designing or injudicious leaders, and refuse to follow other counsels than the dictates of their own consciences and the promptings of their own interests! It is impossible that they can in their hearts cherish any feeling of animosity against those whose only offence consists in having given such a direction to the legacy of slavery, which they inherited from British ancestors, as to offer employment and bread, and luxuries, which were previously attainable by the rich only, to millions of themselves and the poor of the world! Would that they could see in advance the evils which would inevitably fall with a heavy hand upon the toiling millions of their great country, should the mad designs of the Abolition leaders be crowned with success!

Leaving out of question that ridiculous affectation of sentimental philanthropy which is so peculiarly unbecoming and unsuited to the genius of the British character, there ought to be, and but for the influence of unwisely selfish or deluded men, there would be, a feeling of reciprocal sympathy between Great

Britain and the planting States of America. While neither is wholly dependent upon the other, each contributes materially to the other's prosperity. The planting States produce the raw material which England fashions into shape. The planter is, after all, but the overseer for Great Britain, while Great Britain is but the factor of the planter. Without considering the past, if there is any guilt in slavery, it is shared alike by both, for in the products of slave labour they are joint partners. If there is moral turpitude in holding slaves, the guilt of those who knowingly participate in the profits accruing from the wrong, is the same as that of the active agents. By the moral law, as well as by the civil law, all who participate, either as principals or accessories, in any violation thereof, are alike responsible and alike guilty.

Let the real philanthropists of Great Britain and her toiling millions call upon their anti-slavery propagandists to change for a season the field of their labours. Let them take up their abode within the benighted regions of Africa itself, and there devote their time and talents to the work of instilling into the minds and hearts of the natives the great and glorious principles of the British Constitution. When they shall have succeeded in elevating four thousand, ay, four hundred, of its sable inhabitants — its kings and nobles included — to the same rank and to the same condition of comfort and happiness which is now enjoyed by the humblest and most unfortunate of their four millions of fellow-countrymen in America, allow them to return and enjoy in the plaudits of the really benevolent, the rewards to which they would then be so justly entitled. This field would be all the more inviting, because, even though they might fail in gathering and garnering the tempting fruits, it would not be necessary for them to pass through blood and strife, and over the desolated homes of their kinsmen, to reach the scene of their labours.

Although in the course of these letters I have taken advantage of such circumstances as might, even in the estimation of unprejudiced anti-slavery men, relieve the Southern States of all responsibility for the existence of slavery, yet I should be doing an injustice to the South and to my own convictions, were I to rest her defence wholly upon the plea of necessity. Neither will I claim that the shortcomings of those who are their assailants should shield the South from that just responsibility which she owes to God and man for the faithful performance of those duties which Providence has imposed upon her.

It may be a delusion—it may be, as charged, that there is a fanaticism in the South as well as in the North—it may be that the calumnies which malice and ignorance have heaped upon the citizens of the Southern States, and which have penetrated every civilised land, have blinded them to their real faults—yet the SOUTHERNER feels in his inmost heart the consciousness that whatever may be the judgement of to-day, history will record, and posterity will decide, that the Slave States of the American Confederacy have been instrumental in diffusing among mankind as many blessings, with as little of evil or wrong, as any population of similar extent in this or in any other age.

LETTER XI.

Great Britain—her interests in American Affairs—Public mind of Europe excited by misrepresentations against the South—The London 'Times' on Sumner's last speech—'Republican' party of America—Its purposes hostile to the South.

In writing these letters from the Old World, I have been led naturally to discuss the subject at issue between the North and the South in reference chiefly to the attitude occupied by Europe upon the same question. While disagreeing in opinion with those British statesmen who believe that British interests, or the interests of any other nation or people on earth, are injured by the institution of African slavery in America, I have not dared to suppose that they misrepresented the opinions of the British people. Although as a Southerner, I have much to regret and more to resent on account of the unjust strictures directed by them against the institutions and the people of my native country, I have no disposition to turn to account the feeling of irritation which this injustice has very naturally engendered amongst those who have been assailed. I have no desire whatever, even if I had the power, to disparage the claims of Great Britain to the respect of my fellow-countrymen.

I admire the stern and obstinate zeal which she displays in maintaining her rank amongst the nations of the world. But above all, I admire that integrity of character in all the relations of private life which, to their honour be it said, is a distinguishing characteristic of Englishmen. Her history, upon the whole, is a record of great achievements of which the annals of no other nation furnish a parallel. Her governing classes of to-day are more distinguished for their intellectual attainments, and their natural and acquired capacities for discharging the functions of their high position, than any other aristocratic body that ever existed. Their Queen is not only a model sovereign, but more than this—a model woman. There are a thousand sympathies and interests which are common to the two great people of the Anglo-Saxon blood. But Americans should not forget that an apparently dominant party in England have announced that they have a great interest which is in direct antagonism with the chief element of wealth and power in the American Confederacy. The question now at issue between Americans themselves is, shall this element of wealth and power be surrendered?

Although it is well known in America that the present contest between the North and the South is regarded by the British Anti-slavery party with feelings of the deepest solicitude, yet there are perhaps few who are aware of the extent to which this feeling is entertained. The silliest calumnies which are set afloat by the abolition fanatics and presses of the United States are greedily read, republished, and circulated broadcast throughout Europe, and wherever else the English language is read or spoken. The false impressions thus created are instilled into the minds of the children in their very infancy—they are made to imbibe them with their mother's milk. They are taught that the most horrible atrocities are but matters of every-day occurrence in the Southern States; that 'men and women, for pastime, scourge their African slaves to death;' that 'the children of slave-holders are made to participate in these scenes of cruelty until they become as brutal as their parents.' No calumnies are too gross for utterance, or too improbable to be believed. If their truth should be denied, the response is always ready—'We are bound to believe that which the Americans themselves tell us!'

The Southerner, knowing the falsehood and wickedness of these allegations, is almost tempted to doubt the evidence of his own senses. He knows that if there are faults in the treatment of slaves by their masters, they are, as a rule, the reverse of those which are charged by ignorant or malicious commentators. He knows that the feelings of kindness and affection between master and slave are cultivated to an extent utterly unknown to the intercourse of employer and servant or apprentice in his own or any other country. He believes that there are fewer instances of cruelty practised by masters upon slaves in America than even by parents upon their own offspring in any civilised free State of the world; though he is also well aware that when such instances do occur, they are exceptional in both. The Southerner who reads or listens to the recital of these stories in a foreign land is silenced by the very magnitude and enormity of their falsehood! It is true that in England these atrocities are only charged upon the South, yet throughout Europe the geographical divisions are in a great degree lost sight of, and even those who originate them come in as 'Americans' for a share of that obloquy which the malice and hatred of a senseless sectionalism seek to fasten upon a portion of those whom they call their fellow-countrymen.

The political abolitionists of England, while earnest in their efforts to impose upon the ignorance and credulity of Europe by exaggerated and heart-rending descriptions of the horrors of slavery, are still more averse to the frenzied appeals of the abolitionists in the present contest in America between the North and the South. They believe that the abolition of slavery can only be accomplished by lulling the Slave States into a fancied security—that violent denunciation reacts by placing conservative citizens upon their guard—that the true policy is, first to secure the power to control slavery, get possession of the Government of the Federal Union, and then they may, without hazard, strike down slavery and the slave power for ever. In this view of the question, although the defeat of Mr. Seward before the Republican Convention was regretted because of his preeminent services in leading the Northern mind in the direction of abolitionism, yet the more sagacious anti-slavery politicians of England are satisfied that the nomination of a more obscure man will serve more effectually to blind the masses in regard to the ultimate designs of the Republican party. The late speech of Mr. Sumner, of Massachusetts, has therefore been regarded by them with manifest tokens of displeasure. They say that such ebullitions of malignity from those who have been elevated to the position of hero-martyrs are well calculated to arouse the conservative element of the Union to a sense of the real nature of the present conflict, which they insist should only be fully developed after they have succeeded in establishing themselves in power, and that Mr. Sumner's course is like that of an over-confident general of an army who sends to his enemy on the eve of battle a full and detailed plan of his intended operations. A brief extract from a leading English journal will better explain the more judicious, if less honest programme, which is furnished for the Republican leaders: —

It is a part of the destiny of this country, that from its wide-spread dominions and universal interests, the concerns of no State are indifferent to it. *Perhaps the most important foreign question for England is that of American Slavery.* Our relations with the United States, through trade and community of origin, are so close that it is impossible their moral condition should not affect our own. The rivalry which exists between the two countries makes it difficult to discuss any international subject without the chance of giving umbrage. . . . *We have the greatest interest in the decay* of this mighty evil. *The reputation of this country for wisdom* is at stake, for the negroes of the West India Colonies were emancipated *not only* on the ground of humanity, *but on the calculation* that *free labour was more productive* than that of slaves. These islands still lie at the threshold of the American republic, and if the stars and stripes shall ever float over the walls of Mexico and Havana, the British Antilles will be exposed to all the influence of a pro-slavery propaganda. *How important then it is for us* that before these great territorial accessions, which seem inevitable, actually take place, *the system of slavery shall have been modified.* . . . John Brown himself has not done more harm to the cause of abolitionism in Virginia than a man like Mr. Sumner, when he drives the Southern Senators to fury by such a violent and uncalled-for philippic as our American correspondent notices to-day. . . . *We must, in the name of English Abolitionism, protest against* these foolish and vindictive harangues. Scarcely has the frenzy caused by John Brown's outrage begun to die away, than out comes Mr. Sumner with a speech which will set the whole South in a flame. We can well believe *that the prospects of the Republican party* have been already damaged by it. Mr. Sumner is one of that class of politicians who should be muzzled by their friends. . . . We may predict that the man who first gains a victory for the cause of Abolition will be of a very different temper to the Senator from Massachusetts.—*London Times, June* 18.

The influential journal from which I have made the foregoing extract is alike distinguished for its ability and its remarkable versatility. It does not assume to represent the opinions of one man, nor of a political party, nor even of a class. Moreover, it never 'makes war for an idea.' Its chief ambition is, to present itself always to the world as a reflection — a daguerreotype, as it were, of the current public opinion of the day — the rougher and the more uncouth the better, for it disdains to employ those lights and shadows, which, while softening the picture, may render it less startling in its effect upon the beholder. If the likeness taken does not seem accurate in its general outline or details, the indefatigable operator obliterates the impression and takes another, and if need be, another, until the resemblance is thought to be without blemish or defect. Time, or altered circumstances, or both, may bring about a change, in which event, like a faithful photographist, the 'Times' adapts itself to the times, tries it again, and again presents the lineaments of its subject to the world, in the garb which will set it off to the best advantage. I will not quarrel with this versatile operator, albeit the lineaments of the Southern features are painted now in sombre and gloomy and repulsive colours. I will bide our time, for I am sure the day will come when a brighter and a clearer light will shine around the sky-light window of the mammoth daguerrean; and I have an abiding faith that the 'Times' will not then prove a laggard in presenting the picture to the world, in its new, and changed, and more flattering aspect.

But it is with the present, not the future, we have now to deal; and however much the true American may regret that the public opinion of a respectable body of Englishmen is reflected in the spirit of the foregoing paragraph from this leading and influential journal, the subject is one worthy of his serious consideration. We learn from this article that the crime of John Brown, and the blackguardism of Sumner, are only deserving of censure, by the moral code of British abolitionism, because, by exposing at too early a period the designs of the Republican party, the success of the abolition cause, in which England is said to have so deep an interest, will thereby be placed in jeopardy! It is not denied that John Brown and Sumner are both labouring earnestly in that cause which the Anti-slavery party has so much at heart; but they are *indiscreet*. They are exposing the objects of the Republicans *before*, instead of *after*, the Presidential election; therefore such men should be muzzled! We, says this journal, 'have a right to protest in the name of English Abolitionism,' for not only are English interests deeply involved in the overthrow of American slavery, but *the reputation of England for wisdom is at stake*, because the emancipation of the negroes in the West India colonies was not alone on the ground of humanity, but *on the calculation that free labour was more productive than that of slaves.*

There is a frank outspoken boldness in the manner in which the subject is treated for an English audience, very different from the policy enjoined upon the 'Republican' leaders in the United States. Slavery, it is true, is treated as an enormous evil and a crime that should be abated, but it is frankly admitted that the crime and the evil does not consist in its 'inhumanity,' but in its declared antagonism to English interests and English dominion.

The John Browns and Sumners are censured, not because they do not faithfully reflect the sentiments of the Republican leaders, but because such premature disclosures are calculated to weaken the Republican party, before its full strength has been consolidated, preparatory to the final overthrow of the greatest of all the instruments which have contributed to the marvellous growth of the Republic, in all the elements of wealth, prosperity, and power.

This advice of the British abolitionists is certainly prudent, and exhibits much sagacity; but is it honest? If Sumner and Brown really reflect the spirit of the Anti-slavery party, why should not the issue be fairly made up and presented to the people? If John Brown and Sumner have done no wrong, why should they be held up as objects of public censure, as men 'who ought to be muzzled by their friends'? The 'Times' says that British interests are too deeply involved in the issue of the present struggle, to allow that the success of the Republican party shall be placed in jeopardy by its indiscreet friends. But does this constitute any reason why American citizens, who have so much more at stake, shall not consider the question at issue in the true light in which it has been placed by John Brown and Sumner? Were the mere words of Sumner as soft and gentle as the music of the dying swan, would that change the purpose of his party? and though John Browns might cut the throats of their victims while praying for the repose of their souls, or while singing hymns of glory to the Most High, and uttering exhortations to the living to save themselves from a similar calamity, by conforming quietly to the requirements of abolitionism, would it change the true nature of the contest, or should it reconcile the Southern people to the chains which are being forged for them?

In one thing the London journal above quoted has fallen into a grievous error. It urges prudence upon the part of the Republican leaders, for the sake of the great ultimate object which Republicanism has in view. It censures Sumner and Brown for intemperance of acts and speech. The truth is, but for the Browns and Sumners, there would be no Republican party. Blot out of existence the vindictive spirit of such men, and there is no appeal left to the madness of sectional fanaticism. If the leaders of the Northern mind were only to cultivate feelings of kindness and good-will towards the Southern people, there would exist no motive sufficiently strong to urge the Northern people to a crusade against the South. The Abolition party would be reduced to a force so small, that no place-seeking politician would endeavour through such influences to attain to political honours.

I do not believe that all the Republican politicians, much less the Republican masses, desire to be considered as endorsing either Sumner or John Brown. Many, no doubt, hope at the proper moment to stay the tide of sectional hatred, and after having conquered the South by superior numbers, generously propose, upon the fulfillment of certain conditions, to leave them in possession of that which they already occupy. But these should remember that, in the hour of victory, they must press forward, or be left behind in a feeble minority, to be themselves taunted as they have taunted others, with the appellation of 'dough-faces.' If the Republicans are successful, he amongst their leaders who falters in the work of destruction, will only work his own political downfall, without being able to arrest his comrades and followers, maddened by the resistance which they have encountered, elated by success, and thirsting for revenge.

For the true American citizen, who would avert the threatened calamity, there is but one course left open which he can follow with any well-grounded hope of success. All the parties which have nominated candidates for the Presidency profess to find authority in the Constitution for all that they propose to do. Even Mr. Sumner says that the Constitution is upon his side, and that it does not confer any rights upon the slave-holding States in regard to slavery. But it is also a fact, that the hundreds of thousands of abolitionists who frankly admit, that in order to accomplish their purposes the *Constitution must be violated*, and its provisions set at nought—all the leading spirits who pronounce that sacred instrument to be 'a league with death, and a covenant with hell'—all! all! all! are arrayed upon the Republican side, and are fighting their battle under the Republican banner, and have adopted as their candidates the chosen standard-bearers of the 'Republican party.'*

* The most distinguished leaders of the Republican party have already warned us, that, if they come into power they will not regard any constitutional guarantees which oppose the accomplishment of their schemes. Mr. Wm. H. SEWARD, in one of his most celebrated speeches, said :—

'The Constitution regulates our stewardship. The Constitution devotes the domain to union, to justice, to defence, to welfare, and to liberty. *But there is a higher law than the Constitution*, which regulates our authority over the domain.'

Again Mr. Seward says :—

'Wherein do the strength and security of slavery lie? You answer that they lie in the Constitution of the United States, and the Constitutions and laws of the slave-holding States. Not at all. Constitutions and laws can no more rise above the virtue of the people, than the limpid stream can climb above its native spring.'

Salmon P. Chase of Ohio, a leading republican politician, at present a colleague of Mr. Seward in the Cabinet of President Lincoln, was President of a Convention held at Buffalo in 1843, at which the following resolution repudiating an article in the Constitution of the United States was adopted. The reader will be struck with the canting puritanical tone in which the crime of perjury is commended as a holy duty:—

'Resolved that we hereby give it to be distinctly understood, by this nation and the world, that as abolitionists, considering that the strength of our cause lies in its righteousness, and our hopes for it in our conformity to the laws of God, we owe to the Sovereign Ruler of the Universe, as a proof of our allegiance to Him in all our civil relations and offices, whether as citizens *or as public functionaries, sworn to support the Constitution of the United States, to regard and treat the third clause of that instrument*, whenever applied in the case of a fugitive slave, *as utterly null and void, and consequently as forming no part of the Constitution of the United States.*'

It is not wonderful, in view of the sentiments thus expressed by two of the leading spirits of the Republican party, unanimously endorsed by this Convention, superadded to the even less guarded threats of their followers, that the greatest of New England's statesmen, Daniel Webster, should have said :—

'If these infernal fanatics and abolitionists ever get power into their hands, they will override the Constitution, set the Supreme Court at defiance, lay violent hands on those who differ with them in opinion or dare question their infallibility, and finally bankrupt the country, and deluge it in blood.'

The conservative and patriotic friends of the Union, which is but a creature of the Constitution, and which must perish with it, may well ask themselves if they can hope to preserve it in its purity, with such leaders and such associates. If there are those amongst the intelligent promoters of this crusade against the South, who believe that in the hour of victory they can arrest the tide of popular fury in the public mind, let them pause, reflect, and dispel such a delusion.

When they instil into the minds of the people the belief that the only barrier in the way of 'universal equality and fraternity throughout the length and breadth of our continent,' is the slave-holder of the South, can they believe that they can satisfy them of the justice or propriety of allowing the South any longer to keep back the millennium day of that liberty, for whose coming utopian dreamers have been watching and waiting for so many weary years? In short, can they trust that any written compact or constitution can restrain the mad passions of the majority, when that majority is itself the sovereign, and those over whom they are called to exercise sovereignty are strangers to them in blood, are supposed to be opposed to them in interest; whose tastes and whose habits are different from their own, and who, living under a different government, do not even owe obedience or allegiance to the same laws?

Beautifully rounded periods in laudation of the Union will never save it from destruction, if that spirit in the Northern mind which menaces its destruction is not rebuked by both the North and the South. All the constitutions which could be enacted would be powerless to hold together a confederacy of sovereign States, where the animosities of the greater number are a constant menace against the tranquillity, the peace, and independence of the others. Parties may prove what they choose by written parchment articles of agreement, but all such compacts will be powerless to perpetuate a partnership that would be worth preserving, if the members thereof are repelled by a common sentiment of hatred. In this contest, it should be remembered that the North has no domestic interest at stake. It is not pretended that the South desires to interfere, in the smallest degree, in the affairs of the Northern States. No Southern man would accept of any privileges in the common territory which were not enjoyed alike by every citizen of the Republic. The Southern States only ask to be left in the free enjoyment of those rights which the Constitution guarantees to them in common with the States of the North. The South protests against that combination in the North which threatens in its practical results to tax her against her will for the enrichment of Northern manufacturers, without any corresponding advantage to the people of the

Southern States. The South denies that the North has any right, through the instrumentality of a mere majority, to exclude them by prohibitory duties from all commercial intercourse with the nations of the world; thus reducing them to the condition of vassal provinces, without an available representation in the Government to protect their rights. They protest against a political combination of the Northern States having for its object a monopoly of all the powers of the Government, because it would leave the South powerless to protect its rights in the Union, against the aggressions of an irresponsible majority of the Northern people, which would thereafter usurp all the legitimate powers of a majority of the people of all the States. But above all, they demand the right to direct their own domestic institutions in such manner as to them may seem best. They deny that any good could result to either master or slave by the interference of an external Power; but even though this fact should not be admitted, they cast themselves upon their reserved rights of sovereignty, and will resist with every means at their command, all attempts, from whatever quarter they may come, to subvert their laws or to change the relations subsisting between the black and the white races. The defeat of the Republican party would not deprive the North of a single right or privilege of sovereignty, but the success of Abolitionism would place in jeopardy the liberty, the independence, the property, the very lives of the Southern people. While the triumph of that party would seal the bond of hatred between the sections upon the very hearts of the people, too late, perhaps, its misguided followers would find that the fruits of their victory would be death.

LETTER XII.

Influence of Anti-Slavery Fanaticism upon Religion — Bible Authority on Slavery — Increase of Infidelity — Influence of the Clergy for Good and Evil.

In considering the evils which have resulted from the unceasing agitation of the Anti-slavery question, its active influence in producing disbelief or scepticism, in regard to the truths of the religion revealed in the Holy Bible, cannot be overlooked, and should not be disregarded. The fanaticism of anti-slavery has been for many years past, of all other causes, the most fruitful source of infidelity, wherever its baneful influence has become a predominating passion. The philosophical mind may readily trace out the links of the chain which connects abolitionism with infidelity as cause and effect.

Slavery, as a political institution, or as a question involving certain political rights, has been a subject about which there has existed a variety of opinions. An investigation in regard to its influence for good or evil, leads us to consider the circumstances and causes which have produced such a relation between men. There are those, however, who condemn the continuance of such an institution without regard to the causes which brought it into existence, and without consideration of the results which may follow its abolition. Others excuse and tolerate it in consideration of various assigned causes ; while others approve of it on account of its declared advantages, not only to those concerned, but to mankind at large. It may be discussed as any other subject would be, involving the rights of man, and incidentally the question in regard to its moral influence is considered.

The theoretical principle upon which a democracy is founded, is the absolute and unqualified political equality of its citizens. A limited monarchy invests a certain hereditary right in one or more persons to govern the subjects thereof under certain restrictions. An absolute monarchy invests one man with supreme and unquestioned power over the lives and property of his subjects. It does not follow that the monarch employs this power in perpetrating deeds of cruelty upon those over whom he is placed. Within these governments respectively, the inhabitants occupy various relations in regard to each other, which relations are established by the supreme authority of the State. From the earliest period of recorded history to the present time, the relations have been those of proprietor and tenant, noble and vassal, lord and serf, master and slave. Men's minds, as I have said, differ in regard to the political advantages and disadvantages of the various relations thus established between man and man, as well as upon the moral influences of each. The great body of mankind live under the most absolute and despotic forms of government, the rulers of which, as before said, exercise unquestioned power over the lives, the personal liberty, and the property of the subjects. A smaller number are subject to governments in which the power of the monarch is more or less restricted, while fewer still are citizens of democratic governments. The absolute monarch exercises an authority over his subjects far greater than that which is held by a master over his slave; for in addition to the rights which are invested in a master, the sovereign may not only dispose of the life of his subject, but he may delegate his powers to another. The master holds his slave subject to the laws of the land, while the sovereign is himself the fountain of all power. Under very many governments even, in which the rights of the subject are protected by a Constitution, the laws confer upon a creditor the right to dispose of the liberty of his debtor, and instances have occurred, even in the history of our own country, in which white citizens have been sold for a term of years to the highest bidder.

Mankind have discussed the relative merits of these various forms of government, from the beginning of time until the present moment, without having approached any nearer to a satisfactory solution than in the days when the chosen people of God by Divine command bought bondmen and bondmaids from the heathen round about, to inherit them as a possession for themselves and their posterity for ever; or at that interesting epoch in the world's history, when after the terrible upheaving produced by the French Revolution had been calmed for a season upon the field of Waterloo, the victorious Monarchs, under the inspiration of the mystic dreams of a courtesan, established that 'holy alliance' which was to give peace and concord to all the nations of the earth for ever.

The abolitionist of Massachusetts may believe with his whole heart that if the institution of African slavery be blotted out of existence, his native land will have touched the point of perfection in human government; while the extreme monarchists of the Old World may entertain as sincere a conviction that the only existing human institution, more odious than that which is thus condemned by the Yankee leveller, is that very democracy upon which the American Government is founded. Yet who may say that the existence of any one of these different modes of government adopted by man is, *per se*, a sin against God? Has the Almighty ever made such a revelation to man? If so, when, where, and to whom, has the announcement been made? Where has the line of sin been drawn between an extreme democracy and an extreme despotism? If there is no record of any such announcement of the Divine judgement, how impious in man to say that he has penetrated the unfathomable designs of Omnipotence, and has discovered the line of demarcation! How is it that from the creation of the world to near the close of the eighteenth century of the Christian era, the now anathematised institution of slavery has existed, without any discovery having been made by mankind of its criminality or sinfullness in the sight of Heaven? During this period the Messiah himself has appeared upon the earth, and has left to us the record of His mission of mercy, in the sublime and heavenly precepts He has taught us; and yet, during eighteen hundred years, His disciples and followers never gleaned from His teachings a knowledge of the sinfullness of slavery!

Notwithstanding this, men have been found in this wicked age—aye! honoured teachers of our holy religion, who have presumed to announce that the domestic institution of African slavery in America is, *per se*, a crime against the Almighty, and a sin which, without repentance, will consign the offender to everlasting punishment! Pulpits in England and in America have been employed to give effect to this impious doctrine. The deadly sins denounced in the Bible have, in effect, been held as the most trifling vices, compared to the great sin of the slave-holder.

Churches have been set apart, not for denunciations of the sins which were practised by their respective congregations, but of that which, if criminal at all in the sight of God, was the crime of another people! Clergymen have stimulated the passions and the fanaticism of their hearers against the domestic institutions of a distant State, although it could not be pretended that the 'crime and the sin' which elicited their eloquent and frenzied denunciations had ever been, or was likely ever to be, committed by a human being within the sound of their voices. As Peter the Hermit, in the days of the Crusades, preached to all Christendom that the crime of all crimes was to refuse to follow him to the Holy Land, to rescue the sepulchre of Christ from the hand of the Saracens, and that the virtue, the practice of which washed away all sins, was to follow him in his holy enterprise, so have the anti-slavery clergymen stimulated the fanaticism of their congregations against the declared offences of another people, to an extent which has, to say the least, blunted the perception of their own besetting vices and sins.*

* The following brief extracts will serve as an illustration of the spirit which animates these misguided or wicked men.

The Rev. (!) Henry Ward Beecher, one of the most distinguished, popular, and pious clergymen of the North, said in an address delivered by him in his church (see report of New York Evening Post, a Republican journal): —

'I believe that Sharp's rifle is the true moral agency. *There is more moral power in one of these instruments*, so far as the slave-holders are

Whether or not the pulpits of the North have produced the prevailing excitement against the

concerned, *than in a hundred bibles!* You might just as well read the Bible to buffaloes as to those fellows, but they have a supreme respect for the logic of Sharp's rifles. The Bible is addressed to the conscience, but when you address it to them it has no effect — there is no conscience there.'

The Rev. Andrew F. Foss, of New Hampshire, in an address before the Anti-Slavery Society Meeting at New York, May 13, 1857, said :—

'Our fathers placed within the Constitution provision for the rendition of fugitive slaves. *If the Angel Gabriel had done what our fathers did, he would have been a scoundrel for it!* . . . Where slavery and freedom are put into one nation there must be a fight! There never was an hour when this blasphemous and infamous government should have been made, and now the hour was to be prayed for, when that disgrace to humanity should be dashed to pieces for ever.'

The Rev. O. B. Farthington, of New Jersey, upon the same occasion said :—

'We demand justice for the slave, at any price — of Constitution, of Union, of country—our next demand the immediate emancipation of the slave. . . . I believe that the Union effectually prevents us from advancing in the least degree, in the work of the slave's redemption. . . . The Northern people were beginning to see, that the South was divided from them by its system of labour, and by its ideas of human rights. We want to make that gulf of division deeper.'

The Rev. Theodore Parker, in one of his sermons, openly counsels his congregation to violate their oaths. He supposes the case of a man who aids a slave to escape from his master, and who is brought to trial for the offence against the law. He assumes that he has taken the oath as a juror to try the man, and says : —

'If I have extinguished my manhood by my juror's oath, then I shall do my business and find him "guilty," *but if I value my manhood* I shall say "*not guilty.*" Then men may call me forsworn and a liar, but I think human nature will justify the verdict.'

I might multiply extracts of similar import from the sermons, speeches, and letters of the most distinguished Northern clergymen, but these sufficiently indicate the tone and temper of the pulpit. There are, no doubt, many clergymen who would not themselves employ the language above quoted ; but the number is small indeed of the Republican school of the Northern States, who would dare to say that they did not endorse citizens of the Southern States, that it exists to a most fanatical degree will not be denied. That it is the ruling and absorbing passion of multitudes of people is fully established by the fact that the most sagacious, place-seeking politicians have severed their connection with old political parties, and are now sailing on the current of anti-slavery frenzy, as the surest and speediest way to political preferment.

The imagination of a well-meaning man being excited by false or exaggerated pictures of the horrors of slavery, and filled with the idea that the existence of such an institution is a crime and a sin against Heaven, very naturally seeks to find confirmation and authority for such belief in that great Book which reveals the mysteries of the Christian's faith, and which he had been taught to believe was a sacred emanation from on high. He is startled first, by discovering that Abraham held as bond-servants, men and women, born in his house and *bought with his money!* He turns over the pages of the Holy Book, and he reads (Leviticus xxv. 44—46): 'Both thy bondmen, and thy bondmaids, which thou shalt have, shall be of the heathen that are round about you; of them shall ye buy bondmen and bondmaids. Moreover, of the children of the strangers

the sentiments thus declared. We have fallen upon evil times, when the teachers of our holy religion thus debase themselves and their pulpits to a level with the lowest rum-shops and their frequenters.

that do sojourn among you, of them shall ye buy, and of their families that are with you, which they begat in your land: and they shall be your possession. And ye shall take them as an inheritance for your children after you, to inherit them for a possession; they shall be your bondmen for ever.'

Finding nothing in the Old Testament to gratify the cravings of his morbid appetite, he hopes to discover that which he seeks, in the teachings of our Saviour and his apostles—he reads (Ephesians vi. 5, 6): 'Servants, be obedient to them that are your masters according to the flesh, with fear and trembling, in singleness of your heart, as unto Christ; not with eye-service as men-pleasers; but as the servants of Christ, doing the will of God from the heart.'

He searches farther, and finds (1 Timothy vi. 1): 'Let as many servants as are under the yoke count their own masters worthy of all honour, that the name of God and his doctrine be not blasphemed.'

Again, he finds (Titus ii. 9, 10): 'Exhort servants to be obedient unto their own masters, and to please them well in all things; not answering again; not purloining, but showing all good fidelity; that they may adorn the doctrine of God our Saviour in all things.'

In despair he continues his researches, in the desperate hope that perhaps there may still be some words of comfort in the little that remains for him to read. His eye is at length arrested by a passage, bearing an import which startles his very soul. 'Can it be I?' he exclaims! He reads and re-reads (2 Peter ii. 19): 'While they promise them liberty, they themselves are the servants of corruption: for of whom a man is overcome, of the same is he brought in bondage.'

And when he discovers that Paul sends back Onesimus, the runaway slave, to his master, though with gentle words and a request, amounting almost to a command, that he be pardoned for having abandoned the service of his master, and thus fully recognising the master's right, he is tempted to exclaim in the bitterness of his disappointment, 'the apostle of Christ a slave-catcher!'

While his researches inform him that, during the whole period of time of which the Bible furnishes a record, the institution of slavery existed; and that along with the evidence of its recognition by the holy teachers whose writings adorn its pages, there is not a line or a syllable in which it is condemned, either by Christ or his apostles, the terrible doubt crosses his mind. There is a natural struggle between the passion that absorbs him and the religion which his mother taught him. He enters once more, and for the last time, the sanctuary where he had so often in days past listened to the words of love which fell from the preacher's lips, as he laboured to impress upon his hearers the holy precepts of the meek and lowly Saviour. Alas! it is no gentle words of charity that fall upon his listening ear. Instead, thereof, again he hears the confirmation of his own belief: 'Slavery is the sin against God and man which calls aloud for the vengeance of the Almighty.'

He reasons within himself: 'Is not God perfection? Is He not all-wise? If He had made a revelation to man, would it not have enumerated, clearly and distinctly, all the great sins which He condemned? If He had appeared upon earth, would He not, with His own lips have pronounced a sentence of condemnation against the sin of sins which was practised before His eyes?' Fanaticism triumphs! He throws down the Holy Book, exclaiming, 'Give me an anti-slavery Bible, and an anti-slavery God!' These are not my words, but words which have fallen from the lips of an excited abolition orator, and upon the ears of a gratified and approving audience of New Englanders.*

But how could it be otherwise than thus? And

* *'We of the North want an anti-slavery Constitution, an anti-slavery Bible, and an anti-slavery God!!'* The author of this rather startling annunciation of Northern wants has been rewarded, since the accession of the Republican party to power, by a first-class diplomatic mission abroad. The Government to which he was first accredited very properly refused to receive him, but he was subsequently appointed to another, and he now holds the rank at a foreign court, of 'Envoy Extraordinary and Minister Plenipotentiary of the United States of America.'

who can tell how deeply this feeling of infidelity, or at least of scepticism, may have penetrated the hearts of those with whom anti-slavery fanaticism has become a controlling passion? If there are any who are ignorant of the extent to which this sentiment of unbelief is entertained, let him acquaint himself with the proceedings of anti-slavery anniversaries, and note the increasing numbers who openly avow their infidelity.

There is no human engine of good or evil so potent as the clergy — those who are acknowledged as the teachers of religion. In all ages of the world, this influence has been a controlling element among mankind. When it has been worthily directed towards cultivating the feelings of love, and of charity, and forgiveness among men, society has had reason to bless them as benefactors. But when, as has too often been the case, even in the history of our own religion, they have been instrumental in producing strife and discord and heartburnings, and misery, and bloodshed, society has had cause to regret that influence which their sacred calling secured for them.

It is not for me to judge of the motives of those who have contributed so powerfully towards building up that mountain of hatred, which may be said now to be common to a great number of the citizens of both sections of the American Union. Least of all could I say that those motives have not had their origin in a benevolent purpose. The zeal to do good often degenerates into a fanaticism which results in nothing but evil. Fanaticism begets a reverse fanaticism, and to the eye of the disinterested spectator, or to him who beholds from a distance that which is transpiring, the acts of all appear as the acts of madmen.

We cannot but remember that the same sources of discord have existed since the foundation of the Union, and we should likewise bear in mind, that they will exist as long as the Confederation endures! We know that good-will at least, if not congeniality, did once prevail between the different members of the Confederacy, and why may it not exist again? If the clergymen of the entire North would resolve that, for twelve short months, they would preach nothing but Christ, and teach nothing but that which He taught: if they would, in good faith, call upon their congregations to exercise toward all mankind charity and love: if they would denounce, in the spirit of the apostles, the sins which they denounced, who can estimate the amount of good which that one year might bring forth? What a noble field is here presented in which to exercise the duties of a noble calling! How much of wretchedness, and misery, and wickedness, aye, perhaps of bitter strife and bloodshed, they might avert!

LETTER XIII.

Present Attitude of Parties in the United States—Success of the Republican Party will accomplish Disunion—Its Measures examined, &c.

In the preceding letters I have endeavoured to present a brief view of the origin, progress, and developement of the institution of slavery in the Southern States of the American Confederacy. Although I may not hope that the facts I have stated will change the fixed opinions or convictions or long-cherished prejudices of anyone, yet I trust they will not be altogether without influence in directing the attention of true Americans to the importance which attaches throughout the civilised world to the productions of slave labour, as elements in the wealth and power of nations. I am convinced that such an investigation will lead the dispassionate observer to the conclusion that, if the Southern States 'are blinded by their passions to the evils of slavery,' the Anti-slavery party of Europe is not blind to the disastrous effects which its destruction would entail upon the material prosperity of America. That there should be a party in the United States, formidable as to numbers and respectability, cooperating with these in the accomplishment of such a result, either by the force of circumstances or a common sentiment, is well calculated to excite the wonder of mankind. That this party should be sufficiently formidable to present a candidate for the Presidency, with a strong probability of success, founded upon the common action of all the Free States of the Confederacy, and that such should be the issue, and the only avowed issue in such a contest, is a startling fact, the importance of which cannot be over estimated, because it strikes at the very foundation of the compact upon which the Confederacy has been erected.

The subject of slavery, as a question of morals, or political economy, or expediency, or abstract right and wrong, is one which, like all others that affect the interests or passions of men, may be a subject of legitimate discussion, about which mankind may differ, as upon other questions in which the interests of the human family may be involved. The Southern States may naturally seek to remove the prejudices against them, which artful enemies have succeeded in exciting. They may be willing to present their cause at the bar of an enlightened public opinion, as an individual may seek to remove unfounded imputations against his honour or integrity. But the South does not mean thereby to admit that the other States of the Confederacy *have any right to vote away* the political privileges which they claim to have inherited from the founders of the Government, and over which they retained entire sovereignty when delegating certain powers to the general Government.

America has just the same right, if she possessed the power, to subvert the internal laws and customs of England, as the Northern States have to modify, or alter, or in any manner to interfere with, the domestic institutions of the Slave States. All the citizens of the Republic beyond the limits of the Slave States may believe that slavery is a wrong and a sin in the sight of God and man. They may believe that it was a virtue in Europe to establish an institution which it is a crime in the Southern States any longer to tolerate; yet whatever may be their opinions upon the abstract merits of the controversy, or upon the morality or expediency of slave labour, there exists no other external authority than that of violence for any interference with the domestic institutions of the Southern States. This can only be accomplished by illegal means, and would be an act of revolution, which would release the South from the compact of Union.

Do a majority of the citizens of the Free States desire to dissolve the political bonds which unite the Confederacy, or to reorganise the Union upon a different basis from that established by its founders, in order that they may control the domestic institutions of the Southern States? and do they wish by these peaceful means to declare or to accomplish their purpose? The interrogatory seems to assume the possible existence of a public sentiment which at this distance seems almost beyond belief; and yet the dispassionate mind cannot reject the conclusion, that such a feeling or wish lies at the foundation of that party which has entered into the contest for the presidency under the title of Republican.

What are the facts which present themselves to our view in investigating the causes of the present deplorable state of feeling among the citizens of the United States? Upon what special issues does the Republican organisation ask for the support of the Northern States? for it does not expect or desire a single electoral vote in the Slave States. The only issue they present—the only support they ask—the only idea they illustrate, is anti-slavery, pure and simple! designedly and sedulously disembarrassed of all or any side issues. They expect no aid from any except anti-slavery men, and they appeal to no passion, but that of hatred for the slave-holder! In justice to that party, it must be supposed that they have a purpose to accomplish, and that such purpose must be inimical to the Slave States, whether it be through highly protective or prohibitory tariffs, to absorb the profits of slave labour, or to destroy the institution of slavery itself. It cannot be that the leaders would stimulate such a torrent of vindictive passions between the sections of a Confederacy, which in their hearts they cherish, for the mere purpose of obtaining power and place. I give them credit for other motives.

But suppose this to be the true and only object of the politicians, and that these appeals are successful in accomplishing their designs. What would it signify? Could it be interpreted to mean anything but the expression of an abstract wish on the part of the majority of the Confederacy to dissolve the Union, or to reconstruct it upon another basis, which would leave with them the constitutional control of the question of slavery in the Southern States?

Upon the hypothesis that the Republican party has no political purpose to subserve in opposition to the rights of the Southern States, by such an expression of anti-slavery feeling, the force of its significance, as a demonstration of sentiments averse to the longer continuance of the Union, is doubly enhanced. Truthfully interpreted, according to the rules of common reason, such an expression of antipathy to the Southern States, or their institutions, conveying no intimation of a design to give a practical effect to their victory by any act inimical to slavery, would mean, that they had ceased to regard the Union as worth maintaining. After the expression of such a deliberate sentiment of repugnance to the fifteen Southern States, or their domestic institutions, would they not be driven by the force of public opinion without, as well as by their own feelings, to repudiate a longer political association with those whom they had thus formally insulted and pronounced unworthy of respect; or to attempt their subjugation and, if successful, hold them as vassals? Would it not be, in effect, a virtual dissolution of the Confederacy upon the terms previously existing? The unbiassed mind can arrive at no other conclusion, than that such a result would of itself, and in itself, dissolve the union between the two great geographical sections. The chain of the Confederacy would be broken! The fragments might, for temporary purposes, be reunited by a flaxen thread, but its power of cohesion would be gone for ever.

Conservative citizens of the Northern States should not delude themselves into the belief, that this is the mere expression of an idle threat on the part of the South; for the result would be accomplished against the wishes and in opposition to the united protest of the Southern States!

But upon the more plausible supposition, that the Republican party has a political purpose in thus consolidating into one mass the anti-slavery sentiment of the North, without any admixture of other ingredients, it becomes important to discover what that purpose is. Is it that this Anti-slavery party desires to secure the reins of the general Government in their own hands, in order that they may control the institution of slavery within the States? This would involve a palpable violation of the Constitution, and could only be accomplished by violence. The announcement of such a purpose, is of itself an overt act of hostility to the Union, which would be utterly inconsistent with an intention to maintain the existing Confederation. The act of consummation would be revolution. Although this is the avowed object of the extreme abolitionists, and is doubtless the purpose of many who do not give public utterance to their designs, yet it is fair to presume, that those of the Republican party who still cling to the Union and the Constitution as the anchor of safety, have in view the accomplishment of their anti-slavery purposes by other methods. We read in all the Republican journals of the more moderate and conservative school, the declaration of a design to prohibit the farther extension of slavery, by excluding it from the Territories. I presume that I shall not be charged with representing the Anti-slavery party unfairly, when I assume this to be the ground on which every member thereof, embracing every shade of opinion, is willing to stand.

If a proper degree of fraternal feeling existed on the part of the Republican party towards the Southern

States, it might be urged, even if such a prohibition could be legally accomplished, that it would be unkind to the white race, and cruel to the African, to insist upon its enforcement—ungenerous to the citizens of the South, because it would debar the Southern States bordering upon the Free States from abolishing slavery for all time to come. The Northern States were not only permitted to rid themselves of slavery without cost, but also of the slaves, by transferring them to the adjoining Slave States. Here they were purchased by the Southern planters, and by this simple process, these objects were accomplished without involving the loss of a single dollar. The North having thus disposed of its slaves, would it be equitable to deny to the border Slave States a similar privilege? Does there not rest upon the North a moral obligation to leave open this one avenue to the consummation of the same results, should the institution of slavery cease to be profitable, or be rendered from any other cause undesirable? But suppose the number of Africans go on increasing in the same ratio as they have done since the foundation of the Republic; within the lapse of a comparatively brief period, the African population would be equal to the present population of the entire Union. When we add to this the natural increase of the white race, it is easy to perceive that no greater curse could be inflicted upon the posterity of the Southern

States, than thus to confine the Africans for ever within their present limits. It is appalling to contemplate the tyranny which, for the protection of the white race, it would be necessary to exercise over such a multitude of African slaves, confined within such narrow limits; unless, indeed, the ever-menacing danger of insurrection should drive the great body of European races to seek a more secure asylum, and thus leave the country in the possession of the Africans. I know there are those who would say that this is the consummation they desire, but these are madmen with whom it were folly to reason. Let sane men, however, who do not act upon a principle of revenge, or blind hatred, make for themselves an estimate founded upon data already furnished by our history, of the probable extent of the population of the Southern States within a given period, under such a prohibition of emigration. They will find that, like all the radical short-cut roads of abolition philanthropy, it leads not only to evil for the master, but is also cruel and unjust to the slave. The smaller the number of slaves among any given population of the dominant race, the better is their condition, and the more abundant their comforts; while every increase, in reference to the territory they inhabit, or the numbers of the dominant race, draws more closely around them the restraints imposed by their condition of servitude. Intelligent practical anti-slavery philanthropy would seek to expand the area of slavery, when it could be accomplished without increasing the number of slaves, rather than by circumscribing, add to its hardships.

Thus it is ever with the schemes for the amelioration of the condition of the slave, which have their origin in Free States. They are dictated, primarily, by a feeling of animosity to the master, and all end in disaster to the slave, for whom there is such a noisy demonstration of sympathy.

But as I intimated in the outset, the feeling of unkindness or hatred for the South, forms too important and essential an ingredient in the composition of the Republican party to justify any appeal to their magnanimity, or to any sympathies they might be supposed to entertain for the African. The only present defence of the South, therefore, against such an aggression upon her equal rights, rests in the Constitution. So long as the Union is maintained, that is the final arbiter of all disputes. I know that the provisions of that instrument may be violated—I am well aware that by a wide latitude of construction, a false meaning may be attached to certain phrases, yet the undeniable principle which lies at its very foundation, is the equality of the States, and their absolute sovereignty over their domestic affairs.

If these reserved rights were respected in good faith, by all the citizens of the Republic, ages and ages might pass away without the occurrence of a single act which could destroy the harmony and the unity of the Confederation. What a magnificent prospect and reward is thus held out to the true patriot, to restrain within the boundaries of the Constitution his generous efforts to improve the condition, or reform the vices of his neighbours! Alas! there are those who will not brook any restraint which interposes an obstacle to the gratification of their passions or their personal ambition.

If under the Constitution, a dominant section may appropriate for themselves all the property in lands, belonging to the general Government, they may certainly make the same disposition of every other species of property. Upon the same principle they may accumulate a surplus of money in the Treasury, and divide it among the States of the same dominant section. If the Government of the United States may, under the provisions, and according to the true intent of the Constitution, exclude from the Territories any one article which is recognised as property by any one State, then it may prohibit the introduction of any species of property whatever. Even if there were not a Slave State, no statesman in the formation of a charter of Confederation between independent States, however homogeneous might be their internal regulations, would confer upon Congress the power of excluding from the common territories any property recognised as such by any one of the States. If it would be absurd to suppose the existence of any such power in a Confederation of States, having similar local constitutions, how can it be inferred that either the Slave or Free States, which formed the Constitution of the United States, would have authorised the exercise of such power by Congress?

To declare that the citizens of one State shall not enter upon the territory of the general Government with their property, and that the citizens of another State may, strikes down the very corner-stone of the Constitution. It would be a violation of every principle of common justice. For if these Territories are common property—that is, if they have been bought by the common purse, or the common valour of the Confederacy—then there exists no power, except by the exercise of brute force, to exclude any one State from an equal participation therein.

If this exclusion cannot lawfully be made by the Congress of the United States, which might be supposed, at least, to represent the will not only of a majority of the States, but of the people, much less can any inferior power accomplish the same end. For to suppose that a superior can delegate greater power to a subordinate than he possesses himself is absurd, and not to be believed.*

* The 'Inferior Power' here referred to is the Territorial Government and people previous to its admission as a State. The 'Territories'

Neither if such unlawful power is attempted to be exercised on the part of such inferior, can the general Government close its eyes and refuse to see or to redress the wrong. The supreme power is bound to prevent a wrong if within the compass of its means; or failing in this, it must redress the wrong; otherwise it is not sovereign.

I am aware that here is the great stumbling-

of the United States constitute that portion of the public domain which has been acquired by the Federal Government by purchase or otherwise, and which does not lie within the jurisdiction of either State. Whenever a territory acquires a sufficient population, the Government of the United States appoints a Governor, &c., and the said territory has a right to send a delegate to Congress, but he has no vote. It has been the custom to admit these territories as States of the Union whenever they shall have acquired the requisite population, by immigration from the States or otherwise. The only restriction imposed by the Constitution consists in the requirement that the States thus admitted shall have adopted republican forms of government. The ostensible cause of quarrel between the North and the South grew out of this territorial question. The North contended that constituting a majority, they had a right to exclude the South from the territories altogether; that is, they claimed the exclusive right of entering upon these territories with their property, while denying to the South the same privilege. The South, on the other hand, contended that the territories, being the common property of all the States, the citizens of each member of the Union were equally entitled to enter upon the same, with whatever property was recognised as such by their States; and that this equality of rights could not lawfully be destroyed until after the territory had been admitted as a State, and then only by the Government of said State. There was a third party, however, which assumed that while the general Government of the Union could not exclude the citizens of any one State with their property, while such privilege was granted to the citizens of another State, yet they claimed that the Territorial Government appointed by the United States might establish this exclusion. This was simply a middle party, gotten up in order to evade the direct issue, and thus avoid the inevitable disruption which would surely follow if the North should attempt to enforce this exclusion.

block for many honest citizens who, from conscientious motives, from education, or from prejudices, do not desire to legislate in favour of slavery ; or, in the language of the Republican politicians, they are opposed to the establishment by Congress 'of a slave code for the Territories.'

Neither does the South ask for the establishment of a slave code, in the sense in which it is here meant. But the Constitution confers upon them and their property the same rights as are conferred upon the Free States and their property. The citizen cannot protect himself, because he has transferred that right to the Government which, having assumed it, is bound to perform that duty ; otherwise such citizen is an outlaw.

Government is the natural protector of all its citizens. It is bound alike to each. This is the foundation upon which all its powers rest. The government which from inability fails in the performance of this duty, is no longer entitled to the allegiance of the citizen, unless there is a reasonable effort made to redress the wrong. But where the Government refuses to perform this duty, it abdicates, and is no longer the Government.

It follows, therefore, that when the Government of the United States refuses, or fails to protect the South in its equal rights, it abdicates its authority ; and, ceasing to be the Government of the Slave States, cannot rightfully claim their allegiance. By such an act, it becomes only the Government of the States which it protects.

Even though the North might gain a temporary triumph by the abrogation of the equal rights of the South, yet one day or other it would be made to recoil upon herself. However that may be, no other construction can fairly be placed upon the Constitution; and however objectionable may be its provisions, it is the duty of good citizens to conform to them, in letter and in spirit. When they seek to violate or fraudulently to evade its requirements, it is an act of revolution. It is disunion.

LETTER XIV.

A Confederacy could never be established which did not recognise the equality of the States — Position of Parties illustrated — Aggressions of the South and North considered.

Within the Republican or Anti-slavery party there are many who are willing to admit the importance of the Confederacy to the general safety of the whole, but who detest the Constitution which recognises the institution of slavery, and thereby imposes upon the Government the necessity of giving the same protection to the slave-holder and his property as to the Massachusetts manufacturer and his looms. I have already referred to the absurdity of assuming the existence of a government which would not give full and ample protection to all its citizens. I have said — and it will scarcely be called in question — that when a government refuses to protect all its citizens in their constitutional rights it virtually abdicates, and it is no longer entitled to the allegiance of its citizens; and in a confederacy like that of the United States it is, in effect, a dissolution of the Union.

But let it be supposed that, by common consent, and without any popular excitement or unkind feeling between the citizens of the several States, the Union were dissolved into its original elements. The first impulse of many who are now, perhaps, unwittingly engaged in the work of destruction, would be to re-establish some sort of union as a protection against foreign aggression. Let it be supposed that, in accordance with this sentiment, a convention should be called to settle the terms on which the new Union should be established. It assembles: every State is represented; the organisation is completed, and the President announces that all is ready to proceed to the despatch of the business which called them together. Fifteen Slave States and eighteen Free States are represented.

A grave member from Massachusetts rises and says:—'Mr. President,—Before proceeding to arrange the details of the terms upon which these thirty-three independent States may form a Union for purposes of common defence and other great objects of interest to each, it is necessary to declare the terms upon which new States, formed out of the common territory of this confederacy, may be admitted as integral parts of the proposed Union. As I do not desire to awaken any angry or even unkind feelings by making any special reference to certain crimes and sins of enormous magnitude which are tolerated and legalised by fifteen of the States here assembled, I propose to accomplish my purpose in another way. The Constitution of my native State is perfect in all its parts. It is the result of the matured wisdom of the greatest statesmen of this or any other age. Does any member of this Convention find in that charter of our liberties any single provision to which a rational objection can be made?' After a pause, during which there is a profound silence, the gentleman from Massachusetts continues:—'I do not desire, Mr. President, to force this Constitution upon any one of the States here represented; and it would be alike a departure from the great principle of liberty to insist, absolutely, upon the adoption of this Constitution by a new State before being admitted as a member of our Confederacy. I therefore propose to adopt the following article defining the terms upon which new States may be admitted. To wit:—

'ARTICLE I. Any territory of the United States having the requisite population, and complying in other respects with the provisions of the Constitution, may be admitted into the Union as an equal member thereof, *Provided* the said territory has adopted for its government the Constitution of the State of Massachusetts. But if said territory asks for admission under a Constitution with provisions similar to the provisions of the Constitution of North Carolina, it shall not be lawful for such territory to become a State of the Confederacy.'

After the member for Massachusetts has taken his seat, a Republican from New York rises and says:—'Mr. President,—Though there is an entire coincidence and agreement between the distinguished gentleman who has just addressed the Convention and myself, in regard to that sin against God and man which is tolerated, and encouraged, and made lawful by fifteen States here represented, yet I cannot admit that the Constitution of Massachusetts is the only one which establishes and confirms the sublime principles of equality and fraternity which are set at naught by the fifteen States before referred to. The proposition of the gentleman ignores the existence of a North! Like most of his countrymen (I say it with all proper respect, and without designing that the remark shall be interpreted in an offensive sense), the member from Massachusetts can see nothing which is worthy of admiration beyond the limits of his own State. It is notorious that the visions of Massachusetts statesmen are bounded by the view from the summit of Bunker Hill. Let me tell that gentleman that there is a North! a glorious North, proud of her achievements in the past, and ready now to make any sacrifice in defence of her honour and her equal rights. Allow me, furthermore, to declare in direct terms, and in the outset of our proceedings, that the Northern States will submit to no invidious distinctions! They will enter this Union as equals, or not at all! It is well for the gentleman to be promptly undeceived. Massachusetts is not the North, nor is the North Massachusetts. She forms but a small integral part, and to that extent she may ask consideration; but when she demands that hers shall be the model Constitution of all new States, she insults that great North whose very existence she ignores. This self-exaltation may be appropriate enough on Boston Common or in Fanueil Hall, but it is a species of sectional arrogance which is altogether misplaced in the halls of a Convention assembled to form a Union between independent States. I therefore propose a substitute for the proposition before the Convention, and ask for its adoption. It is as follows:—

'Any territory of the United States with the requisite population, &c., &c., may be admitted as a State into the Union, *Provided* the said territory has adopted for its government a Constitution similar in its provisions to the Constitution of any one or all of the eighteen Northern States here represented. But if said territory asks for admission under a Constitution with provisions similar to the provisions of any one of the fifteen Southern States, it shall not be lawful for such territory to become a State of the Confederacy.'

A member from Vermont rises to address the Convention, and says: — Mr. President, — I am a plain, straightforward, out-and-out Abolitionist. I can discover no good likely to result from mincing this question. I have not had the opportunity in my native mountains to acquire the art of expressing my thoughts without calling things by their right names. The two gentlemen who have preceded me deal their blows against vice and crime, without daring to name them, for fear of giving offence Now, Mr. President, I am not afraid to speak my sentiments boldly and above-board. The crime of all crimes, the sin of all sins, the enormity above all enormities, the existing libel upon humanity, which is alike offensive to Vermont and to the Almighty Ruler of all things — is, the crime, the sin, the enormity, of slavery, as legalised by the fifteen Southern States here represented! Our most eminent divines have already made known that before the tribunal of Heaven there will be no mercy for the slave-holder. The churches of the North have announced for him a similar fate; then why should we make Heaven angry, by putting on our kid gloves when we handle the monster? I have therefore to propose, in lieu of the two propositions now before the Convention, the following:—

'The territories of the Union, being the common property of all the States, may be lawfully occupied by all the citizens of the Free States, with their property, of whatever kind. But it shall not be lawful for citizens of the Slave States to reside with their property upon any of the lands which are now, or which may hereafter come into the possession of the Government. No State shall ever hereafter be admitted into the Union whose Constitution tolerates the existence of slavery.'

It is unnecessary to follow up this assumed discussion, or to enumerate the arguments by which the movers and opponents of these respective suggestions would defend their proposed measures. But we may fairly conclude that the representatives of the Slave

States would propose, in lieu of the propositions referred to, something like the following:—

The States forming the Confederacy are in all respects equal. The sovereignty delegated by each to the General Government is the same, and in all other respects the sovereignty of each State within its limits is supreme.

All territories, lands, or other property which may come into the possession of the General Government, being alike the property of all the States, must be held as such. Whenever a territory shall be opened for settlement, it shall be alike free to all the citizens of all the States. Immigrants from any State of the Confederacy may lawfully take with them any property recognised as such by the laws of their own States. The duty of protecting its citizens being an essential condition of sovereignty, the citizens of the respective States shall be fully protected by the Government of the Confederacy, in all their rights in the territories, against all aggressions whatsoever.

Whenever a territory having sufficient population, &c., &c., makes its application for admission as a State in the Union, it may be admitted as an equal member of the Confederacy with whatever Constitution the citizens thereof may adopt, provided it be republican in form. The said Constitution may contain any one or all of the provisions of the Constitution of any one of the original States composing the Confederacy.

It will not be denied that the first three propositions above considered represent fairly the views and opinions of the more moderate and conservative portion of the Republican party, while the latter embraces every claim or demand that any portion of the Southern States have ever made in regard to this subject. The South desires nothing more than the recognition of its equal rights, and it will be recreant to honour and liberty if it ever submit to accept of anything less.

It is scarcely necessary to discuss the probabilities of the formation of a new Confederacy upon any terms which would accord with the principles of the Republican party. Such a consummation would be simply impossible. The Constitution under which we have hitherto lived undoubtedly confers upon the Southern States the equal rights which they would demand under any other which might be proposed. It therefore follows that the Republican party is not only founded upon the principle of opposition to the present Union, but to any other Confederacy which it would be possible peacably to erect upon the ruins of that one which they now in effect seek to overthrow.

Am I mistaken in my opinions in regard to the intentions of the Republican party? Are there any portion of citizens who give it their support, who desire to maintain the present Union upon the terms demanded by the Constitution? In short, do they mean nothing in derogation of the rights of the South, by uniting in the establishment of a great sectional organisation, founded upon the single idea of opposition to the domestic institutions of the South? If they propose no measure hostile to the Slave States, why do they give their countenance to the establishment of a great political Anti-slavery party? Is there any proposition from any quarter to reestablish slavery in the Free States? Has the South ever sought, either directly or indirectly, or does she now seek, to exercise any control over, or in any manner to interfere with, the domestic institutions or governments of the Free States? Does the South deny to the North any right which the Constitution accords? Or does she ask for herself anything more than the recognition of her equality under the great charter of confederation? If to these interrogations there can be none other than a negative response, I repeat, why should there exist in the United States a political Anti-slavery party, if it does not propose some change or modification of the existing institution of slavery, or involve some denial of the rights of the Slave States? Republican partisan leaders would answer, that their organisation was established to resist 'the aggressions of slavery.' I must confess that I find it impossible to conceive what particular acts are here referred to, for, of all the institutions which exist, that of slavery is the least aggressive. When, however, the heated partisan is obliged to furnish an illustration of the nature of these aggressions, he refers usually to the unfortunate collision in the Senate Chamber between a Southern Representative and a Northern Senator. This Senator was attacked and beaten by a Southerner. It is not necessary to discuss the merits of that affair. The act was that of one man; but if the deed was as atrocious as it has been represented, by what harsh epithet may we denounce the crime of John Brown? What is there about Sumner that should excite to a greater degree our feelings of pity or compassion, than the helpless victims of John Brown's brutal propensities for murder? Sumner still lives to utter calumnies which ought to be sufficient to gratify the most morbid appetites of his followers. The victims of John Brown and his confederates are in their graves. Yet, strange and startling truth, the very men and women, who, if their power of performance had been in accordance with the force of their will would have immolated the whole South, to have avenged the 'crime' against Sumner, find but little to condemn in the conduct of that monster murderer, Brown, except *his indiscretion!* His 'zeal,' they say, 'was without *prudence*, but his *motives* were *pure* and *honest!*'

Nothing has occurred within a quarter of a century more significant of the unhappy state of feelings existing in the Northern States against the South, than the effects which the two events referred to have produced in the public mind. And I may add that it furnishes a fair index to the influences which Abolition propagandism has produced upon the morals of its adherents.

I have only referred to this subject to show that the chief aggressions complained of by the Abolitionists, even admitting the propriety of classing the cases referred to in that category, have been exceeded a thousandfold in enormity by aggressions upon the South. At most, they are not of sufficient magnitude to authorise or justify conservative men in giving their support and influence to a party, which can only accomplish its openly avowed designs by a palpable repudiation of the Constitution by which the Union is maintained, and which can only accomplish its measures by the sword. If there are citizens who are in favour of preserving the present Union, but still propose to give their support to the Republican candidates, may I ask them how they can reconcile the two? They cannot accomplish the political object they may propose under the present Constitution, then why should they give expression and form to such abstract desire? Is it to gratify or to give expression to a feeling of hatred against slavery? Let them not delude themselves. Men do not hate vice, but the vicious. They do not hate murder, but the murderer. Neither do men hate slavery, but the slave-holder. Vice, murder, slavery are mere words which convey to the mind the idea of certain acts, which acts must be performed or brought about by intelligent human beings, otherwise no passion of hatred could be excited. Now let me ask the sincere friend of the Union, how he supposes the Union can be maintained, or how he can think that the

Union ought to be maintained, when he and others constituting a majority of all the States of one section, being a majority of the citizens of the Confederacy, declare thus solemnly and formally that they have given their support to the candidate of their choice, with the sole object of giving expression to their feelings of hatred against the citizens of fifteen States of the Confederacy? Can a love of the Union, as it now exists, animate those who cultivate and give expression to such feelings in regard to one entire section of the Confederacy? Or can they expect to excite a feeling of love for any Union whatever, in the breasts of those against whom such an irritating warfare is kept up, on account of the existence of a domestic institution, for the creation of which they are not responsible, the continuation of which has become an inexorable necessity, and the management of which is, and of right ought to be, under their exclusive control?

LETTER XV.

Duty of Citizens — Republican Measures are the results of unfriendly feeling; not the cause — Spirit of the Republican Party inconsistent with a desire to maintain the Union in its integrity.

MAN cannot engage in any work which yields a greater revenue of good than in softening the asperities of his fellow-men against each other. In the present contest in the United States, it is the duty of every good citizen to pause and look steadily and calmly into the probable future of such a struggle. Let him not deceive himself by delusive hopes, but watch the current of passing events, and see with his own eyes in what direction we are tending. Let him pause and listen to the roar of that cataract whose ominous mutterings can now be distinctly heard, even upon the far-away shores of the Bosphorus, from whence I venture to send forth upon their uncertain errand these words of admonition.

It should be borne in mind that there is a feature peculiar to the present attitude of parties in the United States which distinguishes it from all others that have hitherto existed. In the past, parties have been organised in support of and in opposition to certain measures of State policy, which were sustained or opposed without any direct reference to geographical lines. The people naturally arrived at different conclusions in regard to the merits of these measures, and as their judgements or their interests dictated, they have arrayed themselves on the one side or the other. The discussions growing out of these differences of opinion have at times produced more or less of bitterness, and personal as well as sectional unkindness. But it will be noted that these antagonisms originated in the previously existing differences of opinion in regard to questions of public policy. Now, this state of facts is totally reversed. The measures advocated have grown out of a previously existing feeling of animosity, and have no other foundation upon which they rest for support. The proof of the truth of this proposition exists in every man's mind who will consider of this one fact, namely, if every trace of bad feeling, or hatred, or sectional animosity were removed from the breasts of the people, the questions which are now discussed and fiercely sustained upon the one side, and opposed upon the other, would instantly and of themselves disappear.

Without considering the abstract merits of the measures proposed by the Anti-slavery or Republican party, if a contingency could arrive which would remove from the minds of its adherents and supporters all purely personal ill will or exasperated feeling against the Southern people, its presidential candidate could not upon the present issues obtain the electoral votes of three States of the Confederacy. It is impossible that a party in the United States sufficiently formidable to carry a half dozen States, or even one State, could be formed out of citizens who desire to maintain the Union, the inevitable effect of whose measures would be, to take away from the Southern States their equal rights, and to render their domestic peace insecure, unless they were sustained by the passions and prejudices of the electors. The friends of the Union in this contest should act upon this existing fact, that the angry passions which the Republican leaders may make available to their success are not founded upon the measures they propose, but the measures owe their existence to the angry passions. To address these by controverting the policy, the propriety, or the justice of their measures would be fruitless, so long as the feeling referred to exists in their breasts. To eradicate a disease the physician must go to the root of a malady. Those who would labour effectually for the defeat of Republicanism should direct their efforts to remove the unfounded feeling of animosity which has been implanted in the hearts of its supporters. The war of the Allies against Russia brought their armies to Sebastopol. During the pendency of the struggle the besiegers and the besieged erected their fortifications and defences, and planted their batteries, to meet the exigencies which the varying events of the siege brought forth. Peace was finally made, and the works of the defenders as well as of the assailants are now neglected and in ruins. Just as war measures are resorted to by nations when an angry state of feeling exists between them which forebodes hostilities, so stand the parties to the present contest in the United States. The bitterness of feeling which prevails against the South, and the fortifications which are being erected from whence to assail the Slave States, have produced counter defences. Remove the feeling which produced them, and the fortifications and the defences will alike tumble into ruins. Eradicate this sentiment of animosity from the Northern mind, which, while exasperating the South, yields no advantage to the North, and it would be worth more than all the slave codes which the South could ask or a united Congress grant. If the feeling is too deeply rooted to be obliterated, the most stringent laws which could be enacted would be powerless to protect the rights of the Southern States. Let then the friends of the Union and the adversaries of political sectionalism deal their blows at the foundation upon which the superstructure of the Anti-slavery Republican party has been erected. Strike down the corner-stone of the edifice, and the walls and domes and towers will fall into a mass of indistinguishable ruin. This duty, this glorious privilege, I might say, falls upon the true men of the North. Hundreds of thousands have, up to this hour, withstood all the appliances of proffered rewards upon the one hand, and the certainty of political death upon the other. If they should succeed in arresting the calamity which now threatens the Confederacy, a grateful posterity will unite them in their hearts with the fathers of the Republic. If they fail, the consciousness of having discharged their duty will be a reward of far more value than any which would follow their defection from the cause of their country.

Those who would labour with a reasonable hope of success in the great contest which must now soon be decided, should remember that the specific measures proposed by the Republican party are mere outposts or decoys sent forward to draw off the attention of their adversaries from the true point to be assailed. These may be readily overthrown by an appeal to the Constitution, and an exposition of the true principles of equality, which are the foundations upon which the superstructure of the Confederacy has been erected. But of what avail would be this? Others would be proposed; more skirmishing parties would be sent out, which, though driven in, would leave the main body intact, and as strong as at the beginning. Thus would the strength of the national party be frittered away in fruitless contests with insignificant bodies of the enemy, and upon the very ground which that enemy selects.

The only hope of success for the National party which holds out the prospect of a victory that will be enduring in its results, consists in their ability to eradicate, or at least to soften, the spirit of the animosity towards the Southern States, upon which the Republican party alone relies for success. The proposal to exclude the citizens of Slave States from the territories — John Brown insurrections and murders — incendiary publications and incendiary emissaries distributed among the slaves, and the counter propositions of those who are assailed, are all effects, not causes. Remove the causes, and the effects disappear. Let, then, the main attack be directed against the spirit which dictates a wish to inaugurate unfriendly legislation against the South.

A citizen of the North may be conscientiously opposed to the institution of slavery. Be it so. If there should be a proposition to introduce slavery into his State, let him oppose it. But he has no right to assail a neighbouring sovereignty for differing from him in opinion, in regard to the management of their domestic affairs. I know it is contended that in a free country a man has a right to say what he pleases; but the fact is that in a free country, of all others, there is a moral responsibility resting upon each citizen not to exercise that power indiscreetly. A man has the power, and he may also have the legal right, to say and to do many things which are very wrong; but if more evil than good results from what he says and does, he has no moral right to do the wrong. There may be a dozen partners in trade, who have engaged each to contribute to the joint stock an equal amount, and to share equally in the profits. Seven of the twelve may assail the private characters of the five, and that of their families. They may insist that, for fear of spreading the infection of their sins by their example, the women and children shall not be permitted to leave their houses. In furtherance of this good work they may go farther, and say that the children of the five shall not be permitted to occupy or enjoy the use of any of the estates or farms which have been purchased out of the joint profits of the partnership. The power to make such a proposition cannot be questioned. The legal right to ask that such a disposition be made, may be also conceded. But would not such a suggestion be equivalent to a demand that *the partnership be dissolved?* Can it be supposed that the five would consent to continue the 'union' upon such terms, in the face of an agreement that they should be equal partners? Or would a longer continuance of the association be either desirable or proper, after such declarations had been formally embodied and presented, as the only terms upon which the majority would thereafter consent that the business should be conducted?

Whether the causes which should produce this state of feeling be regarded as real or imaginary, would it not be the duty of the seven, in lieu of demanding a proportion of the common estate for their own use, to which they could not justly lay claim, to say, frankly, 'We do not like you personally; we object to the manner in which you are raising up your families; we are shocked by the conduct of your wives and daughters; therefore we propose that the partnership be dissolved, and the estate be equitably divided, according to the letter and spirit of the terms on which it was created?'

So may it be said to the supporters of the Republican party: Your unfriendly and constant assaults upon the Southern States, their institutions, and their people, are utterly inconsistent with the position you occupy to each other as partners and associates. The language of your ceaseless tirades against slavery and the Slave States are carefully collected by the enemies of the Republic, and disseminated in every land where the English language is read or spoken. These are translated into every tongue, and the world exclaims, 'What horrible monsters those Republicans must be, when, according to their own statements, they tolerate a political union with the incarnate fiends who perpetrate such enormities against their fellow-creatures?' If, therefore, nothing can eradicate or soften these feelings, you should act like men who really feel strong moral convictions, and frankly repudiate the political bonds which unite you to so much sin. If you do not urge this as a sequence, how can you expect to secure the respect of mankind by continuing, for mere gain, that confederation which you believe to be a mere 'covenant with hell'? Let every man, then, bring home to himself the true question. The spirit which animates the Republican party, and the feeling of animosity, which is its prime element of strength, is utterly inconsistent with a desire to maintain the present Confederacy, except from the most sordid considerations. Let this issue be fairly and honestly presented; and why should we doubt that tens of thousands, who have drifted into this great gulf of sectionalism, will once more turn their faces towards the shore, and swell the ranks of that civic army which is now engaged in, perhaps, its last struggle for the Union in its entirety, by the preservation of its integrity. Remember that now is the time for action! This occasion lost, and in all human probability all will be lost! Sectionalism once triumphant, no human power can restrain the onward march of the victors towards that goal to which their hopes have been directed. The war of subjugation against the South once inaugurated, who can estimate the terrible consequences of the conflagration which will be enkindled? Let those in the North who believe that, from their superior numbers, there would be an easy victory and a prompt surrender, remember that the South will enter upon the struggle with the conviction, that while defeat *may be annihilation*, submission *would be death!*

LETTER XVI.

The madness of the hour — in Europe the Dissolution of the Union is expected—A few words to Northern Enemies of the South — Conclusion.

AMID the din of arms, and the roar of artillery, and the smoke of battle, and the mad fury of men excited by the contest and eager for blood, there is small hope that the voice of one man calling upon the combatants to lay down their arms, would be either heard or heeded. Neither can I hope that the words of one whose only claim to be heard is, that he is a fellow-countryman, though for a time resident in a distant country, will be listened to by the excited parties to the great, perhaps the final struggle *at the ballot-box*, for the union, the liberty, and the equality of the States, which now moves the heart of the great Republic! It may be that even before we are called upon again to celebrate the anniversary birthday of the Father of his Country—the immortal first President of the Confederacy—opposing armies of his fellow-countrymen may be struggling in deadly strife upon the soil of that Virginia which gave him birth, within sight of the now quiet capital on the banks of the Potomac which bears his name, and upon the very grave where he lies buried! In view of the impending storm, the spectacle now exhibited in the United States is indeed a sad one.

The history of the past teaches us that, at times, nations are seized with a madness which it were even a worse madness to attempt to combat by an appeal to reason. This insanity, if I may so denominate it, though it may have its beginning originally in a sentiment of philanthropy, or even love, terminates by merging every other feeling into the single passion of hatred! It is vain to attempt to deny the startling truth—such is the present aspect of that madness which seems to pervade the people of America! If ever in the inception or progress of this contest, one single element of love or consideration for the slave entered into the thoughts or hearts of the principal assailants in this sectional struggle, it has been supplanted, buried beneath the passion of hatred, which that contest has engendered! * We who are

* Senator Wade, of Ohio, a prominent leader of the Republican party, said, in a speech delivered as far back as 1855 (see 'Boston Atlas'):

'There is *really no Union between the North and the South*, and I believe no two nations upon the earth entertain feelings of more bitter rancour towards each other than these two sections of the Republic. . . . Let us have a Union, or let us sweep away this remnant which we call a Union. I go for a Union where all men are equal, or for no Union at all.'

It may be remarked that among the first serious movements for a formal dissolution of the Union was the petition presented to the Senate of the United States by Mr. Hale, of New Hampshire, at present a prominent leader of the Republican party in the Senate, praying for a dissolution of the Union. Upon the question of its reception, however, there were but three votes in its favour, namely: Mr. Hale;

removed far from the scene of this struggle — far from a knowledge of the under-currents, and personal jealousies of the mere political contest for place and power — see and know full well, that it is not *love*, but *hatred* on which the sectional politician relies for success; and it is that feeling or passion, which gives to the present unfortunate contest its vitality.

Mr. Seward, of New York, the present Premier of Mr. Lincoln's Cabinet; and Mr. Chase, of Ohio, another member of the present Cabinet.

Mr. Wm. Lloyd Garrison, a prominent leader of the Republican party of New York, in a speech in New York, August 1, 1855, said:—

'This Union is a lie! The American Union is a sham, an imposture—a covenant with death, an agreement with hell! and it is our business to call for a dissolution. . . . . If the Church is against disunion, and not on the side of the slave, then I pronounce it as of the devil. . . . Let us give to the winds the rallying cry—"No union with slave-holders, *socially or religiously*, and up with the flag of disunion."'

Mr. Edmond Quincy, a leading Republican of Massachusetts, said, in a church in New York, May 13, 1857:—

'I wish for the dissolution of the Union, because I want Massachusetts to be left free to right her own wrongs. If so, she would have no trouble in sending her ships to Charleston, and laying it in ashes.'

W. O. Duval delivers himself of the following pious and patriotic letter:—

'I sincerely hope that civil war may soon burst upon the country. I want to see American slavery abolished in my time. . . . Then my *most fervent prayer is*, that England, France, and Spain may take this slavery-accursed nation into their special consideration; and when the time arrives for the streets of the cities of this land of the free and home of the brave to run with blood to the horses' bridles, if the writer of this be living, there will be one heart to rejoice at the retributive justice of heaven.'

Extract from Speech of W. Philips, in Boston, in May, 1849.

'We confess that we intend to trample under foot the Constitution of this country. Daniel Webster says that you are a law-abiding people. Shame on us if this be true! If ever the religion of New England sinks as low as its statute-book! But I say we are not a law-abiding community. God be thanked for it!'

There is no practical issue but that of *hatred*. The success or defeat of aspirants for office depend altogether upon the degree of hatred which their appeals may produce in the popular mind! There is no single element of success, and no appeal which can secure success for the Republican party, but that of *hatred!* Americans should not for a moment disguise this fact.

There has been a time in the brief history of the great Republic, when the adherents of despotism in the Old World regarded with distrust and dread, and the lovers of freedom with hope and satisfaction and pride, the progress of the great experiment in democratic government. Now how changed! Both look forward with a confidence, inspired by hope upon the one hand, and by despair upon the other, to a speedy disruption of the Confederacy — civil war—exhaustion — anarchy — and then the repose of despotism.

For myself, while I, as an American citizen, will not admit to be true the declaration of even moderate monarchists of the Old World, that a government founded upon democratic principles bears within itself the germ of its own dissolution — that the turbulence of universal freedom, and the tyranny of mere numbers, or dominant geographical sections, must end sooner or later in the destruction of the liberties of the minority, to be followed by the despotic rule of a single tyrant — yet I confess that the events of the last few years, and the unnatural struggle which they have engendered, involving in its progress no practical issue of good to either, except that of mere sectional domination, and in the future nothing but disaster to both, have made me at least less hopeful of the result.

Never before in the history of any other nation, have we evidence of so rapid a march from the weakness of infancy to the full developement of a hardy manhood, as has been illustrated by the brief career of the American Confederacy. It is the pride of Americans, at home and abroad, to direct special attention to this undeniable truth. Whether that growth in greatness is to be checked, destroyed, or continued, is certainly to a considerable extent involved in the final result of the present controversy. It may or may not be, that the present struggle between men for political power will terminate the contest for sectional supremacy. But whenever it is decided that a *geographical division of the Republic*, owing its cohesion to *sectional animosity* only, and its success to *mere numbers*, shall triumph over its numerically weaker but combined confederates and equals, it were worse than folly, it were madness to suppose, that with unfettered limbs, and the liberty of free action on the part of the oppressed, they would not sever the political bonds which united them to their oppressors.

It is quite true that the mere peaceful dissolution of these constitutional bonds of union and the establishment of smaller and more homogeneous nations, would not of itself abrogate the principle of liberty upon which our free institutions are founded. But such a separation, accomplished under auspices which would leave so much mutual bitterness in the hearts of the people, which, by destroying our unity, would leave us comparatively defenceless as against foreign aggressions, all involving the necessity of large standing armies, make the probability strong that our present form of freedom could not long survive.

How can these calamities be avoided? Madmen may answer, 'By crushing our enemies beneath our heels!' But it is to be hoped that a majority of the citizens of the Republic are not thus held in bondage by their angry passions, and that the voice of reason may yet penetrate the minds of numbers sufficiently formidable to arrest the onward march to such a catastrophe. Let us not surrender until to hope would be fanaticism.

If the will exists, the means are at command to avert such a calamity, without any surrender of political rights, and without any abandonment of matured convictions in regard to politics, morals, or religion. The citizens of the dominant section are called upon simply to deal fairly and justly with their fellow-citizens of the South. They have but to do unto others as they would that others under the circumstances should do unto them. Let patriots make no effort to disguise from themselves or others the true and only questions involved, but in a frank and manly spirit, such as would become the monarchs of a great nation, seek only an equitable solution. The *nature*, the *origin*, and the *objects* of the present struggle we have already considered. We have seen what interests are involved, and *who*, if any, will be the beneficiaries upon a division of the spoils among the victors.

It will be readily conceded, that in a struggle of parties for political supremacy in a confederacy of States, the result of which should be brought about by a combination of certain States composing a section distinguished by geographical lines, and presenting but one single issue, and that issue being an expression of hostility to the domestic institutions of the weaker by the stronger section, and depending for success upon the ability of the latter to create a feeling of hatred for the citizens of the former, could not be regarded otherwise than a menace against the independence and the equality of the States thus assailed. Success, under such circumstances, would of itself amount to a declaration on the part of the majority, of the dissolution of the Confederacy upon the terms previously existing. That which would follow would be nothing more than to arrange the details of separation or reconstruction.

When I say that there is no practical issue involved, except the expression of an abstract feeling, or sentiment, or passion, I of course refer only to that portion of the Republican party who profess that it is not their intention or desire to curtail the equal rights of the Southern States, nor to destroy or attempt to modify the institution of slavery within their respective limits. If this be true, then between them and the South there cannot be an issue, for the most extreme Southerner neither asks nor desires anything more than this. For people of the North who really entertain these sentiments, intentions, or opinions, to unite themselves to the Republican party, could not have any other significance than simply to announce an irreconcilable feeling of animosity against the Southern States. Upon any other hypothesis, why should they combine with those whose avowed or apparent purpose is to destroy the institution of slavery? It must be remembered that this party is founded, by the avowal of its leaders, upon the sole question of slavery. They must have some object, some purpose to accomplish; and we are bound to conclude that this purpose or object, being supported only by men of Anti-slavery opinions, must have some practical Anti-slavery design, and that design must have reference to the Slave States of the American Union, and must contemplate some change or modification, or the destruction of that institution. Otherwise the existence of such a party would be impossible; for it is absurd to suppose that a party can exist without a purpose, at least upon the part of its founders and leaders.

It follows, then, that if the Republican party embraces sane men amongst its leaders, it must have a purpose. Being founded solely upon the single sentiment of Anti-slavery, its purpose must be *inimical to the Slave States.* Now, why should those who have no wish to interfere with the institution of slavery where it exists, and who do not desire to curtail or to destroy the equal rights of the South, give their support to the Republican party, from which they differ, and thus withhold their support from the opposing party, between whom and themselves, on the only practical issue, there is an entire agreement?

Whatever may be the individual exceptions, it must be presumed that those who give their support to the Republican party in the present struggle, do so for the purpose of interfering with the rights of the slave-holding States, or with a view to give expression to a feeling of antipathy or hatred for the people of those States. That such should be the only avowed issues in a great national election for the choice of a President, should of itself awaken the earnest attention of every citizen who in his heart desires the perpetuation of a Union which has been attended with so many blessings. Let no Northern man deceive himself in regard to the results of a victory thus obtained.

If he be a high-minded, honourable man, and will for the moment imagine himself to be a citizen of a Southern State, he would require no other index to the consequences that would ensue than the promptings of his own heart. No threat, no declaration, no warning voice from the South, could add to the firmness of his convictions, in regard to the feeling with which such a sentence of condemnation would be received by those against whom it would be directed, or the consequence which would surely follow.*

* Mr. President Filmore, after retiring from the Presidency, delivered a speech in Albany, in July 1856, from which I extract the following paragraphs. Although the thoughts to which he gives expression are such as would naturally suggest themselves to the mind of every calm reflecting statesman, yet, from his distinguished position, as President of the United States, and as a Northern politician opposed to the institutions of the South, his deliberately-expressed opinions ought to have weight with his fellow-countrymen, who seem madly resolved upon the destruction of the Government. Mr. Filmore said:—

'We see a political party (the Republican), presenting candidates for the Presidency and Vice-Presidency, selected from the Free States alone, with the avowed purpose of electing these candidates by suffrages of one part of the Union only, to rule over the whole of the United States. Can it be possible that those who are engaged in such a measure can have seriously reflected upon the consequences which must inevitably follow, in case of success? Can they have the madness or the folly to believe that our Southern brethren would submit to be governed by such a Chief Magistrate? Suppose that the South, having a majority of the electoral votes, should declare that they would only have slaveholders for President and Vice-President, and should elect such by their exclusive suffrages to rule over us at the North—do you think we would submit to it? No, not for a moment! And do you believe that your Southern brethren are less sensitive on this subject than you are, or less jealous of their rights? If you do, let me tell you that you are mistaken. And therefore you must see, *that if this sectional party succeeds, it leads inevitably to the destruction of this beautiful fabric*, reared by our forefathers, cemented by their blood, and bequeathed to us as a priceless inheritance.'

'I tell you, my friends, that I feel deeply, and therefore I speak earnestly, on this subject; for I feel that you are in danger. I tell you

To the individual exceptions above referred to, or rather to the large class of citizens of the North from whence these exceptions come, the hopeful American can only look for the means of safety from the storm which now threatens to engulf the Republic. So far as regards mere numerical strength, the North is unquestionably the strongest; and if the artful appeals of the Anti-slavery party, and of other enemies of the South, can accomplish a union of the entire North, so far as mere voting is concerned, slavery may be considered as already abolished, and the Slave States prostrate before their more powerful adversaries.

To you, citizens of the North, who have gained much, both in honours and in wealth, from your intercourse with the South, and who are now found in the ranks of her enemies, let me address a few words at parting. You have been made rich by the spoils you have derived from your improvident and free-hearted neighbour. I cannot believe that you are yourselves so mad, as with your own hands to destroy the goose which supplies you, day by day, and year by year, with its golden eggs; but you are exposing it to dangers which, in a few short months, you may

that we are treading on the brink of a volcano, that is liable at any moment to burst forth, and overwhelm the nation. . . . It seems to me impossible that those engaged in this contest can have contemplated the awful consequences of success. If it breaks asunder the bonds of our Union, and spreads anarchy and civil war through the land, what is it less than moral treason? Law and common sense hold a man responsible for the natural consequences of his acts, and must not those whose acts tend to the destruction of the Government be equally held responsible?'

be powerless to avert. The South pours annually into your lap the tribute of its almost boundless resources, for which you pay nothing in return but hard words.* You confide too much in the forbearance and long-suffering of your benefactors. The South has proven to you that she is willing to be fleeced — that she is willing the proceeds of her labours shall build up your palaces, and yield you the means necessary to support them. Be content, and do not, in uncalculating wantonness, place the last straw upon the back of the patient camel.

The South would lavish freely of her wealth and the blood of her citizens to maintain and uphold the dignity and honour of the Union, and she would glory

* Without estimating the tobacco, rice, flour, and other productions of the South, exported to foreign countries from the Southern States, the value of the exports of cotton alone during the last year (1859) amounted to $161,434,923; while the total exports from the North, of every description of domestic produce and manufactures, exclusive of gold and silver coin and bullion, amounted to only $91,783,905. This, however, is not so significant as the disparity in the imports. While the Southern States imported of foreign merchandise only the value of $32,955,281, the Northern States imported to the value of $305,812,849. Whence does the North derive the means necessary to supply this enormous deficiency in its exports, as compared to its imports? What becomes of the enormous excess of exports from the South over its imports? These questions should not be difficult for a Northerner to answer. Under the operations of a most unjust tariff upon foreign merchandise, the South is compelled to resort to the North for the greater portion of the manufactured goods required for its home consumption. The South is thus denied the privilege of trading with her own customers in Europe; and the North, while pluming itself upon its virtuous horror of the institution of slavery, is coolly pocketing the greater portion of the profits resulting from its employment in the neighbouring States of the South.

in its perpetuation to the latest posterity, if it might be preserved on the same principles on which it was established. But if you force upon her the alternative of surrendering her rights, or of withdrawing herself from the Union, be assured that her free citizens will, with one voice, accept the latter, and start forward with hopeful hearts in the new career which will open up before them. You ought to be convinced that the South can do without you, and that her boundless sources of wealth would be augmented, instead of being diminished, by the separation. It is not by any means sure that such a result would follow in that North which, strange to say, seems to have nothing so much at heart as to render a longer union impossible!

You insultingly proclaim to the world that 'the South is a burden' to you, and that 'she herself is so fully satisfied of her dependent condition that she could not be kicked out of the Union'—otherwise you would be gratified if she would take the determination to retire and leave you alone, the glorious champions of liberty, unstained by unhallowed associations. These are harsh words; and it is not surprising that the hot blood of the Southerner should mount with a redder glow to his cheek as he listens to them, and ponders to discover their significance. But may not the words you now so scornfully utter be but the words of the vain boaster? When the hour of consummation would arrive, can you not imagine that some of the golden visions of future prosperity and wealth, which have made tranquil the moments of your repose from the cares of life, would melt away for ever in the presence of the stern reality before you ?

Be assured in time that, if you force upon the South the issue, she can and will pursue her separate career, in whatever direction and with whatever success may be decreed by Providence ; and if you will let her go in peace, she will thank you, and will wish you God-speed, while bidding you a reluctant though an eternal farewell. If, however, your passions, or your pride, or too tardy a consideration of your temporal interests, should make you seek her overthrow, though your number be greater, millions of freemen, with strong arms and chivalrous hearts, will meet you with a bloody welcome when you cross the border. Should the first encounter result in the triumph of the invader, they will, with one voice, pray the God of battles *to prosper the right*, and they will defend their homes and their firesides in every city, on every mountain, and on every plain, from the Potomac to the Rio Grande, and the shores of the Gulf of Mexico; and you will never accomplish your purpose, whether it be to emancipate the slaves or to enslave the freemen of the South, until their last dollar shall have been expended and their last soldier shall have fallen before your victorious legions.

If, however, you still believe that soft words, spoken hereafter, when the crisis comes, will induce the South to forget the past, and shut her eyes to the hard fate which is being prepared for her, do not, let me conjure you, over-estimate your influence in the hour of victory, over the excited politicians, and the maddened, deceived masses, who are respectively your leaders, and instruments. Be warned by the fate of others, who, in times past, have fruitlessly essayed to stay the tide of popular passions, which they themselves had artfully put in motion. The reflection that, in losing all yourself, you compass the destruction of your enemy, will not, in the hour of your affliction, be held to be a sufficient compensation for your own downfall.

Before you drive the South away for ever, remember, that although you are of the same race and lineage, and your governments are founded upon the same general principles, the Slave States have retained an element of conservatism in their domestic institutions, which, however repugnant to your prejudices may be its features, has hitherto reacted upon the entire Confederacy, and has had a powerful influence in preserving the whole from the dominion of that radicalism and license which murders liberty while professing to fight under its banners. Remember, that however happy may be the people who live under the protecting flag of a free government, there lurks in the very heart of every purely democratic republic an element which may be developed in the form of the most hideous despotism. When passion, instead of reason, sits enthroned in its councils, and in the hearts of its citizens, that latent element of tyranny may be developed into acts of more unpitying atrocity than any single despot whose foot has ever pressed upon the necks of slavish subjects, would dare to perpetrate. That dormant principle once aroused to action, farewell to all your hopes of future greatness. You may, in terror or in anger, direct its fury, for a season, against a common foe; you may make desolate their hearthstones, and leave their dwellings in ashes, but as sure as Heaven's laws are always executed, *it will return to fasten its deadly fangs into your own vitals!*

In concluding these desultory letters on the issues involved in the pending contest for the Presidency, I may be pardoned for saying, that no mere party feeling—no wish to promote the success of this or that individual aspirant for the Presidency, on account of any personal predilections for the one, or any unkind feelings for the other, has had the slightest influence in deciding me to write them. Separated by oceans, and continents, and seas, from my native land—standing, as it were, upon the outermost verge of the civilisation of the Old World, beyond which all is darkness—in the midst of decaying empires, whose history, for many centuries, is crowded with the records of dazzling achievements—surrounded on every hand by the melancholy memorials of once powerful kingdoms and republics, whose greatness and whose dominion, annihilated by the sectional dissensions of their own citizens, have passed away for ever; the splendour of whose glorious deeds, in the day of their pride, has only been exceeded by the magnitude of their ignoble fall; whose descendants have for ages lived, and groaned, and died, the despised and slavish subjects of a foreign master; I have asked myself, if the unhappy fate of subjugated and degraded Greece, is but a prototype of that which is in store for the great Confederacy of the New World!

So far as the solution of this question depends upon the preservation of the federal Union, I admit that I am less hopeful than at any previous period of my life. I see the indications of an unswerving purpose, on the part of the North, to obtain a triumph over the South, by means of its numerical preponderance; and well I know the spirit with which the South will meet the issue thus presented.

In view of the impending calamity of a conflict, whose beginning seems almost at hand, but whose end is shrouded in impenetrable gloom; with a vivid appreciation of the disasters which may soon involve us in a common danger, if not a common ruin; in the character of an humble citizen, whose passions have been calmed by the startling proximity of the menacing danger, I have addressed these words, and now send them forth to my fellow-countrymen. That I am a Southerner, by birth, by education, and in all my hopes for the future, I am free to declare; but I am also an American, protected in a foreign land by the flag of the Union, and every day I live I appreciate more highly the value of the great Confederacy which that star-gemmed banner symbolises. Priceless indeed, compared to the pecuniary sacrifices necessary to maintain it in its integrity; priceless, even compared with the blood which might be shed in defending it against a foreign foe; *but detestable as a tyrant, and valueless to freemen, when it can only be upheld by a sacrifice of the honour and the independence of its members.*

LETTER

TO THE

RIGHT HON. HENRY LORD BROUGHAM.

Constantinople, Feb. 1861.

My Lord,—Two events of recent occurrence—trifling in themselves, except when regarded in connection with the peculiar circumstances of the times in which they occurred—have contributed more towards the identification of your Lordship's name with the political convulsion which the year of our Lord one thousand eight hundred and sixty-one is now witnessing in America, and with the anti-slavery movement, in which it has had its origin, than all which you have hitherto accomplished, during your long and brilliant career as an English statesman.

With a zeal which has known no flagging—with a resolution which was appalled by no probable or possible consequences—with an ability which is fully accorded by your adversaries—and with an earnestness which would seem to preclude any doubt of your sincerity, you have laboured for the overthrow of that institution of African slavery in America, which has existed from a period long anterior to the incorporation of the Republic into the family of nations.

In this lifetime labour, however, you have been identified with others of your compatriots, who have exhibited the same pertinacity of purpose, and who have probably acquired a reputation almost equal to your own as the great exponents of English sentiment and English policy.

It has been the fortune of your Lordship, through the instrumentality of the two events referred to, to inscribe your name far above those of your fellow-labourers, in the roll of the recognised exemplars of British sentiment and British policy.

The first of these occasions offered to your Lordship the opportunity, in an assembly of distinguished dignitaries from almost every nation of the civilised world, of proclaiming, in effect, your belief in the equality of the races of man, and the special claim of an African then present to be regarded as a worthy and fit associate for the noble Peers of England.

If your Lordship had been contented with the utterance of this simple expression of opinion, it would probably have been forgotten by those who were your auditors almost as soon as uttered. If by any accident, a representative man of the millions of Anglo-Saxon blood and Anglo-Saxon colour, who have sighed in vain to attain to that social rank and station which you so readily accorded in that august assemblage of princes, and nobles, and statesmen to this sooty African, had bestowed a passing notice upon this paragraph in your lordship's speech, the subject would doubtless have been dismissed, after a brief commentary, with the very natural and charitable observation, that a Peer of England had an undoubted right to choose his own associates, and might be expected to comprehend, better than another, the qualifications and characteristics of those who should be regarded as worthy of such association.

But your Lordship entertained a deeper purpose. You desired to hold up to obloquy a great nation on the opposite side of the Atlantic; and, in order to startle your audience by the magnitude and the enormity of its crimes, you proclaimed the presence of the diplomatic representative of that nation which held in the bonds of slavery millions of a race of people, of which you then and there presented a faithful type, and to whom you assigned an equality of social rank with the noble order of which your Lordship, in the estimation of your fellow-countrymen, is a faithful representative.

Your Lordship's design was skillfully, and artistically, and dramatically executed. To be received and acknowledged as a peer, in such an assembly, was certainly, in your Lordship's estimation, to be placed upon a pinnacle of social and moral elevation which few could hope to reach; while the doom of the slaves upon the plantations of America was a degradation beyond which there was no lower depth. The worthy representative of the oppressed, and the official representative of the hated oppressor, were both present before you. Both were in a foreign land, and both were strangers and your guests. Disregarding these pressing claims upon your forbearance—acting, it may be, upon the conviction that the claims of God and humanity were more than paramount to all other considerations, you held them up, as it were, to the gaze of your audience as representatives of the victim and of the enslaver—of virtue and of vice—of freedom and despotism—of all that was worthy to be loved, and of all that should be hated.

The occasion was one which precluded reply or explanation. The generous, the refined, the intellectual, the noble representative of a despised and down-trodden race, stood revealed before your sympathising audience in all the majesty of injured innocence; while there, too, stood the spoiler—the embodiment of the stupendous crime of his country.

It would probably be presumptuous in me to question the good taste displayed by your Lordship, either in your choice of the occasion, or in your manner of treating one of these stranger guests. I am willing to concede that your Lordship should know better than I the rules of politeness and good breeding proper to be observed in an assemblage of nobles and high dignitaries gathered together in the great capital of the civilised world, and presided over by the Prince Consort of England's noblest Queen. Upon this collateral point I would not dare to make up an issue with your Lordship, the more especially as your audience, by the applause with which it greeted your remarks, has already recorded its verdict in your favour.

The main purpose of your Lordship was achieved — the contrast you suggested startled the world by its magnitude. The irrelevancy of the subject to that which your auditors had assembled to consider, gave to the incident a notoriety which was magnified by its very isolation ; while the event has been perpetuated in the memory of the multitude by the princely character of the audience before whom the scene was so dramatically enacted. From that moment, America has recognised, in the questionable gallantry of your achievement, the qualities which have made you the great champion of British abolitionism.

I will now pass to the second event, which has

served, in a still greater degree, by expanding the field of your operations, to strengthen and to confirm you in the position which, by common consent, had been previously assigned to you. But, before entering directly upon the subject, allow me to refer to an incident which occurred, not a great while ago, at a spot more than 3,000 miles distant from that great centre of civilisation in which your Lordship moves.

A *murderer* in another continent closed a long career of crime under the gallows! There was nothing peculiar in this fact, for such has been often the fate of murderers in England, in America, and elsewhere. But this was a villain of no ordinary stamp. His victims were not stalwart men alone, but defenceless women and little children. He did not slay in the glare of the noonday sun, as a common robber at the head of his band of retainers, but he killed in the quiet hours of the night, and the slumbers of innocence were startled by the death-shrieks of his unsuspecting victims. But his crimes had not their beginning in those for which he suffered an ignominious death. They extended over a series of years; and the last, for which with his life he paid the forfeit, was by no means the worst. I myself have seen and known the unhappy victims of his earlier crimes. I have seen and known the happy wife and mother — happy in the innocence and purity of her life, though humble in her station — and I have seen her again in all the desolation of a childless widowhood. Dreadful, indeed, were the scenes through which that poor woman passed during the brief space of one short night. She was sleeping in fancied security when the spoilers came to her humble log cabin, and passed through the unbarred door to the bedsides of her sleeping husband and children. Your Lordship knows the rest, and I will be brief. They were four when they lay down to rest, that dreadful night. The morning dawned upon the living woman surrounded by the lifeless and mutilated bodies of her husband and children.

The chief criminal in this drama of blood, emboldened by immunity, changed the scene and enlarged the field of his operations. At Harper's Ferry, he again unsheathed his bloody dagger, and again was the hour of midnight made terrible by the death-struggles of his unwatching victims. Am I not right, then, in saying that John Brown was a villain of no ordinary stamp? *Sane* men, in a contemplation of the magnitude of his crimes, have said that he was *mad*, while *madmen* have exalted the *demon* into a *saint*, and mourn for him as a martyr in a holy cause!

It was upon December 3, 1860, that his friends and partisans assembled in the city of Boston, to celebrate the first anniversary of his 'martyrdom.'

Previous to that time, a letter had been addressed to your Lordship by the 'Committee of Managers,' inviting you to be present upon that occasion, and to join in that celebration.

Those who knew the fact that such an invitation had been addressed to your Lordship, were eager to learn in what manner you would respond. The first impression would naturally be, that your Lordship would treat the missive with the dignified silence and disdain with which a nobleman of your Lordship's exalted standing might be expected to meet a gross and studied insult; or, that your indignation, obtaining the mastery of your better judgement, might induce you, in that burning eloquence of words, which your Lordship can so readily command, to hurl back the insult in the faces of your traducers; or, milder and more humane than either, and, perhaps, more in consonance with the gentle manners which might be expected to distinguish those through whose veins flows gentle blood, you would have responded, 'It is not *my sins* but *your insanity*, which has led you to believe that I could hold fellowship with the partisans and admirers of an assassin. Go! you are madmen, and I forgive you.'

These thoughts, I confess, were my thoughts, and that I give them voice here will show to your Lordship that I did not rank you amongst the vicious and blood-thirsty fanatics with whom a common sentiment, upon a single point, had served in some measure to identify you. Besides, I will add, that my high respect for the exalted order to which you belong, as well as the position in which you stand towards the occupant of a throne, induced in my mind the belief that you would, in some manner, exhibit your horror of the crime of assassination, and with such an emphasis that even madmen might never again give expression to the thought that an English nobleman could have any sympathies in common with either assassins or their partisans.

Pardon me, my Lord, if I, in unconscious ignorance, did not estimate, at their proper value, the refined principles of that 'higher law' which have been incorporated among the doctrines of that so-called great humanitarian Anti-slavery party, of which you are so distinguished a chief.

At first view it might occasion surprise that the 'philanthropists' of Great Britain should seem to shut their eyes to the spectacle, and their ears to the wail of woe, which rises up around them from the millions of the unhappy, the destitute and depressed of their own race and kin, while they have only eyes to see, and ears to hear, and tears to shed over the reputed wrongs of a handful of Africans upon the far-off shores of a continent beyond the Atlantic. But it is necessary in charity to remember that the degradation and wrongs of the one are familiar to them from youth to old age. It is an oft-told tale, to which they have become accustomed, familiar, and perhaps indifferent from its constant repetition. They are probably appalled by the magnitude of the evil, and ask to forget its existence and their obligations by the exhibition of redoubled zeal in the cause of those whom their imaginations, excited by heart-rending romances, picture as the victims of sorrow and oppression in a far distant land.

From this brief but not unnatural digression, I will return to the subject of the invitation which was given to you to participate in the celebration in memory of John Brown the great American murderer, who suffered death under the gallows in expiation of his appalling crimes. Permit me to refresh your memory with the first lines of your response to the committee in your own language:—

Sir,—I feel honoured by the invitation to attend the Boston Convention.

Upon reading these few emphatic words, I paused, and re-read the letter of invitation which had been addressed to you, to discover if I had not, in my hasty perusal thereof, misunderstood its import and object. I beg to quote its words:—

My Lord,—A number of young men, earnestly desirous of

devoting themselves to the work of eradicating slavery in the United States, respectfully invite you to meet them in a public convention, to be held in this city on Monday, December 3.

. . . .

It seems to them that the anniversary of the death of John Brown, who was killed in attempting to decide this problem in the mode that he believed to be the most efficient, is an occasion peculiarly appropriate for the discussion of our duty to the race for whom he suffered. . . . . It would be a work of supererogation now to defend John Brown, and a useless waste of time to eulogise him. Leaving both these duties to the coming ages, *let us seek to continue his life by striving to accomplish what he left us to finish.*

It is true, my Lord, that you modified somewhat the only legitimate interpretation of your first emphatic endorsement. True, as 'the representative of the Anti-slavery party in England,' you avowed a wide difference of opinion between those you represented and the promoters of the Harper's Ferry expedition. True, you denied that John Brown was a real martyr. True, you declared your opposition to the encouragement of negro insurrections, because '*they might prove less hurtful to the master than the slave.*' True, you intimated that the surest means of accomplishing your cherished schemes of American negro emancipation was under the form of law, through the instrumentality of a recent political change in the government of the Republic! But preeminent above all other considerations which are suggested by a perusal of your letter, stands forth the declaration that you '*feel honoured* by the invitation to attend the Boston Convention!'

What a spectacle is here presented, and how fruitful a theme for reflection! An English nobleman shaking hands across the ocean and transmitting pleasant messages to *such* an assemblage convened for *such a purpose*!

It is, perhaps, not unworthy of a passing thought, that while some of your admirers have hailed your letter as furnishing evidence of the conservatism and moderation of British abolitionism, many have regarded your slight deviation from the bloody path of an extreme fanaticism as too great a concession to the dictates of an uncalculating and weakly-relenting humanity.

I confess that upon this subject there is a chasm between us, so broad and so deep, that I have not the hardihood to attempt to fill it up. I cannot hope even that anything will ever occur to reduce the breadth of this impassable gulf to smaller dimensions.

But, pardon me, my Lord, if I suggest the possibility that you may not have fully appreciated the deep significance of the first sentence of your memorable letter. Did you reflect upon the powerful influence which your slightest word of encouragement might exercise upon the furious madmen whom you addressed? Do you believe they will fail to infer that while you disclaim sympathy with John Brown's plans of emancipation 'because they are less likely to result in injury to the master than the slave,' you will, nevertheless, regard it as an honour to be invited to attend the celebrations consequent upon the death of other martyrs in the same cause? Do you excuse yourself, my Lord, with the thought that it is only the assassins of slave-holders in America who are worthy to be treated with so much kindness, respect, and forbearance? Have you forgotten from whom, and under whose auspices, American slaves were acquired as chattels? May I be pardoned for saying that in the family of the writer there is a slave, bought and paid for by his ancestor from a British subject in a British province, under the solemn sanction and approval of British laws, and who is now held as a slave under the guarantee of a British title-deed? Should another John Brown, under the pretext of giving freedom to this slave, slay the owner thereof, and for this crime suffer a felon's death, would your Lordship feel honoured by an invitation to attend the anniversary celebration of his 'martyrdom?' Your Lordship has already answered the interrogatory in the affirmative.

The day may come, my Lord, when 'even-handed justice will commend the ingredients of the poisoned chalice to your own lips.' There are more shining marks for the assassin's dagger than the slave-owners of America! Millions of lives stand between the honoured felon and the accomplishment of his bloody work of philanthropy; a thousand times your Lordship might have the privilege of acknowledging 'the honour' of invitations to attend and participate in the celebration of events similar to those which were enacted at Harper's Ferry, and as often might 'English philanthropy' palliate or excuse the crimes in which they had their origin, and still there would be a sea of living blood coursing through the veins of slave-holders! There are millions of the human race who, bound in the chains of political servitude, are ready to believe that they behold but one living man standing between themselves and the liberty to which they aspire! that one life less, and the fetters would fall from their liberated limbs! You may truly believe, my Lord, that no such danger may threaten England's sovereign. Even madmen would not strike at one whose noble virtues have added a brighter gem to the British Crown than was ever placed there by the valour of British arms. But England's best and noblest Queen must die, and be succeeded by sovereigns who may not imitate her virtues. If a British nobleman, of such world-wide reputation for statesmanship and philanthropy as your Lordship, endeavours to instil into the public mind the belief that it is a *real honour* for an honourable man to be invited to join in rendering homage to the virtues, the moral worth, and the philanthropic services of an *admitted midnight assassin*, whose only *virtue*, or *worth*, or *service* in the cause of humanity, whose only claim to distinction above other cut-throats, beyond that notoriety which always attaches to the most revolting murderers, consists in the fact that he killed ostensibly in the cause of the so-called great humanitarian anti-slavery movement of the age; you need not be surprised, if others, who have real or imaginary wrongs to redress, may, while rejecting your peculiar idiosyncrasy, accept this as a means of redress. There are those who from the depths of their bleeding hearts, and for the redress of grievous wrongs which they themselves have suffered at the hands of their own race, would feel and say, 'If this be a real honour, which a British nobleman may covet, how much more honourable to be invited to participate in saturnalia of nobler blood!' May Heaven grant that neither your Lordship nor any other may ever again be called upon to acknowledge the honour of an invitation to join in the celebration of such a feast!

But your Lordship's response has satisfied me that though you may be a *fanatic*, you are not a *madman*. Though you may move fearlessly upon the brink of the precipice, you will not plunge bodily into the abyss into which you invite others to descend. You will not place in jeopardy that which you conceive to be the policy of England, by permitting it to be fully identified with the crime of assassination — the more especially as you imagine that you perceive in recent political events a more effectual means of accomplishing your ends, with less probability of injury to the slave than the master.

I come now, my Lord, to consider a paragraph in your letter, which, containing, as it does, a grave personal charge *against myself*, constitutes within itself my claim and my apology for addressing you. Your Lordship may mentally respond to this announcement, that not the most insignificant thing alive was farther from your thoughts than the unknown writer who now demands and *exercises* the privilege of repelling your unjust imputations — that *he* has never once 'passed between the wind and your nobility,' and that you have, therefore, never given to him a cause of offence.

In order to refresh your Lordship's memory, I beg to refer you to the closing sentences of your response to the Boston Committee. The following is your language : —

In the elevation of your new President, *all friends of America, of its continued Union*, of the final extinction of slavery, by peaceful means, *all friends of the human race must heartily rejoice!* They will, let us hope, find in him a powerful ally, as his country may expect to find an able, *a consistent*, and an honest ruler. I have the honour to be, your faithful servant,

BROUGHAM.*

I have italicised that portion of the above paragraph to which I claim the right of response. While I will not pause to consider the phenomenon which is exhibited in your expressions of friendly regard and sympathy for, and confidence in, an American

* Americans North and South who were acquainted with the state of facts which existed, and the material out of which the party which elected Mr. Lincoln was constructed, were fully satisfied that foreigners who entertained the belief that his success was an event which ought to be hailed with joy 'by every friend of the human race,' would in process of time find occasion at least to modify such opinion. They could hardly have hoped, however, that the developements of a single year would have compelled the noble Lord who gave expression to the above sentiment, to give utterance to the following emphatic declaration: —

'In the House of Lords on August 30, Lord Brougham said he could not refrain from taking that opportunity of directing their Lordships' attention to private accounts which he had recently seen of the progress of the civil war in America. Those accounts disclosed horrors surpassing anything that had yet been made known to the world in the public journals. Thousands on thousands of men were embodied on either side, and while they displayed a courage that was above all commendation, the war, and the malignant passions with which war was always accompanied, appeared to have taken root in every rank of society. The inhabitants of the same village were banded against one another; farmers and proprietors were arming themselves to gratify their animosities; the fury of the strife extended to private families; and he had been informed of one instance in which the father and the son being arrayed on opposite sides, the son was heard to say that he hoped to hear of his father's death.'

. . . .

'He believed that if the civil war should continue, it would be found that slavery was not the worst evil of America, and that that fratricidal war would lay the foundations of more destructive passions than any that had ever arisen out of their unhappy "domestic institution." If the American people had any regard to their reputation in this country, they would at once terminate the frightful struggle; and he could not but believe that the good sense of the more reflecting and of the better-informed among them would soon bring about that most desirable consummation.'

President; yet, I beg to say, that it at least furnishes evidence of a wonderful change in the sentiments of British politicians in regard to the chiefs of the Republic. At the end of a long night of horrors and misrule, your Lordship sees bursting over the horizon the bright and glorious sunshine, which is hereafter to illumine the career of the Republic. By the early light of this dawning luminary you imagine that you behold in the not distant future, the end of that terrible conflict between brothers and fellow-countrymen, which you hope will in its results be less hurtful to the slave than his master. You, perhaps, imagine that in a very brief period the nation which Great Britain failed to conquer with her mighty sword, even in the dawn of its infant existence, will have fallen an easy victim to that subtle policy, by which you and your co-labourers have endeavoured to arm its citizens in a fratricidal war. If the merit of a deed may be measured by its success, I grant that your Lordship may boast that you are upon the point of achieving a greater triumph by the subtle arts of diplomacy, than has ever been won by British arms, during a long and brilliant and bloody career.

In contemplating the possibility of such a catastrophe, one is tempted to exclaim, Was ever nation before so wooed, so won! Your own King Richard had less cause to hope for success, when he sought to win the widow of the murdered Edward. And in surveying the victory you have achieved, you may well recall the words in which he vaunted his victory over the weak Lady Anne, and with a slight change of phraseology, apply them to your own triumph:—

> I'll have her, but I will not keep her long.
> What! I, that killed her husband, and his father!
> The bleeding witness of her hatred by,
> With God, her conscience, and these bars against me,
> And I, no friend to back my suit withal,
> But the plain devil and dissembling looks—
> And yet to win her, all the world to nothing!

Were this communication addressed to my fellow-countrymen, instead of to your Lordship, I might beg them to remember the farewell injunction of the Father of his Country—the immortal Washington:—

> Against the insidious wiles of foreign influence, I conjure you to believe me, fellow-citizens, the jealousy of a free people ought to be constantly awake; since history and experience prove that foreign influence is one of the most baneful foes of Republican Government.

I might pray them to consider that foreign politicians rarely, if ever, mingle in the internal conflicts of a rival Power for any other than selfish purposes. I might say to them, and I might prove, that British anti-slavery fanaticism is but the creature and the servant of British policy, owing its origin and its developement to what was supposed to be a political necessity; and that though your Lordship might *write* as a fanatic, you have never failed to remember *that you are also a British politician*! Yes, my Lord, if I thought that my voice would be listened to in the madness of the hour, I would appeal to my countrymen, with the earnestness of conviction, to resist with all the energy of a determined will, and to repel as an insult not to be forgiven, every effort of the foreigner to embroil them in fratricidal conflicts, even though attempted under the garb of philanthropy. I would say to them that however gratifying it might be to have the sympathies and to win the smiles of the great of other lands, the hopes which may be built thereon will prove delusive; the promises of succour will, in the day of adversity, be forgotten; and all the bright anticipations which may have their origin in such an association will, like the apples of Sodom which tempt the eye of the traveller upon the shores of the Dead Sea, turn to ashes on the lips!

Perhaps, though, your Lordship's visions of the future of the Republic may prove delusive. Perhaps your own unguarded words, written in the first flush of an anticipated but not yet fully accomplished victory, may of themselves induce a momentary pause in the mad career which you and your associates have inaugurated, Perhaps, when they read your Lordship's letter, a *burning thought* of days long past, when as a band of brothers, their fathers by their bloody valour, conquered their independence, may penetrate their hearts. Perhaps the retrospect may reinaugurate once more that feeling of fraternity which animated their ancestors 'in the days that tried men's souls.' Or, if they cannot agree to live together as brothers in one family, that they will, in memory of a glorious past, with all its heart-thrilling associations, in memory of the blood of their sires, mingled together upon many a hard-fought battle-field, consent at least to part as friends. The end may not be yet, my Lord. Out of the *clouds* may emerge a *sun*, more resplendent than even that which seems now to be setting in a starless night.

But your Lordship, plunging into the arena of party politics in America, hails the recent defeat of that political organisation which has ruled and guided the destinies of the Republic from the first moment of its existence to the present day, as an event in which '*all friends of America—all friends of the human race, must heartily rejoice*.'

This is a most harsh judgement, most harshly enunciated—to say nothing of its implied condemnation of the statesmen and citizens who have passed away, and whom we, their sons by blood and inheritance, have been taught to regard as 'true friends of America.' It is certainly, when considered in reference to the source from whence it emanates, a most overwhelming condemnation of the millions of American citizens who struggled to avert its downfall, and who still cling to its fallen fortunes, and to its great distinctive principles as the sheet anchor of the hopes of the Republic. The charge is as sweeping as it is harsh. You will not grant that ONE 'friend of America, or of the human race,' can feel any regret at the occurrence of the event you commemorate.

The Heaven-doomed city of olden time, even after its destruction had been ordained by the fiat of Omnipotence, was allowed a respite from its terrible fate, in answer to the prayer of one *real* friend of humanity, who said: 'Behold, now, I have taken upon me to speak unto the Lord, which am but dust and ashes—peradventure ten righteous men shall be found there;' and the Lord, admitting the doubt, and ever tempering justice with mercy, delayed the execution of his judgement with a promise that if ten righteous men could be found in Sodom, the city should be spared for their sake.

More inexorable in your judgement, though but a man; under the influence of your own antipathies, and upon the testimony of their enemies alone, you condemn unheard millions of your fellow-men, and deny that, amongst them all, there lives one friend of his country or of the human race, whose righteousness might plead, in behalf of his fellow-countrymen, to save them from the doom of Sodom.

While the world may give your Lordship credit

for a more profound knowledge of those subjects which concern the general good of the human race, than the unknown writer who now addresses you, I cannot doubt that an impartial public would decide that an American citizen, whose destiny has been cast within the limits of the Republic, ought to understand as thoroughly, and to appreciate as fully, the qualities which distinguish a 'true friend of America,' as any British statesman, however high his rank, or however exalted his endowments.

This consideration emboldens me to declare, in my right as an American-born citizen, and as the representative of a sentiment held in common by millions of my fellow-countrymen, that it is not *I*, nor *they*, who are the enemies of America. If it must be that one or the other of us, my Lord, is an enemy of the Republic, it is *you*, who, from your high and noble rank, permit your name to be mingled up with those of the openly-avowed friends and followers of assassins! It is you, who, by acknowledging yourself to be honoured by an invitation to participate in demonstrations of respect for one of the foulest murderers whose deeds have found a place in the records of crime, put the lighted torch and the dagger in the hands of the incendiary! It is you, who, from your safe retreat, may laugh to scorn the horrors of such a contest, thus enkindle the flames of a fratricidal war in a distant land, and all *in the prostituted name of humanity!*

You delude yourself, my Lord, if you believe that all 'friends of America' and of the 'human race' share your sentiments of joy upon the occasion you celebrate. Millions of the real friends of freedom in other climes now mourn over the peril which menaces the overthrow of 'the great Republic,' without knowing, or caring to comprehend, the domestic questions which have produced the danger. During eighty-five years, it has been a beacon of hope to the weary and heavy-laden, and should its brightness be now quenched by that dark and clouded night, upon whose gloomy and fitful shadows, we may even, at this moment be gazing, believe not, my Lord, that the announcement of the catastrophe will be a message of joy to the hearts of 'all the friends of the human race!'

I would ask no nobler epitaph upon the tomb of that party, whose defeat your Lordship commemorates as an event which should be hailed with joy by every 'friend of the human race,' than to record, in simple and brief words, this fragment of its history:—

'The political organisation which inaugurated the revolt of the Thirteen American Colonies of Great Britain; which conducted the war of the Revolution to a successful close; under whose auspices the Confederation of Free States was established; and which ruled and guided the destinies of the Republic during the first eighty-five years of its existence, perished in the year of the Christian era one thousand eight hundred and sixty-one. Whether its fall was a consequence of its crimes, its virtues, or its misfortunes, let posterity determine.'

It would be profitless for me to indulge at greater length in the reflections to which the two events I have referred to, and your Lordship's connection therewith, have given birth. I am unwilling to offer to you, my Lord, any defence for the local policy of the political party in America to which I belong. Nor, on the other hand, will I make any attack upon that in whose success your Lordship seems to feel so deep an interest, and whose cause you commend with so much zeal. But, my Lord, you have invited a comparison by which I am willing that my country shall be tested. You have, by the energy of your assaults upon the institution of African slavery in America, indirectly challenged an examination into the manner in which subjugated races have been ruled by your own country, and you seem to invite scrutiny into your own connection, as a nation, with the institution of African slavery in the past, as well as in the present era.

I, in turn, challenge an investigation and a comparison, and I am willing to accept 'all friends of the human race' as our umpires. I am willing that both shall be tried 'by the laws of God and humanity,' and that the enquiry shall have for its object the determination of the question: Which has so governed as to achieve the greatest good, with the least evil, to those over whom Providence or cupidity have called them, respectively, to bear sway? Every friend of the Southern States of America is willing to stand or fall upon the result of such an investigation and comparison.

I have a high respect, my Lord, for the great nation in which you hold so distinguished a rank. I am satisfied that many, very many, of its noblest citizens of all classes deprecate the officious interference of British politicians in the contests of political parties in America. But my friendly regard for individual citizens of your country does not blind me to the fact that English influence has been a principal element in the sectional troubles which now distract my country.

. . . .

The persistent misrepresentations against the Southern American States, which have emanated from the British Abolition party, have excited unjust and wholly unfounded prejudices against my countrymen throughout Europe. I cannot hope that in a day, or a year, these prejudices can be removed by any exposure of that narrow and thoroughly selfish policy which, decked in the garb of humanity, has given tone to the sentiments of Europe upon American affairs. But in the confidence that a returning sense of justice will induce your Lordship to listen to the defence made by one whom you have accused as an enemy to his country and to the human race, I propose, after the lapse of a few weeks, which will be necessarily occupied by other engagements, to do myself the honour of again addressing you.*

I may not hope that the judge who has already pronounced against me, in terms so emphatic, will be induced to reverse his predetermined judgement; but I will not despair of obtaining a reversal of your sentence before a tribunal composed of the 'friends of the human race,' until longer to hope would be fanaticism.

The small grain of mustard seed, which I throw upon the ground, may be choked by the foul weeds amongst which it is cast, and never see the sun; but it may be that from this little seed may grow and 'wax a great tree,' and that beneath its shade, a few, at least, of the noxious plants, from the midst of which it grew, may wither and perish!

I have the honour to be, most respectfully,

Your Lordship's obedient servant.

* The publication of the letters here referred to, is now superseded by those which fill the greater part of this volume. Although they were written antecedently to my announcement to his Lordship, yet, as they cover the points at issue, I submit this volume, with all its admitted imperfections, to 'the true friends of America,' as well as to 'the friends of the human race,' as a redemption of my pledge.

SURVEY OF THE RESULT OF THE PRESIDENTIAL ELECTION AND ITS CONSEQUENCES.

The Governments of the North and South contrasted — Presidential Elections analysed — Votes for President in 1860 — On the Rights of the States to secede from the Union — Ordinances of 1787 and 1790 — Ordinance passed by Congress in 1789 — The United States Government as it is — The Separation must be perpetual — Antagonisms between the North and South — The South will be justified before the World — The South must be Self-reliant.

At the time when the series of letters which occupy the larger portion of this volume were written, the South was making its last appeal to the North for justice, and was engaged in its last great struggle at the ballot-box against its unrelenting adversary. When the letter to the distinguished British statesman which succeeds the series referred to was addressed to that gentleman, the result of the election had been already announced, and the States which had composed the Union were trembling in the balance, between the alternatives of a peaceful separation and a war of subjugation against the sèceding States. It would seem to be proper, in order to complete the connection between the cause and the results, that something should be added upon the subjects indicated at the head of this chapter, as a sequel to that which goes before.

The result of the election for the Presidency of the United States in 1860 — during the pendency of which the preceding series of letters were written in the Old World, and forwarded to America for publication — together with the immediate consequences flowing therefrom, are now events accomplished and ready for the pen of the historian. Never before has any political contest in the New World created so deep an interest throughout Europe, as that which terminated in the installation of one section of the Union, embracing eighteen States, into all the powers of the General Government, and the consequent practical exclusion of the other section, embracing fifteen States, from all participation in the management and control of a Confederacy of which they formed so important a part.

The interest excited by that struggle, in view of the internal changes which it was thought would be likely to follow, have been intensified and deepened into an absorbing passion in presence of the actual consequences which have succeeded swiftly upon the heels of the Northern victory at the ballot-box.

THE GOVERNMENTS OF THE NORTH AND SOUTH CONTRASTED.

All Christendom stands amazed—electrified, as it were—in presence of the stupendous spectacle which is this day presented to mankind in that country which, a few short months ago, was properly regarded as the living embodiment of the principles of freedom.

Eleven of those States have withdrawn from the old Union—have resumed their sovereign powers—and, in the exercise of their inalienable rights, have formed a separate Union, under the style of the 'Confederate States of America.' The four remaining Slave States are ready and eager to unite themselves with their brethren in the Confederate States, whenever they can throw off the chains and shackles with which they have been fettered by the Government of the United States in the exercise of a despotism more ruthless, cruel, and vindictive than any which has marked the career of any civilised conquerors of modern times.

The very first steps taken by the Government of the United States in inaugurating the war against the South, were marked by a duplicity and a vindictiveness unworthy of a great nation. The Southern States, acting upon the belief that the Government of the Union was a Confederacy of sovereign States, sent their Plenipotentiaries to the President of the

Northern United States, to arrange the terms of a peaceable dissolution of the political bonds by which they had been previously united. These Commissioners were authorised to make a fair and equitable arrangement in reference to the existing debt, and the territorial possessions of the Union. Instead of receiving them, and at least stating the grounds of their refusal to consent to a separation, the Government of the United States, under various pretences, evaded any direct communication of its intentions, while actively engaged in secret preparations for commencing the war. Finally, having, as was thought, consummated the necessary arrangements, the Commissioners were informed that the Government would not hold any communication with them; and the intention was announced of immediately reinforcing the fort which commanded the entrance to the harbour of Charleston. It is apparent from the vindictive demonstrations of the Northern mob against Charleston, that the Lincoln Government intended to begin their war of subjugation by the destruction of that city. Thanks to the prompt energy of Beauregard in reducing Fort Sumpter before the arrival of the expected reinforcements, Charleston was saved, and the Government of the United States, foiled in its treacherous attempt, engaged promptly in the work of organising armies for the invasion and subjugation of the entire South.

PRESIDENTIAL ELECTIONS ANALYSED.

It has been so often repeated that the South has had the control of the Government of the United States from its foundation, up to the inauguration of Mr. Lincoln, that the assertion has come to be regarded as an unquestionable fact. In the sense in which this is understood by the world at large, nothing could be farther from the truth, as may readily be discovered by an investigation of the subject.

In considering the Presidential elections, and the causes which have operated in deciding them, the time which has elapsed since the formation of the Government may be divided into two periods: namely, first those which occurred previously to 1825, during which period the men of the Revolution occupied the Presidential office; and secondly, those which have taken place since that epoch, and in the decision of which the old issues were by lapse of time to a great extent superseded by new interests and another generation, which had not participated in the struggle which terminated in Independence. An analysis of the following table will show the error into which the public has fallen in regard to the political preponderance of the South.

FIRST PERIOD				
Year	Elected President	Northern Electoral Votes	Southern Electoral Votes	Total
1789	George Washington of Virginia .	38	31	69
1793	George Washington of Virginia .	73	59	132
1797	John Adams of *Massachusetts* .	59	12	71
1801	Thos. Jefferson of Virginia . .	4 states North	6 states South	
1805	Thos. Jefferson of Virginia . .	86	76	162
1809	Jas. Madison of Virginia . .	61	61	122
1813	Jas. Madison of Virginia . .	30	88	128
1817	Jas. Monroe of Virginia . .	93	90	183
1821	Jas. Monroe of Virginia . .	133	103	236
SECOND PERIOD				
1825	J. Q. Adams of *Massachusetts* .	8 states North	5 states South	
1829	Andrew Jackson of Tennessee .	73	105	178
1833	Andrew Jackson of Tennessee .	132	87	219
1837	Martin Van Buren of *New York* .	109	61	170
1841	W. H. Harrison of *Ohio* . .	151	83	234
1845	Jas. K. Polk of Tennessee . .	103	67	170
1849	Z. Taylor of Louisiana . .	97	66	163
1853	F. Pierce of *New Hampshire* .	158	94	252
1857	Jas. Buchanan of Pennsylvania .	62	112	174
1861	Abe Lincoln of *Illinois* . .	180	. .	180

From the above it will be seen that since the establishment of the Government there have been nineteen presidential elections and fourteen Presidents, of whom seven were taken from the North and an equal number from the South. During the first period, terminating in 1825 with the last of what may be denominated the Presidents of the days of the Revolution, Mr. Adams alone was chosen from the North, while Washington, Jefferson, Madison, and Monroe were all chosen from the single state of Virginia.

During the second period, that is from 1825 inclusive up to the present time, *nine* Presidents have been chosen, of whom six were from the Northern States, and *three* from the new States of the South, two being from Tennessee and one from Louisiana; so that since the election of 1821 not a single president has been chosen from either of the Southern States of the original thirteen.

We discover farther from the above table, that while there have been nineteen presidential elections, sixteen of those who have been elected have received more electoral votes in the North than in the South. *Sixteen have also received a majority of the electoral votes of the Northern States*, while *only three*,—namely, Mr. Jefferson upon his first election, Mr. Madison upon his second, and Mr. Buchanan,—were chosen in opposition to the majority of the North, by Southern States in combination with a powerful Northern minority.

If, then, *the policy* of the South has guided the destiny of the nation up to the election of Mr. Lincoln, this end was attained through the instrumentality of Northern presidents, and with the sanction, aid, and approval of the Northern States, and could not therefore have been sectional or partial. In truth the policy of the South, and of the Government of the United States, when under the direction of the South, has always been unselfish and broadly national, and hence its successful direction of public affairs. It is true that the South has of late been compelled, in order to avert greater evils which were threatened, to yield to the clamours of the protectionists of the North, and especially of Pennsylvania, for high duties upon foreign imports; but that the policy of the Government has never been inimical to the North, by whomsoever governed, is fully demonstrated by the fact, that of the thirteen Presidents who occupied the Presidential office previous to Mr. Lincoln, *twelve would have been elected by Northern votes, even though the South had withheld its votes altogether*; while the only one who would have been defeated by the withholding of all the Southern votes was Mr. Buchanan, a citizen of the North. The reader will understand that although Mr. Jefferson and Mr. Madison each failed to obtain a majority of Northern votes at one election, yet each served two terms, and each obtained for one of these terms a majority of Northern votes.

But the election of Mr. Lincoln opened a new era in regard to Presidential elections. For the first time in the history of the Government a President was chosen by means of votes received upon the North side of a geographical line, and against the unanimous protest of all who lived South of that line of demarcation. An analysis of the votes cast in the election, by virtue of which Mr. Lincoln is now the

President, will show that the precedent thereby established utterly excluded any reasonable hope that the Southern States would ever thereafter be allowed to participate in the administration of the affairs of the Government. They would have been as entirely prevented from any effective intervention, as though they had been the subjects of a Foreign Power.

As will be seen from the following table, Mr. Lincoln received 180 electoral votes, all from the Northern States, while the number cast against him was only 123. Having thus obtained a majority in the Electoral College, he became the President. Yet in the popular vote cast in the choice of electors, amounting to 4,715,270 (estimating the votes of South Carolina at 53,100), Mr. Lincoln received only 1,857,610, while the number cast against him (which were divided between three candidates), amounted to 2,857,670. It will also be observed that in ten of the eleven Seceding States Mr. Lincoln did not receive the vote of a single citizen, while there were cast against him 1,238,285. In the eleventh he received only 1,929 votes, while there were cast against him in that single State 165,294.

VOTES FOR PRESIDENT IN 1860.

Northern States	Electoral Vote		Popular Vote	
	For Lincoln	Against him	For Lincoln	Against him
California	4	. .	39,173	79,667
Connecticut	6	. .	43,792	33,454
Illinois	11	. .	172,161	167,532
Indiana	13	. .	139,033	133,110
Iowa	4	. .	70,409	57,922
Maine	8	. .	62,811	35,107
Massachusetts	13	. .	106,533	62,642
Michigan	6	. .	88,480	66,267
Minnesota	4	. .	22,069	12,730
New Hampshire	5	. .	37,519	28,434
New Jersey	4	3	58,324	62,801
New York	35	. .	353,804	303,329
Ohio	23	. .	231,610	210,831
Oregon	3	. .	5,270	9,140
Pennsylvania	27	. .	268,030	208,412
Rhode Island	4	. .	12,244	7,707
Vermont	5	. .	33,808	9,036
Wisconsin	5	. .	86,110	66,070
In the North	180	3	1,831,180	1,554,191
Southern States				
Alabama	. .	9	. . .	90,357
Arkansas	. .	4	. . .	54,053
Delaware	. .	3	3,815	12,224
Florida	. .	3	. . .	14,347
Georgia	. .	10	. . .	106,365
Kentucky*	. .	12	1,364	144,852
Missouri*	. .	9	17,028	148,490
Louisiana	. .	6	. . .	50,510
Maryland	. .	8	2,294	90,218
Mississippi	. .	7	. . .	69,120
North Carolina	. .	10	. . .	96,230
South Carolina	. .	8	. . .	53,100
Texas	. .	4	. . .	62,986
Tennessee	. .	12	. . .	145,333
Virginia	. .	15	1,929	165,294
In the South	. .	120	26,430	1,303,479
Grand total	180	123	1,857,610	2,857,670

* Kentucky and Missouri have since held partial conventions, and have sent delegates to the Confederate Congress. Maryland is still held

It is manifest that even though an enormous majority of the whole people might be favourable to the preservation of the rights of the Southern States, the Northern sectional party could hold them in subjection; and under the forms of constitutional democratic liberty, and by the sanction of a fallacious popular vote, deprive them of every right and privilege of Free States. He must be indeed blind to the lessons of history, who supposes that the North, seeing its advantage, would ever again have permitted the South to be reinstated in its rights, when by so simple and easy a process they could retain all power in their own hands. Men do not willingly surrender power, except under the pressure of a real or supposed necessity, which, in the case considered, could never exist. Much more is a mere majority disinclined to relinquish its control over another people, against whom they cherish bitter prejudices.

To dispel the delusion of a hope, if it exists in the minds of any, that an appeal to the magnanimity of the North would accomplish the end proposed, it is only necessary to consider *the material* of which is composed that army of voters into whose power we have fallen. First come the sagacious money-wor-

in subjection, as well as Missouri and Kentucky, by an overwhelming military force; but they are only awaiting a favourable occasion to throw off the galling yoke of the Yankees, and join their fortunes to those of their Southern brethren.

shipping Yankee manufacturers, with whom are leagued the iron manufacturers of the great State of Pennsylvania, who seek, through prohibitory or highly protective duties, to draw into their own coffers the profits of the planters. Next, a fanatical priesthood, which declares from the holy desk, during a period of profound peace, that 'one good rifle is worth a hundred bibles' against Southern slave-holders. Next the Radicals, of every hue, both in religious and governmental affairs—advocates of 'woman's rights' and 'free love' —Red Republicans and infidels from beyond the Atlantic, who, having been the curse of their own country, have come over, as the locusts of Egypt, to plant the seed of their radicalism upon American soil; and last, the multitude of thoughtless, or ignorant, or wicked men, whose passions are constantly inflamed by the eloquence of place-seeking demagogues, against those whom they designate the 'aristocratic slave-ocracy of the South.'

It has been illustrated by the election of Mr. Lincoln, against the expressly declared will of the American people,—even admitting that majorities should be endowed with the privilege of voting away the rights of minorities—that by the assent of a majority of the Northern people only, and against the unanimous protest of the Southern States, a mere majority of one section may obtain under the forms of the constitution the entire and exclusive control of the government of both. Admitting that the Northern people are endowed with the virtues and moderation which they claim, and that Northern mobs are humane, and are endowed with the qualities requisite to the administration of a good government, and the enactment of wholesome laws, can any one say, in view of their long-cherished animosity towards the South, that they would be safe custodians of the rights and liberties of the Southern people?

The present attitude of the respective Governments, which are now contending in arms for political dominion over the soil of the South, presents to the philosophical and enquiring mind some curious phenomena. That portion of the late United States, which is spoken of, by superficial observers of passing events, as being 'in a state of revolution,' seceded from the late Union, and formed another, without any change whatever in the internal organisation of the States composing it, and without suspending, for a single instant, the operation of the laws by which the citizens of each had been governed. The acts accomplishing secession and creating a new Confederacy, had no more influence upon the *status* of the citizens than the withdrawal of France and Sardinia from a European alliance, and the formation of a separate compact, would produce upon their subjects.

The Confederacy thus established assumed upon the

instant of its creation the powers which were confided to it by the States composing it, and is now firmly established, not only in the regular exercise of its legitimate functions but in the hearts of the people.

Under the benign administration of this government, the rights of its citizens have been everywhere respected, and the laws have been faithfully executed. The liberty of the press has been maintained inviolate. No citizen held in prison for a political offence has been deprived of his right to a trial before the civil tribunals; and so far from arresting non-combatant subjects of the United States who might be within the limits of the Confederacy, a law has been enacted by the Congress at Richmond, giving to alien enemies forty days in which to make their preparations for departure, and offering them free egress from the jurisdiction of the Confederate States. These are the circumstances and condition of that country which, in common parlance throughout Europe as well as the United States, is said to be 'in a state of revolution.'

On the other hand, the Government of the United States, which is said to be engaged with all its power in putting down the attempted revolution in the States of the South, and in suppressing 'the great rebellion,' is itself in the throes of a terrible revolution. The stupendous encroachments upon the constitutional rights of its citizens, which have marked the administration of the Government since the inauguration of the present President, are without a parallel in the history of any other nation. The liberty of the press has been abrogated, and many journals both secular and religious, which have expressed a doubt in regard to the policy of continuing the war of subjugation against the South, have been either suppressed by the direct orders of the Government or destroyed by mob violence.

An inconsiderate word, uttered in the confidence of private friendship, is employed as a pretext for consigning the offender to a prison. Men are arrested while engaged unsuspectingly in their private avocations—transported to distant fortresses beyond the limits of the State in which they reside—incarcerated in dungeons — deprived of all means of communicating with their friends — and from first to last are kept in utter ignorance of the cause of their arrest and detention; and, as if to complete the parallel between the tyranny inaugurated by Lincoln and that which marked the career of Robespierre and Danton, even women and young girls are arrested and incarcerated, by a simple order from a commanding officer, and without even the forms of law, upon suspicion of disloyalty to the government of Washington. The right of the citizen to petition Congress has been refused, and the petitioners in New York arrested. The writ of *habeas corpus* has been suspended, or rather abrogated, by the sole authority and at the discretion of the President, as to time and place. He has also delegated this usurped authority to his military commanders. All these acts, unheard of in the previous history of the country, and unparalleled in enormity by those of any other government of the present age, are perpetrated, not against those who are said to be 'in rebellion,' but against the citizens and within the legal jurisdiction of 'loyal States,' who profess to be as earnestly desirous of upholding the Government, properly administered, and of reuniting its dissevered elements, as the President himself or his advisers.*

* The only justification which is attempted for these various outrages, is the plea of necessity. This might avail them with mankind if they were defending themselves against invasion, but they are themselves the invaders against an unoffending people, for the avowed purposes of subjugation and virtual robbery. To declare the mere expression of an opinion adverse to the prosecution of such a war to be 'treason,' is against the practice of all civilised nations, and cannot be commended by any friend of liberty.

The following are among the leading newspapers, the circulation of which have been suppressed by order of the government: In New York City, the *Journal of Commerce*, *News*, *Day-Book*, and *Freeman's Journal*; in Pennsylvania, the *Christian Observer*; in Missouri, the *Journal*, *Missourian*, and *Herald*. Those suppressed by the mob are the *Standard* (Concord, N. H.), *Democrat* (Bangor, Maine,) *Farmer* (Bridgeport, Connecticut,) *Sentinel* (Easton, Pa.), and the *Republican* (Westchester, Pa.) The *New York Herald* was assailed by the mob, but was spared on becoming a government paper.

Nothing can more clearly illustrate the utter subjection of the people of the North themselves to the despotism which in a few short months has robbed them of every vestige of their former liberty, than the following extract from the card of the editor, M. E. Masseras, of the *Courier des Etats Unis*, a French paper published in New York, on retiring by

Such having been the conduct of the United States Government when dealing with the 'loyal States,' the treatment administered to those which are said to be in 'a state of rebellion,' or to have sympathies in common with the Confederate States, wherever they have been in whole or in part placed in a state of subjection, may possibly be imagined. The occupation of that portion of the border of Virginia which has fallen under the ruthless dominion of the invaders, has been marked by deeds of the most wanton cruelty, rapine, and violence. Every blade of grass has been destroyed, whole villages and towns have been burned to the ground, and their inhabitants driven forth without pity. Every foot of territory over which their armies have trodden, presents a picture of utter

order of the Government from the editorship of that paper. He says that in future the paper will confine itself simply to the news of the day, as that is all which is permitted, and that he himself will retire until the time arrives when he will be permitted to speak his sentiments. He concludes as follows:—

'To-day as in April—still more than then—I am convinced that war will not save the Union, and that, on the other hand, it will destroy the Republic. I am satisfied that the majority of the nation submits to a war which it does not approve, without believing in the happy termination about which it seeks to delude the people. I am satisfied that the war is the work of a party, who will push it to the last extremity, without hesitating at any means to maintain its supremacy. In all this I see nothing but oppression, ruin, then, as a last consolation, inevitable revolution. And as the situation in which the press is placed only leaves me the choice between blandly praising everything or holding my tongue, I decide upon silence.'

The belief on the part of the Washington Government that such extreme measures are necessary, proves conclusively that there must be a strong feeling of disapprobation on the part of the people against the war.

desolation. Throughout another entire State, the writ of *habeas corpus* has been suspended, and the civil authorities have been entirely superseded by military rule. The commander of this military division — a vain despot, who seems only ambitious of acquiring a wider notoriety of infamy, than any other person engaged in the same occupation — has issued a proclamation, declaring as forfeited, not only the property, but the lives, of all persons who may be found in arms against the Government which he represents.*

* *Extract from Fremont's Proclamation.*—'In order, therefore, to suppress disorders, to maintain, as far as practicable, the public peace, and to give security and protection to the persons and property of loyal citizens, I do hereby extend and declare established martial law throughout the entire State of Missouri. . . . All persons who shall be taken with arms in their hands within these lines shall be tried by court-martial, and if found guilty shall be shot.

'The property, real and personal, of all persons in the State of Missouri, who shall take up arms against the United States, or who shall be directly proven to have taken active part with their enemies in the field, is declared confiscated to public use, and slaves, if any they have, are hereby declared freemen.

'All persons who have been led away from their allegiance are required to return forthwith to their homes. Any such absent without sufficient cause will be held to be presumptive evidence against them: the object of this declaration is to place in the hands of the military authorities the power to give effect to existing laws and to supply such deficiencies as the conditions of war demand.'

The proclamation from which the above paragraphs are extracted, appears to be an exact copy in substance of the proclamation of John, Earl of Dunmore, the last British Governor of Virginia. This state-paper, so celebrated in Virginia annals, must have been the immediate source of Fremont's inspirations. It is to be regretted that the lesson then taught to tyrants, that vindictive and ferocious deeds, in the con-

These acts are done within the limits of a State, four-fifths of the inhabitants of which would hail the

duct of a war, defeat the very objects which they were intended to accomplish, seems to have been lost upon the chief of the present United States Government, as well as upon the tools who are willing to be his instruments in perpetrating the barbarities of a common vengeance. The United States Government may murder its prisoners, and rob them of their property, as both President Lincoln and his military commanders have officially declared they would do; *but mankind would accuse the Confederate States Government of criminal weakness, if it failed to follow the consummation of these threats by a terrible retribution!*

The proclamation of Lord Dunmore, bearing date November 17, 1775, by a mere change of names and dates, would be the proclamation of the Republican general, with only a trifling difference in the mere words. Lord Dunmore says:—

'To defeat such treasonable purposes, that all such traitors and their abettors may be brought to justice, and that the peace and good order of this colony may again be restored, which the ordinary course of the civil law is unable to effect — I have thought fit to issue this, my proclamation, hereby declaring, that until the aforesaid good purposes can be obtained, I do, in virtue of the power and authority to me given by His Majesty, determine to execute martial law, and cause the same to be executed throughout this colony; and to the end that peace and good order may the sooner be restored, I do require every person capable of bearing arms to resort to His Majesty's standard, or be looked upon as a traitor to his crown and government, and thereby become liable to the penalty the law inflicts upon such offences, such as forfeiture of life, confiscation of lands, &c. And I do hereby further declare all indentured servants, negroes, or others appertaining to rebels, free that are willing and able to bear arms; they joining His Majesty's troops as soon as may be, for the purpose of reducing this colony to a proper sense of their duty to His Majesty's crown and dignity.'

The proclamation of the commanding general of the United States in Missouri — the spirit and objects of which have been sanctioned by the President and his Cabinet, and applauded by the people of the North — ought to satisfy the last lingering doubt upon the minds of all, that the intention of the North in the formation of the Republican party was to obtain and to exercise control over the domestic institutions of the Southern States. If a commanding general has a right to give freedom to the slaves, surely the right of Congress to do so cannot be questioned. The advent of a Nero as a deliverance from the despotism of that 'paternal' Government, which has, by its ruthless deeds, banished every vestige of liberty from all territory over which it exercises dominion!

These are not the exaggerated statements of an excited adversary, but facts of public notoriety, every one of which has been derived from official documents which have been authoritatively published in the columns of leading journals in the interest of the Government of the United States.

Nay more, as if the ruler of this once free people were resolved, while destroying the liberties of his subjects, to eradicate every impediment to the exercise of his usurped authority, and to annihilate the last and only remaining bulwark of the people against the encroachments of a central despotism, he has in effect abrogated the sovereign rights of the States—reduced them to the condition of mere counties or townships—and as if to add insult to injury, he pro-

resistance of the South has only hastened the *dénouement* of a foregone conclusion. The only difference between the position which the South would have occupied if she had remained a passive witness of her own enslavement, and her present attitude, consists in this, that in the first instance she would have been degraded by an unresisting subjugation by the North, while now, if she perishes, it is while nobly fighting for all that is dear to freemen; and if she triumphs, all the proclamations of the petty despots who have sprung up like mushrooms under the reign of terror which has been inaugurated by Lincoln, will remain null and of no effect, except as a record of perpetual infamy, against those who have employed the authority confided to them, in attempting to crush out the last vestige of constitutional liberty.

claims officially that the States of the Confederacy never had an independent existence, and that they derive all their powers from that General Government of which he is the chief ruler.*

* *Extract from President Lincoln's War Message to Congress, July,* 1861.—'The States have their status in the Union, and they have no other legal status if they break from this. They can only do so against law by revolution. The Union, and not themselves separately, procured their independence and their liberty by conquest or purchase. The Union gave each of them whatever independence and liberty it had. The Union is older than any of the States, and in fact it created them States. Originally, some dependent colonies made the Union, and in turn the Union threw off their old dependence for them and made them States. Such as they are, not one of them ever had a State Constitution independent of the Union.'

President Lincoln may be an excellent rail-splitter, but it is clear that he is not an expert at hair-splitting. He tears up sovereignties by the roots, and casts them at his feet, without deigning to show to his faithful subjects how he had reached conclusions so adverse to the doctrines universally acknowledged previous to his advent to power. To say nothing of the belief entertained by the States themselves, that they were once sovereign, and that they only delegated a very limited portion of that sovereignty to the General Government, over which, in an evil day for his country, he was called to preside as the chief ruler, mankind will be curious to understand, what disposition he means to make of that act of the British Government, recognising the independent sovereignty of each particular State, which gave to the United States, or rather the States united, their first fully recognised legal claim to independence and sovereignty.

After President Lincoln shall have satisfactorily explained that this recognition did not mean what it declares, the world has a right to ask him how he reconciles the act of war which he has instituted, and is prosecuting with so much ferocity, with the positions assumed in his speech delivered in the Congress of the United States, January 12, 1848, from which the following words are extracted, viz. :—

'Any people whatever, being inclined and having the power, have the right to rise up and shake off the existing government, and form a new one that suits them better. This is a most valuable, a most sacred right. Nor is the right confined to cases where the whole of an existing government may choose to exercise it. Any portion of such people that can,

Strange spectacle of mad ambition! The head of a once free, powerful, and respected nation murdering not only the substance, but the very forms of liberty among his own subjects, that he may employ them the more readily in destroying the liberties of others!

Strange spectacle of wickedness! The President of a once mighty Republic, deriving its powers from the consent of the governed, hurling his armies of mercenary soldiers against eight millions of freemen, living in contented happiness under a government of their own choice, for the purpose of coer-

may revolutionise and make their own, of so much territory as they inhabit.'

In addition to this testimony of Mr. Lincoln, there may be furnished the evidence of one of his predecessors in the Presidential office, that the war which he is waging against the States of the South is in direct conflict with the advice of even the leaders of his own party in the past. It is well known that Mr. J. Q. Adams of Massachusetts, the sixth President of the United States, entertained very strong prejudices against the Southern States, growing out of the fact that in the bitter contest between himself and General Jackson, the Southern planting States supported the latter. After Mr. Adams was defeated for a second term, he entered Congress and contributed more powerfully than any other politician of his day in fanning the flame of discord between the North and the South, yet in the year 1839 he gave utterance to the following just sentiments: —

'If the day shall come, when the affections of the people of these States shall be alienated from each other, when this fraternal spirit shall give way to cold indifference, or *collisions of interest* shall fester into hatred, then the bonds of political association will not hold together parties no longer attracted by the magnetism of conciliated interests and kindly sympathies; and far better will it be for the people of the disunited States to part in friendship from each other, than to be held together by restraint.'

cing them by fire and sword to become his dutiful subjects!

Strange spectacle of weakness! The very people who should defend with their life's blood the rights which are thus set at nought, and who are at once his victims and instruments, rattle the chains which despotism has placed upon their once free limbs, and shout for the war of subjugation against the freemen of the South! They raise their manacled hands towards heaven, and pray that God may prosper their enslaver!

Strange spectacle of madness and folly! Nineteen States of a Union once embracing thirty-four members, without the pretence of a wrong to redress, or an insult to avenge, invade with a great army the territory of their former confederates, murdering their citizens, plundering them of their property, burning their dwellings, committing atrocious violence upon their wives and daughters, and leaving upon the track of their sacrilegious hosts nothing but ruin, and desolation, and woe amongst the inhabitants, and 'all to win back the alienated affections' of those whom they call their brothers!

Of a truth may it be repeated, that while the 'rebellious States' have passed without a revolution or an internal commotion, the period of transition into the new Confederacy, the 'loyal States' which still adhere to the old federal Union, are themselves in the agonies of a revolution involving changes in the organic principles upon which the Government had been previously administered, scarcely less startling in its magnitude than that which was inaugurated by the eloquence of a Mirabeau, in the days of Louis XVI., which terminated by driving the Bourbon from the throne of France for ever.

ON THE RIGHTS OF THE STATES TO SECEDE FROM THE UNION.

So far as it may affect the result of the war in which the two countries are now engaged, a decision confirming the right of the Southern States to withdraw from the late Union would be unavailing. Whether the acts of the now Confederate States be regarded as secession by right of sovereignty, or rebellion by authority of the people, they will maintain their independence by the sword, which they will never return to its scabbard until the last hostile invader shall have been driven from their borders!

Nevertheless, a due respect for the opinions of our fellow-men, and a natural desire to justify our acts and to secure for ourselves the respect, if not the sympathies, of the civilised world, make it a duty incumbent upon the citizens of the South to show clearly the causes which impelled them, in defence of all that they held dear, to sever the political bonds which united them with the States of the North. These causes have already been fully stated, and the opinions of disinterested men everywhere have undergone a revolution, which promises, in due time, to correct the erroneous views which were at first entertained. The impartial historian will declare that the circumstances under which the Southern States resumed their independence, and declared their determination to defend and maintain it by an appeal, if necessary, to the arbitrament of arms, would have justified the adoption of that measure, even though they had previously formed but an integral part of a consolidated sovereignty. But they were not thus bound to their late associates. They joined them in a compact, but they never surrendered to them their sovereignty. They formed with them a Union for certain specified purposes, and delegated certain clearly defined powers, but by express stipulation in the articles of agreement which were concluded between them, all the powers not specifically conferred upon the federal Government were reserved to the States. There was no arbiter appointed to decide in case of a disagreement, so that the right to determine the sufficiency of the causes which impelled them to a separation, was and remained with them, and them alone. The Government of the United States might, or might not, have been stronger and more durable if the States had transferred to it all of their sovereignty; but we are considering what was, and not what might have been. The very name by which the Government was known indicated unmistakably that it was not consolidated into a single State, but was the admitted representative of several sovereignties.* The causes which induced the original States of the Union to guard with so much care their State sovereignty, can

* Lord Brougham, in the Appendix to his treatise on the British Constitution, expresses not only correct views in regard to the nature of the Union between the States, but he echoes what was the almost universal opinion of American statesmen, up to the period of the election of the present President, Mr. Lincoln. Upon this subject this distinguished author says:—

'We may remark that there are two ways in which the federal relation subsists among States. The one which may be termed the *proper* federal Union is where two or more States, having their separate governments for all domestic purposes, are united by a central government, which regulates their mutual relations, as members of a political community, but does not interfere with the functions of the several governments *and their authority over the individuals who are their subjects*, unless in so far as those functions, and that authority may affect the federal relation; *and it is of the essence of this Federal Union, that its different members should have equal rights, and that all should bear a part in the central administration* . . . Of this kind were the federal unions of Ancient Greece, and in modern times, that of Germany, Switzerland *and the United States of America.*'

. . . .

'There is not, as with us, a Government only and its subjects to be regarded; but a number of governments; of States having each *a separate and substantive, and even independent existence*; originally thirteen, now six and twenty, and each having a Legislature of its own, and laws differing from those of the other States. *It is plainly impossible to consider the Constitution which professes to govern this whole Union, this Federacy of States, as anything other than a treaty*, of which the conditions are to be executed for them all; and hence, there must be certain things laid down, certain rights conferred, certain provisions made, which cannot be altered without universal consent, or a consent so general as to be deemed equivalent for all practical purposes to the consent of the whole.'

be readily discovered by considering the peculiar circumstances in which they were placed. The territory embraced an extent of country large enough for two empires, each one of which would have rivalled the greatest Powers of Europe. There already existed an antagonism between the Northern and the Southern States, and their domestic institutions were still more widely at variance. If these Governments had been consolidated into one, slavery might have been abolished, or made universal, throughout the whole. The States therefore retained their sovereignty, for the reason, amongst others, that they desired to avoid giving any pretext to the General Government for attempting to control their internal affairs.

One is almost tempted to smile at the flippant insolence with which the Northern people charge the Southerners with being in a state of rebellion against them! In America they call it 'the rebellion of the Southern States,' but in Europe they speak of it as 'the rebellion of the Southern provinces.' There is no doubt that the North is labouring to accomplish this end, but as it has never yet had a beginning, the South can scarcely be said to be in rebellion against anything, except *the intentions* of the North to enslave her. There are those, however, who speak of the rebellion of the Southern States against the Government of the United States, without considering that such a thing, under existing circumstances, is absurd and impossible. If there were a Monarch upon the throne, there might be a rebellion among his subjects, but the people were the sovereigns of the late United States, and to say that the people of the South are in rebellion, is to say that the sovereign has rebelled against himself, which is absurd. Moreover, suppose that the North is right in declaring that the Government of the United States was the representative of a single sovereignty, namely, the people of all the States. The people of the Southern States have refused to constitute any longer a portion of the sovereignty of the whole, and having separated themselves from all political association with the North, it follows that the Government of the United States is the agent of the Northern people alone; and, as the Southern people cannot be in rebellion against themselves, if it may be said that they are in rebellion against the Government of the United States, and the people are the sovereign, it follows that the South must be regarded as in rebellion against the North. This would assume that the Southern people were never sovereign, but that they were subject to and owed allegiance to the North. We do not find this in the bond.

To satisfy the intelligent mind that the Southern States, in refusing to remain any longer as an integral part of the Federal Union, are only acting in the exercise of a right which they had never alienated, it is only necessary to glance at the history of the formation of the different governments composing it, and of the articles of agreement which were at different times entered into between them. Always these compacts were made for the express purpose of insuring 'domestic tranquillity,' and providing for the 'common defence.' Never up to the period when Mr. Lincoln assumed the direction of public affairs as President of the Union, had it been claimed by a prominent politician, not to speak of a party, that the States possessed only such powers as they derived from the General Government.

It may be readily understood that foreigners might be deceived in regard to the actual distribution of powers, because they only come in contact with the common agents of the several States acting in the name of 'the United States of America.' The world has been so long accustomed to the sound which falling upon the ear, calls to mind the American Government, that the true signification of the words are lost to the sense; whereas the words composing the name were intended to convey an idea, and have a significance,—namely, that many sovereign States had for certain purposes leagued or United themselves together. The French at first properly understood that the words conveyed an idea, as well as designated a government and a country, by calling the Confederacy 'Les Etats Unis,' words which in sound have no resemblance to 'United States,' but which express their quality and value.

If the different States of Germany were to enter into a league for mutual protection, conferring upon a Congress of all the States the power to make treaties with Foreign Governments, and to regulate the intercourse of the different States with each other, each, however, expressly retaining its sovereignty in all other matters appertaining to government, it may readily be imagined that in process of time, foreign nations might forget the true significance of the words 'United States of Germany,' and regard them as a consolidated sovereignty. Thus has it been in regard to 'the United States of America,' whereas in their very essence the words are utterly opposed to the idea of a single sovereignty.

Acting upon the erroneous idea that the States of the Confederacy had surrendered and merged their sovereignty into that of the Union, foreign Governments have withheld their recognition of that independence in the sovereign States, which, although partially dormant and not previously called into action in their intercourse with foreign nations, nevertheless remained perfect and entire, whenever they might choose to reassert its existence.

During the war between the thirteen colonies and Great Britain, the Articles of Confederation, which created 'the United States of America,' were adopted, and the Government thus created was inaugurated. Two years previous to this event, that is on July 4, 1776, the thirteen colonies made their celebrated Declaration of Independence, through their delegates in Congress assembled. It would almost seem as though in this eloquent declaration its framers foresaw the state of things which existed in 1861, and endeavoured to provide for the peaceful separation of aggrieved States from the Union which they were about creating. It expressly declares and avows the principle that 'Governments are instituted among men deriving their just powers from the consent of the governed;' that 'whenever any form of Government becomes destructive of these ends, *it is the right of the people to alter or to abolish it*, laying its foundation on such principles and organising its powers in such form, *as to them shall seem most likely to effect their safety and happiness.*' After referring to the reluctance which has been manifested by mankind to engage in revolutionising an established Government, it continues:—

> But when a long train of abuses and usurpations, pursuing invariably the same object, evinces a design to reduce them under absolute despotism, it is their right, it is their duty, to throw off such governments and to provide new guards for their future security.

It was not until July 9, 1778 that the first Constitution, or Articles of Confederation of the United States, was adopted. Let us examine the terms upon which this Union was created, and see if we can discover a single feature thereof which would imply a want of sovereignty in the members composing it, antecedently to the formation of the Union; or the slightest intimation that in framing the Union for certain specified purposes, they intended to surrender their individual sovereignty. The following are the words of that instrument: —

Articles of Confederation and Perpetual Union between the States of New Hampshire, Massachusetts Bay, Rhode Island, and Providence Plantation, Connecticut, New York, New Jersey, Pennsylvania, Delaware, Maryland, Virginia, North Carolina, South Carolina, and Georgia.

Art. I. The style of this Confederacy shall be, the United States of America.

Art. II. Each State retains its SOVEREIGNTY, FREEDOM, and INDEPENDENCE, and every power, jurisdiction and right, which is not by this Confederation ***expressly delegated*** to the United States in Congress assembled.

Art. III. The said States hereby severally ***enter into a firm league of friendship*** with each other, for their common defence, the security of their liberties, and their mutual and general welfare; binding themselves to assist each other against all force offered to, or attacks made upon them, or any of them.

Art. V. *sec.* 4. In determining questions in the United States in Congress assembled ***each State shall have one vote.***

Art. VII, *sec.* 5. The United Statesin Congress assembled shall have authority, &c., to appoint a 'committee of the States,' and such other committees and civil officers as may be necessary for managing the general affairs of the United States, &c., and to ascertain the necessary sums of money to be raised for the service of the United States, &c., *transmitting every half year to the respective States* an account of the sums of money so borrowed or emitted, &c.

Art. IX. *sec.* 6. The United States in Congress assembled shall never engage in a war, nor grant letters of marque and reprisal in time of peace, nor enter into any treaties of alliance, nor coin money, nor regulate the value thereof, nor ascertain the sums and expenses necessary for the defence and welfare of the United States, or any of them, nor emit bills, nor borrow money on the credit of the United States, nor appropriate money, nor agree upon the number of vessels of war to be built or purchased, or the number of land or sea forces to be raised, nor appoint a commander-in-chief of the army or navy, *unless* nine States assent to the same.

Art. XIII. Every State shall abide by the determination of the United States in Congress assembled, *in all questions which by this Confederation are submitted to them.* And the articles of this Confederation shall be inviolably observed by every State, *and the union shall be perpetual* : nor shall any alteration at any time hereafter be made in any of them, unless such alteration be agreed to in a congress of the United States, and be afterwards confirmed by the legislatures of every State.

Could human language have been employed which would have more clearly conveyed the idea and the fact of the reserved sovereignty of the States composing the league? Would it have been possible to have formed any league, offensive and defensive, which could have preserved with greater precision the independence of the parties composing it? Four facts are clearly deducible from these Articles of Confederation.

1. That the parties to the compact were independent sovereignties.

2. That they did not by the compact surrender their sovereignty to the general government.

3. That the restrictions contained in section 6, article 9, rendered it almost impossible to successfully administer the government of the Union.

4. *That those restrictions might all have been removed*, and the powers therein conveyed have been exercised by the general government, without any surrender whatever of the sovereignty of the members composing it.

The next important historical incident bearing upon this point occurred about four years and a half after the adoption of the foregoing Articles of Confederation.

The war was over. The thirteen united colonies had achieved their independence, and that independence was about to be formally recognised by their former sovereign. Was this recognition based upon the idea of a consolidated sovereignty? No such thing. The independence *of each of the thirteen States* was specifically admitted by King George III., as will be seen from the following:—

Extract from the Provisional Articles signed at Paris, November 30, 1782, by the Commissioners of His Britannic Majesty and the Commissioners of the United States of America.

Art. I. His Britannic Majesty acknowledges the said United States, that is, New Hampshire, Massachusetts Bay, Rhode Island and Providence Plantations, Connecticut, New York, New Jersey, Pennsylvania, Delaware, Maryland, Virginia, North Carolina, South Carolina, and Georgia, *to be free, sovereign, and independent States, and that he treats with them as such* ; and for himself, his heirs, and successors, relinquishes all claim to the government, proprietary and territorial rights, of the same and every part thereof.

These were the articles of the provisional treaty, which was to be ratified only after the conclusion of peace between Great Britain and France. On September 3, 1783, the 'definite treaty of peace' was concluded in the following words:—

In the name of the Most Holy and Undivided Trinity :

It having pleased the Divine Providence to dispose the heart of the most serene and most potent Prince George III., by the Grace of God King of Great Britain, and France &c., and of the United States of North America, to forget all past differences and misunderstandings that have unhappily interrupted the good correspondence and friendship which they mutually wish to restore, they have agreed upon and confirmed the following Articles :—

Art. I. His Britannic Majesty acknowledges the said United States ; viz., New Hampshire, Massachusetts Bay, Rhode Island and Providence Plantations, Connecticut, New York, New Jersey, Pennsylvania, Delaware, Maryland, Virginia, North Carolina, South Carolina, and Georgia, to be free, sovereign, and independent States; that he treats with them as such, and for himself, his heirs, and successors, relinquishes all claims to the government, propriety, and territorial rights of the same, and every part thereof.

But it was not alone in Great Britain that the true relations between the general Government and the States composing it, were understood. If any Government ought to have comprehended better than another the nature of these relations, it was France, when she made her first alliance with those States, and espoused their cause against England. The treaty of amity and commerce entered into between that Government and the United States is as follows:—

The Most Christian King and the Thirteen United States of North America; to wit: New Hampshire, Massachusetts Bay, Rhode Island, Connecticut, New York, New Jersey, Pennsylvania, Delaware, Maryland, Virginia, North Carolina, South Carolina, and Georgia, willing to fix in an equitable and permanent manner, &c.

In the 'treaty of alliance' between the United States and France, the same States are recognised individually, as parties thereto, although the treaty was entered into with plenipotentiaries of these States, acting in the name of the United States. After peace had been declared, and the independence of the United States had been fully recognised by their former sovereign, the same States were still recognised as parties to the treaties between the

United States and other foreign governments. The treaty of amity and commerce concluded with Sweden, April 2, 1783, begins as follows:—

> The King of Sweden, of the Goths and Vandals, &c., and the Thirteen United States of North America; to wit: New Hampshire, Massachusetts Bay, Rhode Island, Connecticut, New York, New Jersey, Pennsylvania, Delaware, Maryland, Virginia, North Carolina, South Carolina, and Georgia, desiring to establish in a stable and permanent manner the rules which ought to be observed relative to commerce, &c. &c., have agreed upon and signed the following Articles.

The States-General of the United Netherlands also, on October 8, 1782, entered into a treaty with the thirteen American States in their separate capacity, the plenipotentiaries of the United States Government being the parties representing the American States.

It must be remembered that all these treaties were made after the establishment of the Government of the United States, and that the said Government exercised then precisely the same powers in regulating the intercourse of the States with foreign powers as at present. About the same period of time treaties were made with other Governments which did not enumerate specifically the separate States composing the Union; but it is apparent that the world understood that the 'United States' was composed of separate and independent sovereignties. Although the articles of agreement between the

States have been changed in some particulars since that date, yet so far as concerns their intercourse with foreign Governments, and their separate sovereignty, the provisions remain unaltered. The States composing the Union did not send special representatives abroad, notwithstanding which their independence was recognised. A portion of these States having withdrawn from that Union, now, for the first time, send their delegates to these same Governments which have, by the most solemn treaties, recognised their separate right to independence, and they withhold that recognition because another portion of those same States interpose objections thereto. When these powers of Europe recognised the sovereignty of Virginia, Georgia, North Carolina, and South Carolina, they certainly did not mean to declare that they would withdraw that recognition at the instance of Massachusetts, New York, and the other Northern States. However this may be, it is a truth which cannot be controverted, that the Southern States above named have done no act since, nor have they entered into any contract or alliance, by which they have forfeited any right of sovereignty which was conceded by George III., or which was recognised by France and other nations. Before and at the time of this recognition, they formed a part of the 'United States,' and they continued to occupy that relation to the other States until their withdrawal from the

Federal Union in 1861. If they were sovereign and independent in 1783, they are sovereign and independent to-day. Governments may decline now officially to *recognise* the fact, from considerations of policy, but *they cannot gainsay its existence* without denying the validity of their own solemn treaties, or showing, when, how, or where that sovereignty has been, since that period, forfeited or relinquished. This they cannot do, though they may subject the entire history of these States to the closest scrutiny. And yet these Governments persist, in effect, in holding the South as in a state of rebellion against the North, and call it '*neutrality!*' This they certainly have the power to do. They may even go farther, and permit their flags to be insulted upon the high seas, and their ships to be seized by Northern cruisers, within sight of their own ports, and excuse the outrage out of consideration for the 'natural irritability of the United States Government;' but while their forbearance may not be called an act of intervention in favour of the North, it cannot be denominated an effective neutrality.

We thus discover that, from the beginning, the States claimed to be sovereign and independent; that they subsequently reasserted that independence when they created the government of the United States; and that finally, at the close of a seven years' war, the independence and sovereignty of each State was specifically recognised, by their former sovereign, although the United States Government had been then in operation during a period of nearly five years.

The Government of Great Britain then declared and agreed that it would treat with these several States, each as 'free, sovereign, and independent.' What offence has been committed since that time against England, by the States of Virginia, North Carolina, South Carolina, Georgia, and other Southern States, that the British Government now refuses to recognise the act of George III. acknowledging their independence? The United States Government existed then, as it existed afterwards. Upon what principle does Great Britain now act, when her Government, repudiating the separate recognition of George III., will only acknowledge the Southern States as dependencies of the North. It is true that the Southern States are less powerful in numbers and in population than those of the North. It is true that the North has threatened to wage war against England, if the British Government should re-affirm the act and acknowledgement of George III.; but do these constitute a sufficient cause for the refusal of a great and powerful nation to recognise a mere fact, which they had previously acknowledged in the most formal manner, and which it is manifestly unjust to withhold?

But turning from this partial digression, let us examine what subsequently follows, bearing upon the question of state sovereignty.

More than nine years after the Government of the United States had been established, that is on September 17, a convention of the Representatives of the States, presided over by George Washington, adopted the present Constitution, and submitted it to the 'States,' not the people of the United States, for their ratification. The 7th, and last article, is in the following words:—

Art. VII. 'The ratification' of the conventions of *nine States* shall be sufficient for the establishment of this Constitution, *between the States so ratifying the same*. . . . In witness whereof we have hereunto subscribed our names.

(Signed) GEORGE WASHINGTON, President,
and Deputy from Virginia.
(And others.)

Does not even this brief and closing article of the Constitution of the United States recognise to the fullest extent the sovereignty of the States? That it was a compact between THE STATES, as independent sovereignties, is proven by the fact that it was submitted to *the States* for approval or rejection. If it had been a compact entered into by the people of all the States, would it not have been submitted to the people, and not to the States, for their ratification?

We also find another important fact contained in

this brief article, namely, that the present Constitution and Government of the United States was formed by the SECESSION OF NINE STATES OF THE UNION from their colleagues, notwithstanding they were bound by their previous compact in the following strong language:—

Art. XIII. . . . The articles of this Confederation shall be inviolably observed by *every State*, and *the Union shall be perpetual; nor shall any alteration at any time hereafter be made* in any of them, unless such alteration be agreed to in a Congress of the United States, and be afterwards *confirmed by the Legislatures of every State.*

We thus discover that the first united government of the colonies of Great Britain was *founded in rebellion* against their previously acknowledged sovereign, and that the late and present Government of the Union was formed by a secession of a portion of the States composing the first Union. It was not until several years after this secession of nine States, that the other States gave in their adhesion to the Government created by the seceders. We deduce also, from the foregoing pregnant article of the Constitution, other most important facts bearing upon the question under consideration. The framers of this instrument, with the immortal Washington at their head, affirm that the ratification of nine States 'shall be sufficient for the establishment of the Constitution *between the States so ratifying the same;*' thus fully recognising the right of the remaining States to continue as a separate sovereignty under the old Constitution. 'Coercion' is not dreamed of or hinted at; nor did it enter into the thoughts or minds of the framers of the Constitution, that the other States had not the same right to continue under the old government, that they had to secede therefrom and establish a new one; and they also considered, that in each the right was undoubted, perfect, and inalienable.

It is often declared, by the supporters of a consolidated government, that the present Constitution does not in terms confer the right of secession. Neither did the old one from which George Washington seceded. It would have been absurd to have incorporated such a clause in either; but it may be said that the present Constitution contains no clause so restrictive, or so utterly opposed to any change in the government, as the 13th article of the first confederacy, the language of which is quoted above.

The question here suggests itself, did George Washington and the other framers of the Constitution believe that they had, and did they have, the right by the assent of '*nine States*' only, to abolish the old Constitution, and establish a new one, notwithstanding the restrictions of the 13th article? These interrogatories can only be answered in the affirmative. They were simply resuming, for their

States, that sovereignty which had never been surrendered. It is true that the league or confederation was declared by its terms to be perpetual; but such are the terms of almost all treaties of amity between nations. It is true that they also agreed and pledged themselves not to alter the conditions of that league without the consent of 'all the States.' This consent being impracticable under the then existing circumstances, George Washington and his associates determined, for their States, to secede from the old Union and establish a new one, which they did. And it is under the government thus formed that the Northern section of that confederacy are now waging their war of subjection against the seceding States of the South, with a vindictive ferocity only paralleled in enormity by the magnitude of the injustice which they are perpetrating against a people who have never wronged or attempted to wrong them. If the Southern States had no right to resume their sovereignty and establish a new government, after having been excluded from all practical participation in the government of the Union to which they belonged, much less right did George Washington and his associates have for seceding from the old confederacy and forming a new one, in violation of the express terms of their compact, and without a pretence that they had a wrong to redress or a right that was endangered.

Let us for a moment consider the provisions of the Constitution thus inaugurated by secession, and under which the Government of the United States has continued with but little modification up to the present moment. Although the unnecessary restrictions imposed upon the action of the Federal Government under the sixth section of article nine (above quoted), of the old Constitution or league, were partially removed in the second, yet it is impossible to discover in the new Constitution any single clause which intimates that the sovereignty of the States individually was thereby impaired. On the contrary, in every essential particular, the reserved rights of the States are the same in both. By the new as by the old compact, *each state* as such was to be entitled to two senators, without reference to population. Thus the little sovereignty of Delaware, with its population but little exceeding *one hundred thousand souls*, has always exercised in the Senate of the United States —without the sanction of which body no law could be enacted or put in force—the same power as the great state of New York, with its population of nearly *four millions*. Moreover, although the restrictions as before observed, contained in the old articles of confederation, were partially removed, yet it will be seen by the following provisions that all important acts of the President were to be ratified, not by the people, not by the Congress of the United States, the lower branch of which is the representative of the people of the States, respectively, but by *two-thirds in some instances, and a majority in all others, of the senators representing the States.*

Art. II. *sec.* 2. The President, &c., by and with the advice and consent of the Senate, shall have power to make treaties, provided two-thirds of the senators present concur; and he shall nominate, and by and with the advice and consent of the Senate shall appoint, ambassadors, other public ministers and consuls, judges of the Supreme Court, &c.

A further examination of the provisions of the Constitution will show, still more conclusively, that the powers of the general government did not affect, nor were they intended to affect, the sovereignty of States, any more than a treaty for the accomplishment of the same purposes would impair the sovereignty of any two governments which might enter into such stipulations.

The following are defined to be the duties and the powers of the Courts of the United States:—

Art. III. *sec.* 1. The judicial power shall extend to all cases in law and equity arising under this Constitution, the laws of the United States, and treaties made, or which shall be made under their authority; to all cases affecting Ambassadors, &c.; to controversies to which the United States shall be a party; to controversies between two or more States; between a State and citizens of another State; between citizens of different States; between citizens of the same State claiming lands under grants of different States, and between a State, or the citizens thereof, and foreign States, citizens, or subjects.

This enumeration covers all the powers claimed or exercised, by virtue of the Constitution of the United States, over the respective States. So far from conveying the idea of a want of sovereignty on the part of the States, every single sentence asserts and establishes the contrary. The sovereignty of the States, and not of the people of the United States, as a unit, is distinctly and unmistakably announced and acknowledged; and the Government of the United States presents itself in its real character, simply as umpire between the States, so long as they recognise its authority and claim its protection.

But even these self-evident truths were not sufficient to satisfy all the States, and hence an amendment was subsequently added to the Constitution in the following words:—

Amendment, Art. X. The powers not delegated to the United States by the Constitution, nor prohibited by it to the States, *are reserved to the States respectively, or to the people.*

But however conclusive the above recited facts are in establishing the sovereignty of the States, and the right of each to withdraw from the Union, even according to the Constitution of the United States, yet there exists proof still more conclusive in the Constitution of each and every State of the late Union.

Not only were the States bound by the Constitution of the United States, but also by their own separate

Constitutions. In fact, the latter form a part of the general compact, and to understand the relations of each to the whole, it is necessary to consider them all. It is clear that no State could be admitted into the Union if its Constitution was in conflict with the provisions of the Constitution of the United States. Hence, when a State asks for admission into the confederacy, its Constitution is first submitted to the Congress of the United States, and if it is 'Republican in form' and 'contains nothing in conflict with the Constitution of the United States,' such State is admitted as a member of the Union.

Let us now briefly examine the provisions of the Constitutions of the States engaged in this most cruel, unjust, and inhuman war. Massachusetts stands in the front rank of the States which uphold and sustain the United States in its bloody butchery of the Southern people, who it is not intimated have committed any other offence than to withdraw peacefully from a hated Union, whose existence they conceived to be incompatible with their liberty or happiness.

Constitution of Massachusetts. Declaration of Rights, Sec. 4. THE PEOPLE OF THIS COMMONWEALTH *have the sole and exclusive right of governing themselves, as a free, sovereign, and independent State,* and for ever hereafter shall exercise and enjoy every power, jurisdiction, and right which is not or may not hereafter be by them *expressly delegated* to the United States of America in Congress assembled. *Sec.* 7. . . . The people alone have an incontestible, unalienable, and indefeasible right to institute government, *and to reform, alter, or totally change the same,* when their protection, safety, prosperity, and happiness require it.

Part II. *Frame of Government.*—The people inhabiting the territory formerly called the province of Massachusetts Bay do hereby solemnly and mutually agree, *with each other,* to form themselves into a free, sovereign, and independent body politic, or State, by the name of the Commonwealth of Massachusetts.

Under this Constitution, Massachusetts is now one of the States of the United States, and with these solemn declarations of her own sovereignty and independence, and of the right of her people to abolish their government, 'whenever their safety, prosperity, and happiness require it,' the Puritan inhabitants of this commonwealth are carrying fire and sword, and spreading desolation and death, in the Southern States, because they have asserted for themselves the same right of self-government which Massachusetts claims for her own citizens.

New Hampshire declares in her Constitution that — The people inhabiting the territory formerly called the province of New Hampshire do hereby solemnly and mutually agree, with each other, to form themselves into a free, sovereign, and independent body politic, or State, by the name of the State of New Hampshire.

Bill of Rights, Sec. 7. The people of this state have the sole and exclusive right of governing themselves as a free, sovereign, and independent State, and do and for ever hereafter shall exercise and enjoy every power, jurisdiction, and right pertaining thereto which is not or may not hereafter be by them *expressly delegated* to the United States of America in Congress assembled.

The State of Vermont is even in advance of Massachusetts in the zeal with which she has entered into the war against the South, although her Constitution is even more explicit, if such were possible, in asserting her own sovereignty.

Constitution of Vermont, Art. V. The people of this State, by their legal representatives, *have the sole, inherent, and exclusive right* of governing and regulating the internal police of the same.

Art. VII. . . . The community hath an indubitable, unalienable, and indefeasible right to reform or alter government *in such manner as shall be by that community* judged most conducive to the public weal.

Art. XIII. The people have a right to a freedom of speech, and of writing and publishing their sentiments, concerning the transactions of government, and therefore the freedom of the press ought not to be restrained.

Art. XXI. No person shall be liable to be transported out of this state *for trial of any offence* committed within the same.

Art. XXX. Every person of good character who comes to settle in this state, *having first taken an oath of allegiance to the same,* may purchase, hold, transfer land, &c.

The Constitution of Connecticut declares:—

Declaration of Rights, Sec. 2. All political power is inherent in the people, and all free governments are founded upon their authority, *and they have at all times an unalienable and indefeasible right to alter their form of government, in such manner as they may think expedient.*

I might go on making further extracts from the Constitutions of the Northern States, but it will be sufficient to say that those of each and every State of the United States now engaged in the prosecution of this war contain provisions precisely similar in import, and generally in language, to those I have quoted. All affirm their right to alter or abolish their government, whenever they may so desire, without the consent or approbation or counsel of any other state or person. Nay more, they pronounce and declare that the right in question cannot be alienated. Moreover, they each assert that they are free, sovereign, and independent, and that they will exercise the same except when such right is specifically transferred to the United States. But they are themselves to be the judges of the time, cause, and manner of changing or abolishing their respective existing governments.

Out of the millions of human beings who, from foreign lands, are watching with interest the progress of this terrible conflict most inappropriately called a civil war, how few there may be supposed to be who would wish success to the Northern invaders, if they knew the facts above recited.

Having examined the Constitutions of the Northern States, let us glance for a moment at the provisions incorporated in the Constitutions of the Southern seceding States. The Constitution of Virginia, in the 'Bill of Rights,' declares:—

Sec. 3. Government is or ought to be instituted for the common benefit and security of the people. Of all the various modes or forms of government, that is best which is capable of producing the greatest degree of happiness and safety. . . . Whenever any government shall be found inadequate, or contrary to these purposes, a majority of the community hath an indubitable, unalienable, and indefeasible right to reform, alter, or abolish it, in such manner as shall be judged most conducive to the public weal.

Sec. 14. The people have a right to uniform government, and therefore *no government separate from or independent of the Government of Virginia ought to be erected or established within the limits thereof.*

I may add an important fact, which shows clearly that the United States Government was not disposed to deny the right thus claimed. When the Government of Virginia granted to the United States the lands on which Fortress Monroe and the Navy-yard at Portsmouth were erected, it was expressly stipulated that while the property was vested in the United States, the sovereignty of the soil was retained by Virginia.

The State of Tennessee was formed out of territory ceded by North Carolina to the general government, upon condition that the said territory should be admitted as a State into the Union, after acquiring sufficient population. The Constitution framed and adopted by this State, and under which it entered the Union by assent of the Congress, declares:

Whereas the people of the territory of the United States south of the river Ohio, *having the right* of admission into the general government, as a member state thereof, &c., do ordain and establish a Constitution or form of government, *and mutually agree with each other* to form themselves into *a free and independent* State, by the name of the State of Tennessee.

Declaration of Rights, Sec. 1. The people have *at all times an unalienable and indefeasible right to alter, reform, or abolish the government,* in such manner as they may think proper.

Without multiplying extracts, it is sufficient to add that every Southern State claimed the rights herein asserted, in the Constitutions by virtue of which they were admitted into the partnership of the Union.*

* The right of secession has been distinctly affirmed and admitted by almost every President, and in turn by almost every State of the Union, since the celebrated Resolutions of Virginia and of Kentucky in 1798. The former were drawn up by Mr. Madison, and the latter by Mr. Jefferson. The first Kentucky resolution was as follows :—

'1st. *Resolved,* That the several States comprising the United States of America, are not united on the principle of unlimited submission to their general government, but that by compact under the style and title of a Constitution for the United States, and of amendments thereto, they constituted a general government, for special purposes, delegated to that government certain definite powers, reserving, each State to itself, the residuary mass of right to their own self-government; and that whensoever the general government assumes undelegated powers, its acts are unauthoritative, void, and of no force; that to this compact each state acceded, as a State, and is an integral party; that this government created by this compact was not made the exclusive or final judge of the extent of the powers delegated to itself, since that would have made its discretion and not the Constitution the measure of its powers, but that, as in all other cases of compact among parties having no common judge, each party has an equal right to judge for itself, as well of infractions as of the mode and measure of redress.'

This was the interpretation given to the compact of the Union by Jefferson and Madison, and the fathers of the Union. To come down to the interpretation of more modern times, it may be stated that Van Buren, Polk, Pierce, Buchanan, and perhaps others, were elected respectively to the office of President upon platforms embracing *specifically* the above recited resolution. It will be remembered that upon this

It would be absurd to suppose that the Government of the United States did not fully recognise

declaration of principles Mr. Pierce received the votes of every State in the Union except four, and two of those have time and again given their adhesion to the same principle.

To show how this subject and the subject of coercion was regarded by the framers of the very Constitution under consideration, I close with the following extracts from the debates in the Federal Convention for forming a Constitution, 1787 :—

'Mr. Edmund Randolph, of Virginia, presented a series of resolutions as a basis of a form of government. The sixth resolution suggested, amongst other matters, that the National Legislature ought to be empowered to "call forth the force of the Union against any member of the Union failing to fulfil its duties under the articles thereof." See Madison Papers, vol. ii. p. 732.

'Mr. Madison observed, that the more he reflected on the use of force, the more he doubted the *practicability*, the *justice*, and the efficacy of it! when applied to people collectively, and not individually. A Union of the States containing such an ingredient seemed to provide for its own *destruction*. The use of force against a State would look more like a declaration of war than an infliction of punishment; and would probably be considered by the party attacked as a dissolution of all previous compacts by which it might be bound. He hoped that such a system would be framed as might render this resource unnecessary, and moved that the clause be postponed. This motion was agreed to unanimously. See Madison Papers, vol. ii. p. 761.

'Mr. Patterson, of New Jersey, moved a series of resolutions, as a basis of a plan of government. Ib., vol. ii. p. 863–867.

'His sixth resolution suggested, "That if any State, or any body of men in any State, shall oppose or prevent the carrying into execution such acts or treaties, the Federal Executive shall be authorised to call forth the power of the Confederated States, or so much thereof as may be necessary, to enforce and compel an obedience to such acts, or an observance of such treaties." Mr. Patterson's whole plan, including the sixth resolution, was voted down.

'Col. Alexander Hamilton said, "The great and essential principles necessary for the support of government are" five in number, which were respectively enumerated and commented on by him. The fourth was "*Force*, by which," he said, "may be understood a *coercion of laws, or coercion of arms*." After commenting on a coercion of laws, he continued, "A certain portion of military force is absolutely necessary in large communities. Massachusetts is now feeling this necessity, and making provision for it. But how can this force be exerted on the States collectively? *It is impossible. It amounts to a war between the parties*." Ib., vol. ii. p. 881.

'Col. George Mason said, "He took this occasion to repeat that, not-

and admit the binding force and validity of the claims thus put forth by every State of the confederacy. The States in their individual capacity

withstanding his solicitude to establish a national government, he never would agree to abolish the state governments, or render them absolutely insignificant. They were as necessary as the general government, and he would be equally careful to preserve them." Ib., vol. ii. p. 914.

'Mr. Luther Martin agreed with Col. Mason as to the importance of state governments: he would support them at the expense of the general government, which was instituted for the purpose of that support. . . . At the separation from the British Empire, the people of America preferred the establishment of themselves into thirteen separate sovereignties, instead of incorporating themselves into one. To these they look up for the security of their lives, liberties, and properties; to these they must look up. The Federal government they formed to defend the whole against foreign nations in time of war, and to defend the lesser States against the ambition of the larger. They are afraid of granting power unnecessarily, lest they should defeat the original end of the Union; lest the powers should prove dangerous to the sovereignties of the particular States which the Union was meant to support, and expose the lesser to being swallowed up by the larger. Ib., vol. ii. p. 915.

'Mr. Madison said, "It had been alleged (by Mr. Patterson) that the confederation, having been formed by unanimous consent, could be dissolved by unanimous consent only. Does this doctrine result from the nature of compacts? Does it arise from any particular stipulation in the Articles of Confederation? If we consider the Federal Union as analogous to the fundamental compact by which individuals compose one society, and which must, in its theoretic origin, at least have been the unanimous act of the component members, it cannot be said that no dissolution of the compact can be effected without unanimous consent. A breach of the fundamental principles of the compact by a part of the society would certainly absolve the other part from their obligations to it. If the breach of *any article, by any of the parties*, does not set the others at liberty, it is because the contrary is *implied* in the compact itself, and particularly by that law of it which gives an indefinite authority to the majority to bind the whole in all cases. This latter circumstance shows that we are not to consider the Federal Union as analogous to the social compact of individuals: for if it were so, a majority would have a right to bind the rest, and even to form a Constitution for the whole; which the gentleman from New Jersey would be among the last to admit. If we consider the Federal Union as analogous, not to the social compacts among individual men, but to the conventions among individual States, what is the doctrine resulting from these conventions? Clearly, according to the *expositors of the law of nations*, that a breach of *any one article, by any one party, leaves all the other parties at liberty to consider the whole convention as dissolved*."'

presented themselves to the States in their united capacity, each one claiming for itself sovereignty, and the right to abolish the government whenever their interests or happiness might demand its exercise. These State Constitutions formed a material part of the compact of the Union, and they are unanimous in their justification of the Southern States, for practically enforcing that independence to which each one declared itself entitled. It is not necessary to decide whether the causes which existed were sufficient to justify the apprehensions of the South in regard to the intentions of the North. It is not a question whether they would have been happier to have continued the old partnership, for this was a subject about which they and they alone had the right to decide. And the Northern States having each asserted the same claim to abolish their governments, and having by implication conceded the same right to each member of the Union, they remain wholly unjustified for their ruthless war against the South.

ORDINANCES OF 1787 AND 1790.

The independence and sovereignty of the States has been fully recognised and acknowledged, by the General Government of the Union, upon almost every page of its history, up to the very moment of time when the Northern States, in the pride of their superior power at the ballot-box, attempted to subvert the same, and establish in lieu thereof the sovereignty and despotism of a Northern mob.

The recognition of this sovereignty in the respective States, by the Government of the United States, is so fully conceded in the Congressional proceedings consequent upon the cession by Virginia, to the Government of the Union, of the vast domain known as the 'North-Western Teritory,' and the cession by North Carolina of the territory now embraced within the limits of the State of Tennessee, that of itself it affords proof conclusive to any one who will take the trouble to investigate the subject, that it is *the North*, and not *the South*, which is to-day in rebellion against the principles upon which the Union was established. Even these isolated and incidental proofs of the *status* of the States, in reference to the general government which they established, are sufficient to prove the justice of the cause in which the South is now engaged; but these, in connection with the overpowering testimony before adduced, establish conclusively the following facts—

1. That the States were sovereign; that they never surrendered that sovereignty, and that said sovereignty was fully recognised by the Government of the Union, in all its acts.

2. That while a state of the Union might violate and set at nought the articles of confederation, and might thereby subject itself to such retaliatory measures as might be adopted in a case where one government had violated its treaty obligations with another, there could not arise a contingency in which the entire people of a state, acting in obedience to the Constitution and laws of said state, could be properly said to be in a state of rebellion against the Government of the Union.

3. That those States which have violated or threatened and attempted to violate every principle or compact upon which the Government of the United States was created, are the States of the North, and not the States of the South.

4. That the acts of the Northern United States Government, in declaring as confiscated for their use all the property of the citizens of the seceding Southern States, and pronouncing against all of said citizens *the penalty of death* for what is declared to be 'treason against the Government of the Union'—which is now only the Government of the North—has inaugurated

principles, in the conduct of the war now raging between the North and the South, as repugnant to the recognised laws of honourable warfare, as they are violative of every principle of honesty, humanity, or even common decency.

5. That while it may not be expected that foreign nations will intervene, upon the one side or upon the other, for the purpose of aiding either one of the belligerents, yet it is a duty which the great governments of the civilised world owe to themselves, and to the dictates of an enlightened humanity, *to demand that the war waged by the North against the South shall be in accordance with the principles recognised by all civilised nations.* It is a well-known fact that the Northern Government has only refrained from inflicting the penalty of death upon the prisoners who have fallen into their hands by the retaliatory measures which the Confederate Government was prepared to inflict upon Federal prisoners. Yet this position of the parties has only postponed the execution of the bloody code which has already been adopted in their laws by the action of Congress, under the approval of their President. The fortunes of war may at some period of time deprive the Confederate Government of all means of retaliation, in which event none can doubt that this bloody and barbarous law will be carried into effect, unless the great governments of the world, which claim to be at the head of

civilisation, shall first have required the United States Government to conduct their war against the South upon the recognised principles of civilised warfare. The South asks no aid from abroad, either in men or money. She is ready for any and for all the sacrifices which in the Providence of Heaven she may be called upon to suffer; but a brave, honourable, and chivalrous people, defending the integrity of their territory, and the once happy though now desolate homes of their wives and children, against vastly superior numbers and a worse than barbarous foe, have a right to demand, in the name of humanity and in the name of civilisation, that they shall be treated as men and not as wild beasts, or outlaws, whom every man who encounters may slay.

At the close of the War of Independence, the limits of the State of Virginia embraced an extent of territory as large as that which is covered by one-half the governments of Europe combined. The populous and wealthy State of Kentucky formed but a small part of this vast empire. Virginia consented that this portion of her domain should be stricken off, and formed into a separate State. The General Government of the Union being then poor, and with scarcely strength to sustain itself, implored the States having large territorial possessions to transfer a portion thereof to the general use of all the States. Virginia responded to this call for aid by an act of prodigal generosity, the magnanimity of which was only exceeded by its uncalculating and unselfish improvidence. The whole of that vast territory now embraced within the limits of the five great Western States of Ohio, Indiana, Illinois, Michigan, and Wisconsin was, upon certain named conditions, transferred to the Government of the Union, thus to continue during a necessary period of transition, after which it should be divided into five parts, each one of which should be admitted into the Union as an equal sovereign State. By a still greater exhibition of magnanimity she consented that, in the territory thus voluntarily surrendered, slavery should not exist, thus depriving her own citizens of the right of immigration, with their property, into the ceded territory. We have not an example, in all history, of such an unselfish and improvident act of self-immolation for what was conceived to be the general welfare of the country. But for this surrender of territory, Virginia would have been to-day more powerful than all New England combined, and the war for the subjugation of the South would never have been attempted.

Let us consider for a moment the effect produced by this act of more than imperial munificence upon the cold-hearted Northerners. Instead of honouring her for the noble self-sacrifice, they have taunted her with the diminution of her wealth and power which was a necessary consequence. Instead of defending her against the unjust imputation of a relative decline in power because she had not kept pace with the rapid progress of some of her sister States, they have been foremost in assigning the existence of this fact to the demoralising influence of the institution of slavery. In the records of civilised nations can there be found a parallel to such injustice and ingratitude? Yes! there is one instance of ingratitude against this same noble mother of ignoble States more atrocious even than that which we have been considering. The very children for whom she thus bountifully provided, and to whom, without a sigh of regret or a single misgiving, she assigned out of her abundant resources the great empire of the West, as a possession for them and their posterity for ever, are now foremost amongst the invaders of her soil! With their impious feet they are trampling upon the mother who bore them! With a joyful alacrity they have dashed upon the territory she had reserved for herself, and with fire and sword have carried desolation, war, and death alike into the palaces of the rich and the cottages of the poor!

Let us turn from this spectacle of wickedness and depravity to the subject from which I have been tempted for one moment to digress.

Not only do the facts connected with this great cession of territory establish the recognition of the sovereignty of the States by the Government of the Union, but they also prove that the General Government conceded that the territories were the common property of all the States, and were held for their benefit ; and that the right of the South to enter thereon with their property was precisely the same as that which was afterwards claimed by the Northern States as exclusively appertaining to their citizens. These acts also furnish evidence that all the Northern States bound themselves to restore fugitive slaves to their owners, although at a later period they repudiated that obligation. In order not to fatigue the reader with unnecessary details, I will extract from the official records only such portions as are important to a correct understanding of the facts. The great 'Ordinance of 1787,' accepting the cession of the North-Western Territory upon terms agreed upon by Virginia, was adopted in Congress by *the unanimous vote of all the States, and with but a single dissenting voice among the delegates.* In the extracts which will be found below from this ordinance the words to which the attention of the reader is more especially directed are printed in italics.

ORDINANCE PASSED BY CONGRESS IN 1789.

Whereas the General Assembly of Virginia, at their session commencing on the 20th day of October 1783, passed an Act to authorise their delegates in Congress to convey to the United States, in Congress assembled, all the right of that commonwealth to the territory north-westward of the river Ohio : and whereas the delegates of the said commonwealth have presented to Congress the form of a deed proposed to be executed pursuant to the said Act, in the words following:—To all who shall see these presents, we, Thomas Jefferson, Samuel Hardy, Arthur Lee, and James Munroe, the underwritten delegates for the Commonwealth of Virginia in the Congress of the United States of America, send greeting:

Whereas the General Assembly of the Commonwealth of Virginia, at their session begun on the 20th day of October 1783, passed an Act, entitled 'An Act to authorise the Delegates of this State in Congress to convey to the United States, in Congress assembled, all the right of this commonwealth to the territory north-westward of the River Ohio,' in these words following, to wit:

'Whereas the Congress of the United States did, by their Act of the sixth day of September, in the year one thousand seven hundred and eighty, recommend to the several States in the Union having claims to waste and unappropriated lands in the western country, a liberal cession to the United States of a portion of their respective claims, for the common benefit of the Union: and whereas this commonwealth did, on the second day of January, in the year one thousand seven hundred and eighty-one, yield to the Congress of the United States, for the benefit of the said States, all right, title, and claim which the said commonwealth had to the territory north-west of the river Ohio, subject to the conditions annexed to the said Act of cession. And whereas the United States in Congress assembled have, by their Act of the thirteenth of September last, stipulated the terms on which they agree to accept the cession of this State, should the Legislature approve thereof, which terms, although they do not come fully up to the propositions of this commonwealth, are conceived, on the whole, to approach so nearly to them as to induce this State to accept thereof, in full confidence that Congress will, in justice to this State for the liberal cession she hath made, earnestly press upon the other States claiming large tracts of waste and uncultivated territory the propriety of making cessions equally liberal, for the common benefit and support of the Union.

Be it enacted by the General Assembly, That it shall and may be lawful for the delegates of this State to the Congress of the United States to convey, transfer, assign, and make over unto the United States in Congress assembled, *for the benefit of* THE SAID STATES, all right, title, and claim, as well of soil as jurisdiction, which this commonwealth hath to the territory or tract of country within the limits of the Virginian charter, situate, lying, and being to the north-west of the river Ohio, *subject to the terms and conditions contained* in the before recited Act of Congress of the thirteenth day of September last; that is to say, upon condition that the territory so ceded shall be laid out and formed into States, containing a suitable extent of territory, and that the States so formed *shall be distinct Republican States, and admitted members of the Federal Union,* HAVING THE SAME RIGHTS OF SOVEREIGNTY, FREEDOM, AND INDEPENDENCE as the other States.'

. . . .

Resolved, That the United States in Congress assembled *are ready to receive the deed* WHENEVER THE DELEGATES OF THE STATE OF VIRGINIA are ready to execute the same.

The delegates of Virginia then proceeded, and signed, sealed, and delivered the said deed, whereupon Congress came to the following resolution:—

The delegates of the Commonwealth of Virginia having executed the deed; *Resolved,* That the same be recorded and enrolled among the acts of the United States in Congress assembled.

Resolved, That it be, and is hereby recommended to the Legislature of Virginia, to take into consideration their act of cession, and revise the same, *so far as to empower the United States* in Congress assembled *to make such a division of the territory* of the United States lying northerly and westerly of the river Ohio into distinct Republican States, not more than five nor less than three, which States shall hereafter become members of the Federal Union, and have the same rights of SOVEREIGNTY, FREEDOM, AND INDEPENDENCE as the original States.

[According to order, the ordinance for the government of the territory of the United States north-west of the river Ohio was read a third time and passed.]

It is only necessary to refer here to two articles of this ordinance, for the purpose of showing the nature of the compact thus made, and the obligations respectively assumed by the parties thereto. They are as follows:—

> It is hereby ordained and declared that the following articles *shall be considered as articles of compact* between the original States and the people and States in the said territory; and for ever remain unalterable *except by the common consent*, to wit:
>
> . . . .
>
> *Art.* VI. There shall be neither slavery nor involuntary servitude in the said territory, otherwise than in the punishment of crimes, whereof the party shall have been duly convicted. PROVIDED ALWAYS, *that any person escaping into the same, from whom labour or service is lawfully claimed* in any one of the original States, *such fugitive may be lawfully reclaimed*, and conveyed to the person claiming his or her labour or service as aforesaid.

Although North Carolina generously ceded to the Union that great extent of territory south of the river Ohio which is now embraced within the limits of the sovereign State of Tennessee, she did not by an act of self-immolation, as was the case with Virginia, nurture into life a viper which should in the end turn its deadly fangs upon her own bosom. The territory was ceded by North Carolina, and was accepted by the unanimous voice of all the States in General Congress assembled, with the following distinct and emphatic provision, to wit: '*Provided that no regulations made or to be made by Congress* SHALL TEND TO EMANCIPATE SLAVES.'

The great State of Tennessee was the result of this compact. The daughter has grown stronger and more powerful than the mother, but, with her million and a quarter of inhabitants, she stands side by side with that mother in defending their common right to independence. Situated as she is upon the frontier of that galaxy of Southern States whose gallant deeds have everywhere elicited from generous minds the tribute of their admiration, she has already been made to endure, at the hands of a ruthless enemy, what no other State but noble old Virginia has been called upon to suffer. Her armies have been decimated upon the field of battle; her territory has been invaded with fire and sword; the streets of her cities have been desecrated by the footsteps of the hated Yankees, with their legions of mercenaries gathered from the scum of every civilised land; thousands of her citizens have been driven into exile, or consigned to Northern dungeons; yet the day of her deliverance and the day of vengeance will come, though she will never imitate the atrocities which have marked the career of her invaders. She is prepared to accept whatever destiny may befall her, provided it is shared alike by her Southern sisters, but never will she consent to abandon the cause of the South while the foot of a hostile invader presses upon the soil of a Southern State.

The impartial mind can discover, in almost every act or part of an act of the General Government as illustrated by the proceedings to which I have thus briefly referred, a full recognition of every claim or demand which has been put forth by the South. It will be seen that the Northern States voluntarily and unanimously, through the action of their accredited representatives, consented to incur certain obligations by which long before the secession of the Southern States they refused to be governed; in contempt of which they combined in the election of Mr. Lincoln; and which they continue to repudiate, notwithstanding the clear letter of the Constitution and the laws. They consented to the surrender of 'fugitives from labour,' and afterwards repudiated the obligation! They consented to regard the territories as the common property of all the States, to be held in trust for the common benefit of each, and they afterwards claimed them for their exclusive use and benefit, denying to the South the privilege of an equal participation therein. They treated with the States of the

South as independent sovereignties, deriving from them their sole right to the domain upon which five of their largest States have been erected, and they now deny that the States from which they have derived their title-deeds were ever sovereign, and affect to treat the citizens of these same States as rebels against their lawful authority! They entered into a solemn compact with the Southern States, at the instance of North Carolina, that they would '*never make any regulations which* WOULD TEND *to the emancipation of slaves*,' and they have now enacted a law to set them free; not as a boon to the slaves, whom they despise, not even professedly in the interests of humanity, but for the gratification of their malice and hatred against the master! They profess to be fighting for a restoration of the old Union, while denying that the States composing it ever possessed that sovereignty which was essential to the validity of its former existence. They profess to be battling under the banner of the Constitution, while violating all its most sacred provisions; and to be warring for the establishment of the principles of liberty, while attempting to subjugate eight millions of freemen, by means which Robespierre or Danton would have blushed to employ.

But the question of slavery, its morality or immorality, its justice or injustice, its policy or impolicy, has nothing to do in deciding upon the great issue involved between the North and the South. The United States has always been a Slave Power, and would offer to-day any guarantee for its perpetuation of slavery, which the South might demand as a condition of its return to the Union. If the South succeeds in establishing its independence, it will be nothing more than the same Slave Power shorn of half its strength.

The civilised nations of the world may, through fear of incurring the hostility of the Government of the Northern United States, or from considerations of self-interest, decline to recognise the right of the Southern States to the independence which they claim; they may wink at the violation of the laws of nations and of honourable warfare; they may refuse to listen to evidences of the unlawfulness of a blockade which is producing misery throughout the civilised world — yet impartial posterity will decide that the war waged by the North against the South, whether considered in reference to the causes which produced it, or the manner in which it has been conducted, involves a more flagrant violation of the principles of justice, honour, honesty, decency, and good faith, than has ever marked the conduct of any civilised nation of ancient or modern times.

The only pretext upon which the Northern United States may justify the unprovoked war which they are now waging against the Southern Confederacy might, with equal propriety, be employed by England, or France, or Russia, if either of these powerful nations should attempt the subjugation of all Europe, upon the ground that the existence of other nations upon its borders was a constant menace against the integrity of its own dominions.

THE UNITED STATES GOVERNMENT AS IT IS.

The moral spectacle which is exhibited to the civilised world by the United States Government, even apart from the bloody horrors of the desolating war which it is now waging, is enough to arouse in the bosom of every true lover of liberty an agony of grief and shame. Through seven long and dreary years, the immortal founders of that government continued in arms against a mighty foe, in defence of the great principle that the people had a right to determine the character of the government under which they lived.

They won the victory after a long and doubtful struggle, and forthwith proceeded to establish their own political institutions, upon the great principle which they had proclaimed during the progress of their struggle.

Let us for a moment glance at the political condition of the nations of the earth at that turning point in the world's history. It was scarcely more than three quarters of a century ago, and many who were living then are living still. Of all the nations of the globe, there was not one holding a high rank which recognised the right which was thus proclaimed by a handful of Americans, as inalienable to the people. All Europe held that the source of all legitimate earthly power was the monarch, and that the monarch derived his authority from the Almighty. If the people came into the possession of any rights, they were indebted therefore to the gracious sovereign who conferred them. Now how changed! England, which was the adversary of America in that contest, big with great results, proclaims to-day from the Throne, from the Parliament and from the people, its adhesion to that great principle. The empire of France — that mighty France, which proclaims to the world that she will go to war for an idea, or fight for an abstract principle of right or justice, is ruled over by the third Napoleon, in conformity with the will of the people, deliberately proclaimed at the ballot-box. Victor Emmanuel is the elected King of Italy, recognised as such by some of the Great Powers of Europe, upon the specified grounds that he was the chosen of the people. The King of Sardinia ceded to the Emperor of the French his right to the sovereignty of Savoy and Nice. These little principalities, hid away amid the rugged and barren slopes of the Alps, were only incorporated into the empire of France after the question of transfer had been submitted to the people to be affected by the change, and ratified by their votes. And even the Sultan of Turkey, in obedience to the demand of the Great Powers of Europe, headed by the autocrat of Russia and the Emperor of Austria, has conceded to the people of Moldavia and Wallachia, and other Christian principalities within his dominions, the right to elect the prince who may rule over them.

The people, upon the various occasions referred to, may or may not have exercised wisely or even independently the privilege which was conceded to them, but the principle and the right is granted and acknowledged by the very fact of claiming to exercise authority by virtue of the sanction thus accorded. The governments of Europe do not submit the election of their rulers to the people at stated periods, but the great point has been gained, that the people have an inherent right to be regarded as the original fountain of power. The consequence is that almost all the governments of Europe profess to exercise dominion in the interests of their subjects, and with their approbation.

At the very moment when the enlightened public sentiment of mankind has recognised the validity and binding force of the sacred principle for which the fathers of the American Republic contended single-handed, only eighty-five years ago, against the opinions and practice of the whole world, their degenerate descendants are waging an exterminating war against eight millions of freemen, in order to compel them at the cannon's mouth to surrender the government of their free choice, and come under the dominion of a power which in the depths of their hearts they abhor. The vain pretext that the armies of the Union are hurled upon the South in order to relieve the majority of its people from the tyranny of a minority which holds them in subjection, will no longer avail them, since the terrible routs of Manassas Plains, and Bethel, and Oak Hills. The world will say with truth, whatever way its sympathies may run in the contest, that there can exist *but one impulse, and one heart*, amongst a nation of eight millions of people, whose armies can successfully meet and vanquish in battle the hosts which eighteen millions of their own race, acting under the impulse of an undivided purpose, can direct against them.

THE SEPARATION MUST BE PERPETUAL.

Whatever may be the fluctuating fortunes of war, every intelligent observer, who will calmly survey the attitude of the two parties in the struggle, must see that it can only terminate in the establishment of the independence of the South. The North declares in the face of the world that it is fighting for the restoration of the old Union, a result which, in the very nature of things, is not only improbable, but impracticable. Even though their victorious armies should desolate every district, and destroy every village and every city within the limits of the Confederate States, and carry mourning into every dwelling, the consummation of such a purpose would be still farther removed beyond the verge of probability. Every vestige of a Union sentiment, upon the part of the people of the South, has been already burned out of their hearts, and seared over as with a red-hot iron, by the vindictive deeds and no less atrocious designs of their former confederates. It could never have entered into the thoughts of those who inaugurated this war of subjugation, that the South would ever again receive as brothers the ruthless foe, whose hands were dripping with the blood of her murdered children.

It is absurd to attempt, by force, to compel a people to enter or return to a political union, whose existence can only begin or be perpetuated by consent. It is scarcely to be credited that any portion of the Northern people can now look to any other end to the present conflict than the complete independence, or the utter enslavement and subjugation, of the South to a military rule.*

* In corroboration of this fact, the reader has but to refer to the speeches and writings of the recognised leaders of that party about the time referred to. In order not to encumber this note with an unnecessary

When such is the issue, and the only issue presented, the South knows well that, whether the war endures for one year, or five years, or a generation, she must fight on until her victorious legions establish her independence.

And why should such a result be deplored by any friend of liberty? The old federal Union had played its part upon the political stage—it had answered the purpose of its creation, by sustaining the power

number of proofs upon this point, I will extract some brief paragraphs from a journal which has always been recognised as the leading anti-Southern paper in the United States.

From the *New York Tribune* of Nov. 26, and December 17, 1860.

'We hold with Jefferson to the inalienable right of communities to alter or abolish forms of government that have become oppressive or injurious; and if the cotton States shall become satisfied that they can do better out of the Union than in it, we insist on letting them go in peace. The right to secede may be a revolutionary one, but it exists nevertheless, and we do not see how one party can have a right to do, what another party has a right to prevent. Whenever a considerable section of our Union shall deliberately resolve to go out, we shall resist all coercive measures designed to keep it in. We hope never to live in a Republic, whereof one section is pinned to the residue by bayonets. . . . . If ever seven or eight States send agents to Washington to say "We want to get out of the Union," we shall feel constrained by our devotion to human liberty, to say "Let them go!" And we do not see how we could take the other side, without coming in direct conflict with those rights of man which we hold paramount to all political arrangements, however convenient and advantageous.'

From the same of May 1, 1861.

'But nevertheless, we mean to *conquer* them—[the Confederate States] not merely to *defeat*, but to CONQUER, to *subjugate them*. But when the rebellious traitors are overwhelmed in the field, and scattered like leaves before an angry wind, *it must not be to return to peaceful and contented homes!* They must find POVERTY at their firesides, *and see* PRIVATION *in the anxious eyes of mothers and the* RAGS *of children*. The whole coast of the South, from the Delaware to the Rio Grande, *must be a* SOLITUDE, save from the presence of a blockading squadron, so that no relief shall come in to the beleaguered people from the sea. It is in the power of the West literally to *starve her into submission*.'

of the infant Government until the Republics which formed it had attained to manhood. The great continent of North America was never designed, by the wisdom of Omnipotence, to form but a single, undivided, and indivisible Power. The State of Texas, alone, embraces territory sufficient for a vast empire. The old Union has had its day, and it has passed away for ever. No human agency can restore it to life. It has perished by the fiat of Omnipotence, and by the unchangeable will of the people of the South.

ANTAGONISMS BETWEEN THE NORTH AND SOUTH.

The North and the South are of the same race, speaking the same language, but they are, and always have been from the beginning, two peoples. Circumstances, coupled with a once existing political necessity, for a time united them, but they never mingled. They were as oil and water preserved for a season in the same bottle. Confined upon every side, and shaken up with a sufficient degree of violence, they pass through and through each other, creating an ugly, excited compound, covered with froth and filled with bubbles. But remove the external force, give both an equal chance and a moment's quiet, and they separate upon the instant, under the influence of a mutually irresistible repulsion.

'Puritanism'—a word of terrible significance, both in English and in Anglo-American history—is not developed into fanaticism by a long process of incubation. It does not confine itself wholly to subjects directly connected with religion, but it is infused into all the details of every-day life. It is an active element in peace or war, in private or in public station, in the writing of a book or in the manufacture of a 'Yankee notion.' It sings psalms of gladness upon the deck of the slave ship, to commemorate the conversion of its heathen victims to the 'only true and living faith,' while it marches forth its armies to invade the territory and spill the blood of its unoffending 'brethren,' under the inspiring strains of 'Old Hundred,' chaunted by a thousand voices to the cadence of their own foot-fall.* It is born fanaticism, fully matured in all its hideous proportions, at the very instant of its conception. It has shown itself capable

* An illustration of this characteristic quality occurred in the streets of Washington when the New England Regiments, amongst others, were ordered into Virginia, in anticipation of a great battle and a decisive victory. Having been drawn up in line, the men were addressed by the clergyman. He told his 'fellow soldiers' that they must remember they 'were not fighting the battles of *men*, but of the King of kings.' They had girded around them 'the sword of the Lord and of Gideon, and they were going forth to fight against the heathen in the name and for the sake of that beloved Saviour, Jesus Christ, who had bled and died for them upon the cross at Calvary.' A prayer was offered up imploring the blessings of Heaven upon them, and upon their holy cause; after which, to the tune of 'Old Hundred,' the troops took up the line of march across the Potomac, to the battle-fields of Bull Run and Manassas Plains!

of great achievements both for good and evil; but even in its blandishments it strikes terror into the hearts of those on whom it fondles. It appeared first in England in the form of a great pestilence of living men professing to be heaven-descended. They went forth to battle with shaved heads, but strong arms, and unconquerable hearts, and they varied the monotony of killing their fellow-men by singing psalms over their victims. The wickedness of England may have induced the All-wise Ruler of the Universe to visit it with this pestilence, and the result may have been a purification, but the medicine was not the less nauseating to the patient. It performed its work there, and partially disappeared; although leaving seed which took root and which has not even yet been eradicated. In the meantime, a sufficient number for a colony took their flight to the bleak and barren coasts of New England, where it still rules and reigns without a rival. Leave it alone to operate upon itself, and it developes great achievements; but whenever it is brought into contact with others, it exhibits the same spirit which, under the direction of Cromwell, shivered the power of his royal rival for regal honours. It is a pestilence which was doubtless sent upon the earth for a wise purpose, but a merciful Providence surely never designed that its power should be perpetual in any one country. Eternal punishments are only inflicted by our benevolent Father in heaven, in the eternal world.

The 'Puritan' exiles, who established themselves upon the cold, and rugged, and cheerless soil of New England, and the 'Cavaliers,' who fixed their destinies in the ever-blooming, smiling, sunny South, did not bear with them from the mother-country to the shores of the New World any greater degree of congeniality than existed amongst them at home, previous to the commencement of their perpetual exile; and there has been but little perceptible change in their relations since. The infusion of the best blood of the French Huguenot, who sought a refuge in the South, with that of the Anglo-Saxon Cavaliers, may have added to the impetuous temperament of the Southerner, but it did not bridge the gulph which separated him from the Puritans of the North. It does not matter which was or is the better, or which the worse. Others may settle those points according to their tastes, their judgements, or their prejudices, *but they are different*—always have been, and always will be.

The one drowned or burned women, according to the tastes or humours of their judges, on satisfactory proof that they were witches, holding nightly communications with the Evil One; the other would have been charmed to make the acquaintance of these curiously gifted ladies, and would have bestowed upon them more than a due share of their proverbial hospitality. The one will employ force, if necessary, to convince an adversary of his error; the other cares but little whether his fellow-men believe as he does, if he is permitted the full and free enjoyment of his own opinions. The one wishes to compel every man to enter the gates of heaven by the road which he points out as the right one; the other does not care how his neighbour gets there, so he himself is allowed to go in his own way. The one will not smile when he is happy; the other will not smile at any other time. The one would look sternly, and ask you what you meant by calling him a gentleman; the other would be angry if you called him anything else. The one would destroy the character of his adversary by cruel defamation, or by insidious speech, but he will not fight his enemy; not from a lack of courage, but upon principle; the other is loth to insult a gentleman by words, but he is ever ready to take 'or give satisfaction' for an insult. The one is scrupulously observant of all the external forms of piety; the other, if he has any religion in his heart, does not care to make a display of it before the world. The one is prudent, cautious, and calculating; the other inclined to be reckless, rash, and improvident. Each is great in his own way, each is capable of achieving glorious results, each is brave, each can worthily fulfill a high destiny, but in different fields, and upon diverging lines. What God in His wisdom and in the exercise of His inscrutable will has put asunder, let none attempt to join together. The New England Puritan fled from the home of his fathers in order to enjoy unrestricted freedom of religion upon the barren rock of Plymouth, but he whipped the Baptists who followed after him, for non-conformity, and drove them away into the deeper depths of the great forest. He made bondmen and bondwomen from the heathen round about him, and bought and sold them like cattle in the market, 'for the glory of God and the spread of His holy word;' but his descendant would to-day, if he were allowed to follow the bent of his inclinations, adjust the rope around the neck of the Southern slave-holder, exhort him to repentance for the sin of holding his fellow-man in bondage, say a prayer, sing a psalm, let fall the drop, and after being assured that his victim no longer breathed, would retire with the belief that he had acquired another claim to the joys of Paradise.

These contrasts indicate the adverse principles under the influence of which the public sentiment of the respective sections is developed or directed, in reference to all the affairs of life. Circumstances may and do modify, and no doubt in many instances change, these sectional or, more properly speaking, national characteristics. The spirit of the Cavalier has even made strong inroads upon the very soil, and in the very temples of the descendants of the Roundheads, but the spirit of Puritanism in its most strongly defined and most aggressive features is, and always will be, the predominating power from whence the North will derive its inspirations; for if it were otherwise, New England would emigrate to another Plymouth rock, where her strong-minded men and women could enjoy in undisturbed quiet, that liberty of conscience, and freedom of action, and supreme control, which they never concede to, or share with, any others of their fellow-men.

On the other hand, the Puritan may emigrate into the South, and sometimes he adopts the tastes and habits of his new associates, and is lost by being merged into the mass by which he is surrounded; but, as a general rule, he is and remains an exotic. The improvident prodigality of the Southerner is an ever-present temptation for him to remain a little longer for the augmentation of his worldly stores; but ever his eyes wander back under the promptings of his heart to the land of wooden nutmegs, from whose soil he hopes to rise, when called to enter upon the realities of the other world.

Each ought to be, and would be all the happier for the separation, if the Northern people could but divest themselves of their insane ambition to govern the South. They once possessed all they should have desired, and might easily have retained their hold, but in mere folly or wantonness they madly threw away from them for ever the golden possession, as a child breaks its toy and casts it at its feet. For long and weary years, they have absorbed the lion's share of the profits of slave labour, while denouncing the South to the world as barbarians for the sin of holding slaves. They have grown rich upon the spoils wrung from the South by means of protective tariffs, while taunting them with their poverty. They have denounced them to mankind as a hideous reproach to the enlightened age in which we live, while they have proclaimed themselves to be at the head of the advancing columns of progress and civilisation. If they believe to be true the smallest fractional part of what they have said, and have a proper self-respect, they should hail the separation as a deliverance, instead of fighting to bring them back. It is too late. The deed is past recall. The South can brave any danger, look death in the face without fear, and accept with reasonable composure any destiny which Providence may order, except that of entering again into a political union with those whose unkindness and injustice towards them, when they were at peace, have only been exceeded by their atrocities in war*—a war which they wan-

* A war of invasion is at all times attended with horrors to the invaded, even when the lawlessness of the troops is restrained by the exer-

tonly commenced, not because they believed they had right, but upon a calculation by arithmetical rules that

tions of the high officers, but the civilised world may be able more fully to comprehend what the Southerners have been called upon to suffer, when they consider that many of the chiefs of the Northern Army seem to be engaged in a rivalry wherein each of them appears to rest his claim to the gratitude of his fellow-countrymen upon the amount of evil he may inflict upon the inhabitants of the South, men and women, who fall within his power. Butler has probably succeeded in obtaining for himself a wider notoriety of infamy than any other Federal General, and has therefore been the recipient of greater demonstrations of respect from his fellow-countrymen: but, as far as it is known to the public, Butler has only murdered one citizen in cold blood, while sending other gentlemen to work with ball and chain upon his fortifications, and imprisoning ladies on account of the peculiar colours of the ribbons worn upon their bonnets. In a drunken frolic, as some of his friends aver, he threatened to turn loose his army upon the ladies of the city of New Orleans. But while he has been blustering, some of his brother Generals have been openly conniving at atrocities at which the heart becomes sick, and which the pen refuses to portray. When it is admitted that a commanding officer informed his soldiers, upon entering as conquerors into a town which had no means of defending itself, that during 'two hours he would shut his eyes,' the tale of woe and of horror is already told. Let us pass over this, and turn to another species of atrocity, which, if less revolting, shows the nature of the war which is waged against the South, the material of which the invading chiefs are composed, and the hopeless future which looms up before the Southern people if they should fail in their efforts to shake off their oppressors.

The following is an extract from the testimony of Col. Norton, of the 21st Ohio Regiment, before a Committee of Congress, in reference to General Mitchel, who commands the Federal forces in Northern Alabama. It is selected at random from a mass of testimony of similar import:—

'I claim, in the first place, that General Mitchel took possession of cotton in a rebel fortification, and sold that cotton for three cents per pound to a man by the name of Clark, when he was offered seven cents per pound by a man named Fuller.

'I charge Col. Turchin, and the officers and soldiers under his command, with having committed outrages and depredations upon the people of Limestone county, and the county west to Tuscumbia, in that they have stolen horses, mules, bacon, corn and fodder, from the inhabitants, without receipting therefor or giving any account of the same. I charge that they have plundered houses, taken from them ladies' wearing they were the strongest; not because they had any hope by such means to restore the departed Union upon the terms previously existing, but as a mere gratification to their pride and ambition. No! The chain of the old Union is broken, and the links are cast into a bottomless sea where no line can ever reach them.

As distinct nations the North and the South may, by respecting each other's rights, learn to appreciate each other's virtues—for both possess qualities worthy of admiration—to respect each other's strong convictions; to smile at each other's foibles, and to thank Heaven, from the depths of their hearts, that they do not resemble each other! They could only be held

apparel, gentlemen's clothing, and have broken furniture and windows, broken locks of drawers, and destroyed everything in and about various premises. I charge them with committing . . . . with stripping rings from ladies' fingers, cutting bacon upon parlour carpets, piling meat upon pianos, and being quartered in houses when they should have been quartered in their tents; robbing citizens upon the highway, breaking open safes and stores, breaking jars and everything generally in drug stores, in two or three instances. They have also taken away horses, mules, buggies and harness.

'I further state that General Mitchel knew of these things; that I took written statements to him on two occasions; that I introduced committees of citizens to him for the purpose of getting some redress for these grievances or a cessation of them; that he paid no attention to them, or rather failed to stop the depredations up to the time the brigade was ordered to march to another section of the country. In proof of these charges I will submit the sworn statements of the citizens who suffered under this treatment, as well as the statements of officers of the army who were cognizant of the facts. These sworn statements will be submitted to the committee whenever they ask for them.

'General Mitchel required of those who applied for permission to buy cotton, that they should give him one cent per pound on all they bought for the privilege of buying.'

together hereafter, under the same government, by the bonds of a common despotism. No true lover of liberty can desire that such should be the fate of either. In order that nations should be free and happy, whether they be monarchical or democratic, there must be homogeneity amongst their respective subjects. Where this bond of union exists, they are almost always virtually free and contented, whatever may be the form of government under which they live. The world abuses Austria, composed of its dozen different languages, for not conferring upon her subjects the rights, and privileges, and guarantees of the English Constitution; whereas, if they wish to establish their point, they should first condemn Austria for being an empire at all. There are periods in the history of weak nations, when it is better they should be held together by the ligaments of a common government, in order, by their joint strength, to be able to repel external enemies, and thus avoid falling victims, in detail, to an unscrupulous and ambitious foe—just as the North and the South have been united, during their infancy and weakness—a period which both have long since passed. But whenever, and only when, a country is united together by the bonds of a common sentiment, a common sympathy, a common interest, a common language, and a common history, the people may look forward, without apprehension, to a common destiny. If ambitious men should refuse to render, or, afterwards, should rob them of their liberties, the people have but to bide the proper time, and, if they are worthy to possess them, day by day, year by year, or generation by generation, they will recover, or take possession of them, as the English people have done; or they will seize upon them suddenly, as did our forefathers, and once more enter quietly and smoothly upon the fulfilment of their destiny.

It is not only not necessary that nations should be very great, or very powerful, in order to be free and happy; but it is always to be apprehended that the possession of great strength will create a disposition to employ it, by invading the liberties of others; which event is very naturally followed by the loss of their own. If a people is strong enough to offer a successful resistance against external enemies, even though they may not have the physical strength to make successful aggressions upon the liberties of others, they have all the force necessary to maintain a government which will secure their own happiness, and the respect of mankind.

Such is precisely the attitude occupied by the Confederate States of America at this very moment; but, unlike any nation of the Old World having a population of like numbers, never yet has there been for any other people so glorious a prospect of a bright and a happy and a great future! In a war for defence we have a million of men upon our muster-rolls, all of whom possess those manly qualities, and have been inured to those habits of life, which make soldiers who are to be relied upon in the hour of peril. As for a war of aggression, we will never wage it, except in self-defence. Our pursuits are chiefly agricultural, and one of our principal products is sought after by all the civilised nations of the world. They will come with their money or their manufactures to buy it, and with their ships to take it away. They will never make war upon us, because it would diminish our production; we will never make war upon them, because no reasonable cause of quarrel can arise. Nations which are competing with each other in the sale of manufactures make war upon each other; but between an agricultural and a manufacturing country, each being always the customer and never the rival of the other, to engage in war would be almost impossible. We have to-day a population four times as great as that of the thirteen colonies when they achieved their independence. It is nearly seventy per cent. greater than was that of the whole United States during the last war with Great Britain. It is greater than was the entire population of the United States in 1828. Our exports to foreign countries are greater than the entire exports of the United States previous to 1856, and more than the average of the whole during the last twelve years.

Although our population, including all the Slave States, is only about 12,000,000, against 18,000,000 in the Northern States, our exports are nearly the double of theirs.

The mind becomes dazzled by a contemplation of our magnificent domain. We could receive half Europe into our embraces, and still have an empire to spare. If we acquire no more territory, we have now 850,000 square miles, which embraces an extent of territory equal to that occupied by France, Austria, Prussia, Spain, and Great Britain combined.

We have a productive soil, and strong hands and arms to work it. We have the Government of our choice, and stout and willing hearts to maintain it; and, with the approval of Heaven, we will maintain it at all hazards, and at whatever cost of blood, or treasure, or present comfort. The property and the lives of our citizens have been offered up upon the altar of their country, as freely as they would bestow a draft of cold water from the sparkling fountain upon the thirsty traveller on the way-side. If they do not themselves live to enjoy the ripe fruits of their labours, they know that they will live for ever in the hearts of a grateful posterity; and whatever may be now the public sentiment of their fellow-men, who have been misled by the misrepresentations of their enemies, as sure as the sun shines mankind will one day do justice to their motives and applaud their deeds.

THE SOUTH WILL BE JUSTIFIED BEFORE THE WORLD.

We may here note one of the agreeable results which will immediately follow the complete establishment of the Confederate States Government. There exists among the people of all civilised nations a very natural desire to secure the respect of their fellow-men. The South has hitherto, from her unfortunate political associations, been constantly and grossly misrepresented by those who professed to be fellow-countrymen. These slanders, after receiving the proper embellishment at the hands of that numerous class of newspaper writers and bookmakers, in Europe, who thrive by pandering to the passions or practising upon the credulity of their readers, are employed in creating or fostering that public sentiment of the Old World against the Southern people, which has not a single truth for its foundation.*

*As specimens of the peculiar character of the 'facts' relied upon by the European adversaries of the South to support their cause, as well as of their moral sentiment, the reader's attention is directed to the following characteristic passages, in a late London publication, from the pen of the 'Professor of Jurisprudence and Political Economy, in Queen's College, Galway.' In the same book may be found recorded the bloody story of the Yankee's scalp before referred to, with all the embellishments necessary to give a dramatic effect to the striking narrative. The author says :—

'Some explanation perhaps is needed why in the foregoing sketch no mention has been made of *one of the most signal acts of heroism in modern times*—the attempt of John Brown to open a guerilla warfare against slavery in Virginia. The enterprise, however worthy of being recorded, having yet originated exclusively *in the noble heart of the man who conducted it*, and having been carried into operation without the connivance of any considerable party in the United States, could not

Whatever prejudices may have been excited abroad against the people or the Government of the United

properly be included in a sketch of which the object was to trace the workings of those parties. . . . .

"Actions of the just
Smell sweet in death, and blossom in the dust."'

There are, perhaps, few readers throughout the civilised world who are not familiar with some of the events which brought the name of this monster murderer, John Brown, prominently before the world: none, perhaps, beyond the limits of the radical Anti-slavery party, who have not been thrilled with horror at the recital of his crimes. He was an obscure man, residing in the State of New York, when, according to the author above quoted, 'he conceived in his own heart, without the concurrence of any considerable party,' the bloody career which, after a long course of crime, was terminated under the gallows. I have already referred in another part of this volume to some of the more monstrous crimes which marked his first appearance before the world as a midnight assassin. The greater number of his victims were not even slave-holders. Many of them were poor, harmless, and inoffensive. He killed them in their beds at night, not only men, but children! He seemed to be governed by an uncontrollable thirst for the shedding of blood. At length he took up his abode in a peaceful and quiet village in the State of Virginia, and having gathered around him a few desperate wretches, who were doubtless inspired chiefly by a hope of plunder, he suddenly, at night, rose upon the unsuspecting inhabitants, murdered a number of them, but failing in his efforts to induce the negroes to join him, he was arrested, tried, and executed. These murders were not perpetrated during a period of civil commotion or war, like that which now exists, but in the year of our Lord 1859. All was peace and calm and quiet throughout the State which he selected as the scene of his atrocities.

When this fiend, covered with the blood of his innocent victims, appealed to the party spirit of Northern abolitionists for support and countenance, upon the ground that he murdered in their cause, it was possible to suppose that he might find a small number of inconsiderate and wicked men, with hearts sufficiently corrupt to accord to him their sympathies; but that in the enlightened kingdom of Great Britain there could be found men and women, occupying a high rank, and professing to be the leaders in every movement tending towards human progress; teachers of morality and religion; and even professors in colleges, instituted for the enlightenment of the young; who would proclaim their reverence for the character, and their admiration for the crimes,

States, whatever insult offered by the Northern press which foreigners might wish to resent, they had the

and their sympathy for the fate of the bloodthirsty assassin John Brown, would be too monstrous for belief, if we did not find it recorded by their own hands, and bound up for preservation and transmission to posterity. And these are the men who affect to shudder at what they denominate the sins of the Southerners, and to weep over the reputed wrongs of the black men upon the American continent, who of all their race least require the sympathies of their fellow-men!

The entire volume from which the foregoing morsel has been abstracted, is made up of monstrosities and absurdities which cannot fail to elicit smiles from even its sympathising American readers. The author's 'facts' are evidently derived in chief from the files of the more reckless section of the New York sensation press, published upon election day, for the enlightenment of ignorant foreign voters; but it is only fair to add that the deductions are all his own. My purpose in referring to this book will be fully achieved by one more extract, in which the 'Professor of Jurisprudence and Political Economy' defines the nature and character of the different classes which make up the dreadful compound of Southern society.

The author says:—

'Four million slaves have thus come into the possession of masters *less than one-tenth of their number*, by whom they are held as chattel property, *while the rest of the dominant race*, more numerous than slave-holders and their slaves together, squat over the vast area which slave labour is too unskillful to cultivate, where by hunting and fishing, by plunder or by lawless adventure, they eke out a precarious livelihood. . . . The mean whites, as has been shown, are the natural growth of the slave system. . . . They will for a time, indeed, *when pressed for food*, their ordinary resources of hunting or plunder failing them, hire themselves out for occasional services; *but so soon as they have satisfied the immediate need*, they hasten to escape from the degradation of industry, and are as eager as Indians to return to their wilds. . . . In the Southern States, no less than five millions of human beings are now said to exist in this manner in a condition little removed from savage life, eking out a wretched subsistence by hunting, by fishing, by hiring themselves out for occasional jobs, by plunder. Combining the restlessness and contempt for regular industry peculiar to the savage with the vices of the *proletaire* of civilised communities, these people make up a class at once degraded and dangerous, and, constantly reinforced as they are by all that is idle, worthless, and lawless among the population of the neighbouring States, form an inexhaustible preserve of ruffianism, ready at hand for all the worst purposes of Southern ambition.'

What response may a Southerner make to enlightened men, in regard to such a stupendous misstatement of facts? He might say, with truth, ever present retort of the horrors of American slavery, as reported by those who were themselves American

not only in regard to these, but to almost every material allegation in the whole book, that if the author had been engaged, for a consideration, to represent a condition of society diametrically the reverse of that which in reality exists, he could not have employed human language which would have more effectually accomplished his task. This, however, would only suggest to the uninformed reader, that there was an issue of facts between the Queen's College Professor and a Southern citizen. Leaving this point undecided, let us test his statements by the rules of common reason. Is it not most inexplicable, if true, that so vast a preponderance of the dominant race should follow such dangerous and laborious modes of obtaining a precarious existence, when they may, without restraint, 'squat over the vast area which slave labour is too unskillful to cultivate,' and thus appropriate to their own use all the rich products of that favoured land?

Five millions of the inhabitants of that prolific land, 'flowing with milk and honey,' when 'pressed for food' emerging from their fastnesses to satisfy the cravings of hunger by 'hiring themselves out for occasional services!' Fishermen upon those great rivers and mountain streams teeming with their scaly denizens, in despair of obtaining another nibble, abandoning their hooks, and starting forth upon their predatory expeditions to kill and plunder! Hunters in those grand old primæval forests, abounding in wild buck and pheasant and rabbit, where there are no game laws, and where each man's park is as extensive as a European principality, reduced to the deplorable necessity of robbing their fellow-men to save them from starvation! 'Squatters over the vast area, which slave labour is too unskillful to cultivate,' too indolent to grasp the luscious fruits which nature has provided for them, until want of food and the approach of starvation compel them to seek elsewhere for the material necessary to sustain life!

Without relying upon the well-known fact, that there is not a nation under the sun where an unarmed stranger may pass with so little cause for apprehension of robbery or molestation, as in the country so improperly described by this author, where are these five millions of robbers, when aroused from their accustomed lethargy by the pangs of hunger, to find victims upon whom to exercise their predatory calling? Certainly not from among the wealthy governing class of slave-holders, else they would, in view of such an ever-present danger, adopt some stringent means for their protection; whereas it is a well-known fact, that previous to the commencement of the present war, there was not to be citizens. Thus has the South been a target for the shafts of the world, without having any means of

seen a single soldier nor an armed policeman in the whole South. What a benefactor to European governments our teacher of political economy might become, if he would only go South and learn from personal observation how four millions of slaves pining for their deliverance, and five millions of semi-savage plunderers and vagabonds, may be governed by less than half a million of masters without the employment of musket, sword, or soldier!

Assuming that our author derives his figures from correct data, we have in the States of the South four millions of slaves ready to turn upon their masters, five millions of roving worthless mean whites, and four hundred thousand lords, upon whose shoulders rests the responsible duty of governing and controlling this mass of ignorance and vice! We ought properly to deduct that immense Union element which we are informed by the Washington Government pervades the 'better class of Southerners;' but that it would leave our author minus a single controlling spirit to direct the movements of his army of vagabonds, and me without an excuse for continuing this note.

Let us look for a moment upon the grand achievements of this handful of Southerners. With a 'glance of the eye,' they reduce to abject submission the four millions of slaves, who are 'waiting and sighing for the day of their deliverance.' They crush beneath their iron heel that 'great Union element, which is prevented by terror alone from joining the ranks of the North!' With a frown they bring the five millions of dissolute vagabonds to their knees, and with a single word convert this idle thriftless mob of semi-savages into fully armed ready drilled regiments, of as gallant soldiers as have ever shouldered muskets, mounted war steeds, or drawn swords in defence of any cause! They send forth four millions of cotton bales, which give employment to the looms of the world, and thus feed and clothe hundreds of millions of the human race! In the midst of these labours, they are called upon to defend themselves, their homes, and their firesides against an army of 700,000 men, fully armed and equipped, and directed by a powerful and enlightened nation. Neither daunted nor discouraged, they enter upon the unequal struggle, under a government scarcely a month old, without a ship, without money, without a soldier, and without arms, or the means to make them. They are shut out from intercourse with their fellow-men by the blockade of their ports, with the assent of the Governments of the world, which, while declaring 'neutrality,' in effect deny the Confederates all access to their markets, while supplying every want of their enemy.

defence. Never yet has any country been so unfairly treated by the civilised world as the planting States

Under all these disadvantages, the flag of the Confederacy has waved in triumph over every great battle-field of the war, and they still maintain themselves with a heroic gallantry which has extorted the admiration even of their foes.

As if the author had not sufficiently magnified the greatness of this handful of Southerners, he gravely proposes, in the event it becomes manifest that the South is going to triumph in the war, that the civilised world should interpose to save the North from falling a victim to the arrogant dominion of the organised barbarism of the Slave Power! It is clear that the imagination of the astute Professor of Political Economy, having been wrought up to a pitch of frenzy by a recital of the astounding achievements of the Virginia 'Merrimac' and the 'Arkansas,' discovers in every Southern soldier a ready-made iron-clad ram, fully armed with a dozen ten-inch rifled cannon, and with all steam on, ready to pounce down upon the Lilliputian hosts of the grand Yankee army!

The mind very naturally reverts to the deluge of pamphlets and newspaper articles which preceded the war, all claiming that slavery had so enervated and enfeebled the white population of the South, in soul and body, that they would be utterly incapable of resisting for a day the earnest assaults of a few regiments of Yankees and foreign mercenaries. Perhaps there are few intelligent readers in Europe or America who do not remember how the North deluded itself with this theory; and how their European allies of the fanatical Anti-slavery school endeavoured to stimulate the North to commence the war by promising them an easy victory over the effeminate and unwarlike Southerners. Now they are able to prove with equal certainty, and by a process of reasoning just as infallible, that the inevitable tendency of the institution of slavery is to impart such a martial vigour and energy and indomitable power of will to the dominant race, as to render it at least possible that the result of the present war will be the utter subjection of the modest, unassuming, gentle, and pious Yankee nation, unless the civilised world should interpose to save it from the organised barbarism of the Southern slave-holders.

How blessed above all other institutions of learning is the Queen's College of Galway, in the possession of such a profound professor of jurisprudence and political economy! What a treasure of knowledge for the favoured youths who have the good fortune to be brought up at the feet of this modern Solon! The merchants and manufacturers and politicians of Europe learn from his teaching, that the enormous surplus of of America. The Southerner who can have the patience to peruse the books and newspaper articles

agricultural and planting products of the South — greater in value, *per capita*, than the surplus products of any other nation — are furnished to the world by a population more than one-third of whom are slaves, and eleven-twelfths of the remainder 'worthless, idle, roving, semi-savage vagabonds, who earn a precarious subsistence by hunting, fishing, and plunder!' Nay, more; the professors of the art of war are gravely informed that out of this mass of barbarism has been constructed and organised that vast and gallant army which has successfully defended Richmond, Charleston, Savannah, Mobile, and Vicksburg; and which has planted its victorious standard upon the bloody battle-fields of Shiloh, Bull Run, Manassas Plains, and the Chickahominy!

Certain authors, like fourth-rate sculptors, can only execute a work by attempting to imitate something that is already in existence. It is easy to imagine that the 'Queen's College Professor of Jurisprudence and Political Economy,' before writing his book, had studied deeply, under the inspiration of a glass of punch, the life and character of the renowned Baron Munchausen. But, like nearly all imitators, he only succeeded in copying the vices of his model. His solemn asseverations are as monstrous and as improbable, but there the parallel ceases — the wit is wholly wanting. Admit as facts the premises laid down by the author of the Baron's life, and there is a beautiful simplicity and an air of probability in all that follows, which in all its parts challenges the admiration of the reader. Grant the truth of the Galway author's premises, and the only inferences which may be derived therefrom are so utterly monstrous, that the intelligent and unprejudiced reader must mentally exclaim on rising from a perusal of his book —'what a libel upon Munchausen!'

Though we may not be surprised that such a book as the one under consideration should have been written, since it can find readers who relish its tale of horrors, yet the Southerner has reason to be astonished at the easy credulity, the unreasonable prejudices, or the vitiated tastes of those who find a gratification in listening to such self-evident slanders and misrepresentations. We may well understand that there should be a class in Europe who witness with pleasure the dissolution of the great Confederacy. We know that a party exists in Great Britain — a relic of the past — who believe that upon the downfall of the institution of slavery in the South, Great Britain, by means of her vast possessions in India and elsewhere, may be able to supply the world with those tropical productions which have been hitherto furnished by the planting States of which are circulated throughout Europe in reference to the South and slavery, is astounded not less at the

America; and although we may well doubt whether such hopes would be realised, or whether, in any event, mankind would be the gainer thereby, yet we cannot reasonably ask that this class of politicians should not employ all legitimate means to promote the end they desire to see accomplished. But surely a generous European foe, in view of events which are now transpiring upon the American continent, should for the moment at least suspend the promulgation of those calumnies which have in times past been so successfully employed in stimulating the prejudices of mankind against the Southern States of the late American Union. They may possibly have the effect of irritating those against whom they are directed, but surely the day has passed by when the enlightened public sentiment of Europe may be influenced by such stupendous drafts upon its credulity as signalise the literary effusions of the 'Professor of Jurisprudence and Political Economy in Queen's College, Galway.'

In concluding this reference to the unreliability of European books, written by authors under the influence of long-cultivated prejudices, who pretend to describe the condition of a country more than three thousand miles distant from them, and of which they know nothing from personal observation, it may not be out of place to refer to other errors, which prevail in many quarters where we might hope to find a more correct knowledge of the facts. It is often asserted in Europe, and is believed by many, that the Southern States desired to force the institution of slavery into the Free States! It is most difficult to establish a negative, yet the history of parties or of legislation, or congressional proceedings, may be searched in vain for any record of such a purpose. No intimation of such a desire has ever been made in any deliberative body in the South; and if any single Southerner has ever given expression to such a desire, it has never come under my observation, although I may say that I have had the fullest and the freest intercourse, during my whole life, with those statesmen and politicians of the South who have been supposed to represent the public sentiment of their section.

It is also asserted that the North has upon several occasions compromised its rights in order to satisfy the unconditional demands of the South. So far from this being true, the reverse thereof is the fact. The South has most unwisely compromised away many of its rights, in order to obtain greater security for the remainder. The most extreme Southern party has never demanded for the South anything more than a right to control their own domestic institutions within their own limits — to participate as an equal partner in the lands purchased by the United States out of the common fund, and to magnitude of the falsehoods which obtain ready credence, than at the easy credulity which accepts them as truths. The happy, contented, well-fed, well-clothed slaves are represented as miserable, half-starved, over-worked wretches; the Southern gentlemen and ladies, as ferocious, cruel, and depraved; and the great body of the Southern people as unlettered savages, having certainly the features of humanity, but the low instincts of brutes. Every fixed opinion which is entertained by the general European public in reference to the Southern States and the institution of slavery is founded at best upon theories

reclaim their property when found within the Northern States in accordance with a specific stipulation and requirement of the Constitution! The South has never demanded more than this, and they could not submit to anything less.

It is also charged that the South has sought to reopen the African slave trade. That this measure has some advocates is true, but it is also true that this party in the North is much stronger than in the South, and in both it may be declared with truth that the almost universal public sentiment is opposed to it. The Southern States, as has been shown, during almost an entire century stood solitary and alone amongst the nations of Christendom in their opposition to this traffic. They abolished it in defiance of the wishes of almost all Christendom, and they oppose it now for the same reason that they opposed it then: namely, that the traffic would be opposed to their interests. They do not pretend that in this they are influenced by any other than selfish considerations for themselves, and from motives of humanity for their civilised slaves. So far as the subjects of the King of Dahomy are concerned, the Southerners are well aware that it would be a mercy to accept them as slaves, and train them up to the ways of civilisation; but they are not so unselfish as voluntarily to undertake the task.

The South asks nothing more from the civilised world than that its opinions shall be founded upon truths, and not upon falsehoods or perverted facts.

deduced from isolated and distorted facts, or upon an utter perversion of truth. If we may judge of their knowledge in regard to the South, by the character of the books from which they may be supposed to derive their information, Europe is almost as ignorant to-day of the practical operation of the domestic institutions of the Southern States, as of the manners, customs, and habits of the antediluvians. It may not be doubted that many intelligent gentlemen of the Old World are better informed, but it can only be expected that the truth will break upon the multitude by slow degrees, when we succeed in freeing ourselves from all political association with our Northern Confederates. For the most selfish and unworthy purposes, they have endeavoured to isolate the South from all communication with the outer world, and at this very moment of time, when they are imploring and endeavouring to force the Southern States back into the Union, and when they would freely give every guarantee for the indefinite perpetuation of slavery which the South could ask, they have the audacity to present themselves before Europe as the friends and champions of the enslaved Africans! The tricks and falsehoods which have hitherto served to delude the world in regard to the Southern people, will lose half their force after the South shall have established her independence, and separated herself from those who, under the garb of brothers, have ever acted the part of enemies. We may reasonably hope that the nations of the world will take a more practical view of the question of African slavery, and that they will see and admit the difficulties which would attend the developement of their schemes of emancipation.

As the Southern States have been misrepresented in reference to their domestic institutions, so in regard to suggested aggressions upon the territory of our neighbours. Cuba — rich, fertile, ever-blooming Cuba — was spread out invitingly before our eyes. Northern cupidity would have clutched the tempting prize, and the South would have taken in the bait of an augmentation of its political power, if Spain could have been induced to sell. But there was no Southerner of intelligence so blind as not to perceive that the acquisition, however valuable to the North, would have resulted in a heavy pecuniary loss to the South, because we could not have competed with her successfully in productions common to both. The South, like a drowning man, was willing to grasp at any straw which would, by adding to her political power in the government, have enabled her to make a few more feeble struggles to maintain herself against that storm of sectionalism and fanaticism by which she was at last overtaken; but it was well known that the only beneficiary would be the North.

These causes of irritation to European Powers have all been charged as the 'aggressions of the slave power;' whereas, if the Southern States had been left to themselves, and had been free from constraint, while they would have been perfectly indifferent to any acquisitions which Spain might choose to make among the barbarous inhabitants of the American islands, who have shown their utter incapacity to govern themselves, the Island of Cuba, however desirable as an acquisition of political power in the Senate, to counterpoise the strength of the North, would have been one of the last possessions they would have coveted. Now that we are and will remain free, sovereign, and independent upon our own soil, each of us will be judged by mankind by our own acts, and not by the interested or malicious representations of the other. The world will be surprised to find how egregiously it has been misled in regard to the characteristics and qualities of the people of the South.

THE SOUTH MUST BE SELF-RELIANT.

Nevertheless, in the prosecution of the war in which the people of the South are now engaged, however gratifying it might be to have the sympathies of good men everywhere, we neither seek, nor desire, nor expect any foreign aid from any quarter of the globe. If we cannot win our own liberties by our own unaided efforts, we could not maintain them if they were bestowed upon us as a free gift. If other nations choose to recognise our just claim to independence, we will give them the right hand of friendship; but we do not desire them to fight our battles. If they should think proper to withhold that recognition, it will not occasion us the loss of a man nor a single element of success which we now hold; and although it would be folly to deny that their persistent refusal to invest us with the rights which would attend our recognition as a nation, does not increase our hardships by stimulating the North to increase its barbarities, yet we will prove to them by the result that we are capable of maintaining ourselves, single-handed and alone, now and in all time against all our enemies.*

* The Great Powers of Europe are already committed to the recognition of the Southern Confederacy by their action in regard to the secession of Belgium from the mild and beneficent Government of the Netherlands. In this case, the principle that a nation had an undeniable right to create, and live under, a government which they believed would promote their own happiness and interests, was conceded by all Europe, and Belgium was permitted to withdraw from Holland by the very same Great Powers which united them together, on the ground of a political European necessity. One of the most distinguished and able diplomatists of Holland stated to me that the party which had been most opposed to the severance of the kingdom was now fully satisfied that the separation was an act of wisdom, and had undeniably added to the prosperity of both, while no European interest had thereby suffered detriment.

While the Confederate States may not expect that European governments will recognise the fact of their existence as an independent sovereignty while they may have reason to believe that the act would be

It is in no boasting or vain-glorious spirit that we utter this declaration and defiance; but because we

inimical to their interests, yet we might reasonably have hoped that, in adopting the policy of neutrality, they would have devised some means by which that neutrality would have been real. Up to the present moment this has not been the fact. While the South is rigidly denied all access to Europe for supplies of arms and other munitions of war, the United States have supplied themselves with all they required from European markets. In truth, the effect of the neutrality of the Great Powers of Europe has been to supply the United States with all they required for the conduct of the war, while virtually denying the same privilege to the Confederates. It has served to build up the navy of the former, while it has effectually checked, if it has not wholly prevented the Confederates from establishing a navy. In addition to these great advantages, it has enabled the United States to procure the very best material for her army out of the discontented and desperate adventurers and mercenaries of Europe, who are ever ready to sell their swords to the highest bidder, while from this source not a single recruit has been added to the armies of the South. The best blood of the native Southerners has been poured out in exchange for that of the vilest rabble that perhaps ever before formed so large an army. The neutrality of the Great Powers has, therefore, had precisely the same results as though they had entered into a league of friendship with our enemies. This, however, is but a natural result of the relative conditions of the parties to the war. While the sympathies of individuals sometimes run with the weak, the Governments upon whom the responsibility rests, generally find most to admire in the strong. In addition to this, the people of the United States have adopted the policy of governing other Powers, by infusing a wholesome terror of the consequences of any act which may not accord with the views of the Washington Government. Never yet has any other nation, however great, beenso insolent or so overbearing; and the more meekly her insults are received the more she threatens. The belief is really entertained in the United States, that if the Washington Government should order the confiscation of every foreign ship found sailing within fifty leagues of a Confederate port, some of the Great Powers would submit with becoming resignation to the award of an American tribunal. The Great Powers only very recently made a treaty in which they declared that they would not recognise an ineffectual blockade. The uninitiated outside world imagined that if vessels might come and go with perfect freedom into one-third of the ports of the South, and if nine of every ten attempting to run the blockade at the other ports should succeed, that such blockade know that 8,000,000 of men, who are determined to be free, cannot be subjugated by any force which may

was not effectual. But it has been virtually decided that the words of that treaty referred rather to the intentions of the blockading party, than to the capacity to enforce it. Besides, there was the potent argument that cotton was scarce in Europe, hence the proof that the blockade was effectual, without considering that the Confederate States entered into the war with scarcely a ship of any kind. But of far greater significance than this quiet submission on the part of other governments to a notoriously inefficient blockade, is the fact that they should recognise this blockade at all. The United States have hitherto utterly denied the right of a nation to blockade its own ports, and Europe acquiesced in the enforcement of their views against a weak and tottering government. Now, that same government declares half a continent over which it assumes the right of sovereignty to be in a state of blockade, and the great commercial Powers acquiesce in the act. Thousands of their own subjects are starving for want of that material from which they are illegally deprived, and yet their own governments refuse to give them any relief. They admit that they are innocent sufferers from the war; that the people of the United States were under a tacit agreement to supply the looms of Europe with cotton, and that they should not be punished for the acts of the Southern States; that the blockade under the circumstances was a violation of neutral rights, besides being inefficient; yet they say in effect—the United States threaten us with war and extermination if we seek to protect our rights, and it is better therefore to 'bear the ills we have than fly to others that we know not of.' Europe has yet to learn that the United States are not always in earnest when they threaten to destroy all who cross their path. Besides, it is by no means sure that a great nation saves anything in the end by submission to insult and wrong. In the present case it is clear that, if European Governments had insisted firmly upon the enforcement of their rights, the United States Government would have submitted, as it did in the *Trent* case, when it discovered that France, Spain, Prussia, and all the other Great Powers were ready to sustain England. No intelligent observer of the progress of the war entertains a serious doubt that if other Powers had enforced their rights, and if the neutrality of Europe had been made to operate alike upon both the belligerents, the United States Government would long ago have been compelled by the Confederate States to acknowledge their independence. However the conclusion of a peace between the two sections of the Republic might grieve a certain class of heartless politicians in Europe, yet the great be brought against them. We do not conceal from ourselves the mighty odds arrayed against us. We know that our enemies are powerful and vindictive. We know that they have attracted to their bloody standard the debased, and the dissolute, and the radicals of every land. Princes without kingdoms, renegades without a country, infidels without a religion, revolutionists without principle, adventurers without honour or honesty, criminals and refugees from foreign lands—in short, the very scum of Europe—all have flocked to the scene of carnage, and instigated by the Puritans of New England, and led on by ambitious demagogues, are eager to despoil us of our wealth, to desolate our country, and to murder our people. Yet we know, also, that *our cause is just*, and this knowledge steels our hearts, and nerves our arms, for the great and unequal conflict.

But let us not, while relying upon the justice of

mass of mankind throughout the civilised world would have had occasion to rejoice. The South has never sought the aid of foreign Powers, and she never will, unless the tide of events should indicate the fruitlessness of a struggle which at present seems ready to crown her heroic sacrifices with success. Then, if she asks for aid, she will offer a full equivalent for the services to be rendered. I have been impelled to this cursory glance at the attitude of European Governments, to show to my fellow-countrymen that they have nothing to expect from other Powers, not even the enforcement of an effective neutrality. There are Governments, however, which have sought to do us justice, and though obstacles may have been interposed to prevent the accomplishment of their purpose, they are nevertheless entitled to our gratitude for their good intentions.

our cause, leave any means untried which may aid in the accomplishment of our deliverance. Let us look the danger full in the face, and prepare ourselves for every sacrifice of life and property which may be necessary to secure our independence. Above all, let us not rely upon receiving any aid from without. The sympathies of mankind are more often with the strong than the weak, and governments especially which have no direct interest to subserve are slow to ally themselves with a cause, however just, which has not demonstrated its ability to sustain itself without their aid. When we prove our capacity to stand alone without help, the world will not be slow to recognise the fact. Although we are fighting the battle of real liberty and conservatism, against the radicalism of a mere mob, led to battle under the influence of a fanaticism which cannot be satiated but by the destruction of all who interpose to impede its despotic rule, yet the burthen has fallen upon our shoulders, and we cannot expect that others will voluntarily come forward to share the dangers and the penalties of resistance. There is, perhaps, not a single disinterested intelligent observer of the bloody drama now being enacted upon the American continent, who is not satisfied that the North is waging this war for the purposes of dominion, conquest, and plunder; and that, under pretence of love for the slave, the attempt to overthrow the institution of slavery is only the employment of a means, to the accomplishment of their hostile intentions against the independence of the South.

Visions of viceroyalties, over subjugated provinces, and governorships of conquered cities, are held out as inducements to the ambitious Yankee; confiscated plantations, worked by semi-enfranchised Africans, are the promised rewards to be bestowed upon the conquering soldiers; while foreign mercenaries, many of them the most depraved and dissolute outcasts from Europe, have been stimulated by money bounties, high pay, and indefinite promises of the spoils of victory, to swell the invading hosts.

It may be that we shall pass through a long night of horrors before we are able to drive back our relentless foe; but let every Southerner remember, that it were better far to be the vassals and subjects of any single foreign despot who bears a sceptre, than to fall under the dominion of the mob-multitude who would be our masters if we should unhappily be subjected to the Northern invaders of our once happy homes.

No people have ever had more unmistakable evidences that they were guided and directed by an overruling Providence, which smiled upon their undertaking, than have the people of the South since the commencement of their great struggle. To crown all, we have been blessed with the most bountiful crops that have ever before been garnered in recompense for the toils of the husbandman. While our free citizens have shouldered their muskets and have gone forth to fight the battles of their country, the Africans are contentedly working in the fields. Faithful and true to the interests of their masters; watching with kind solicitude over the unprotected women and children who have been left with no other defence than their fidelity afforded; rejoicing in the successes, or mourning over the reverses of the Southern armies, of which they are themselves a chief element of strength by means of the products of their labour; resisting alike the promises and the threats of the Yankee invaders; they have put to shame the enemies of the South, who predicted their unfaithfulness, and have taught mankind a lesson of experience, in regard to the influences and nature of the institution of slavery in the Southern States, which it is to be hoped will be more instructive than the speculative theories which have hitherto formed the basis of public opinion.*

* If any real sentiment of humanity, or consideration for the welfare of the African race in America, animates disinterested foreigners whose sympathies are enlisted in favour of the North, in the present struggle between the dissevered members of the late Confederacy, the events developed during the progress of the war should satisfy them that their hopes can never be realised under such auspices. That it is possible for the present relations between the master and slave to be broken up, by the annihilation of the white race, may not be questioned. It may even be granted that the Yankees may seize upon and occupy the plantations made vacant by the murder of their present possessors; but who can

Never yet in the past history of nations has an ignorant or a servile population been subjected to

believe that the cold-hearted, cruel, and avaricious Northerner would prove to be more lenient in his exactions upon the Africans than those who at present control them? The Northerners are proverbially more cruel towards the blacks than any other nation of the civilised world. Even the small number who are living amongst them in the enjoyment of nominal freedom, are not treated with the humanity which is accorded to beasts of burthen, and the conduct of both government and people since the war commenced, precludes the hope of any change in their conduct towards the degraded race. They first declare that they do not intend, under any circumstances, to interfere with the relations of master and slave. Next they propose to free the slave as a punishment to the master. Again they propose to inaugurate a servile war, in order that they may accomplish their fiendish designs against the Southerners. Now their government proposes to employ the slaves, as menial labourers in their camps, as hewers of wood and drawers of water, and diggers of ditches. But in all this we discover no approximation to that 'equality and fraternity,' which they would have the world believe is the purpose they seek to accomplish. The isolation of the poor African is intensified and perpetuated by the degradation of the offices assigned to him; and in the very act of being called upon to sacrifice his life in their service, he is reminded that his heart's blood, even in death, must not be mingled with the blood of the white man.

We remember with pleasure the conduct of the American Colonies during the war of Independence. Even Massachusetts repudiated the employment of Africans to aid them in their unequal struggle against the mother-country, as will be seen by the following resolution adopted by the 'Committee of Safety': —

'Resolved, That it is the opinion of this Committee, as the contest now between Great Britain and the Colonies respects the liberties and privileges of the latter, which the Colonies are determined to maintain, that the admission of any persons, as soldiers, into the army now raising, but only such as are freemen, will be inconsistent with the principles that are to be supported, and reflect dishonour on this colony, and that no slaves be admitted into this army upon any consideration whatever.'

But there is still higher authority to show that even in the most gloomy period of their struggle, the fathers of the revolution refused to employ the Africans to aid them in securing their independence. Washington himself in 1775 instructed the recruiting officers not to enlist Africans in the service of the United States.

At a council of war held at head-quarters, October 8, 1775, present similar temptations, which have produced such small results. The Yankee invaders, by demoniac appeals

General Washington, Major-General Putnam, Brigadier-General Gates, and others, the question was proposed:—

'Whether it would be advisable to employ negroes in the army, and if there be a distinction between such as are slaves and those who are free. It was agreed unanimously to reject all slaves, and by a great majority to reject negroes altogether.'

A Committee of Conference, consisting of Mr. Franklin, the Governor of Rhode Island, the Committee of the Council of Massachusetts and others, met at Cambridge, October 18, 1775, to confer with General Washington as to the best means of recruiting for the army. On October 23, the question arose:—

'Ought not negroes to be excluded from the new enlistment, especially such as are slaves? All were thought improper by the council of officers.

'Agreed that they be rejected altogether.'

In general orders, November 12, 1775, Washington says:—

'Neither negroes, boys unable to bear arms, nor old men unfit to endure the fatigues of the campaign, are to be enlisted.'

At a subsequent period the rigour of this exclusion was somewhat mitigated in consideration of the fact that the British Government might otherwise succeed in enlisting the negroes into the armies of the enemy. But there was no period of time when the numbers in the service of the United States exceeded ten or twelve hundred men. Of these there was one regiment of slaves consisting of about three hundred from the State of Rhode Island. Although the colonists numbered only three millions of souls arrayed in rebellion against the greatest Power on earth, yet they scorned to win their liberties by the employment of a degraded race. Now the Northerners, with a population of eighteen millions, confess that without the assistance of the Africans they cannot subdue eight millions of Southerners. The following general order issued by the present Governor of Rhode Island, presents a striking contrast to the part acted by his predecessor in that office in 1775:—

STATE OF RHODE ISLAND AND PROVIDENCE PLANTATIONS.

'Adjutant General's Office,
'Providence, Aug. 4, 1862.

'The 6th Regiment, authorised by the Secretary of War, under date of October 23, 1861, and orders issued therefor from this Department, No. 103, Dec. 28, 1861, will consist entirely of coloured citizens. Enlistment will commence immediately. Camp will be established under direction of General Robbins, who is directed to organise the regiment.

'Our coloured fellow-citizens are reminded that the regiment from this to their passions, have invited them to imbrue their hands in the blood of their masters, and to banquet

State in the Revolution, consisting entirely of coloured persons, was pronounced by Washington equal, if not superior, to any in the service. They constitute a part of the quota from this State, and it is expected they will respond with zeal and spirit to this call.

'The Commander-in-Chief will lead them into the field, and will share with them, in common with the patriotic soldiers of the army of the Republic, their trials and dangers, and will participate in the glories of their successes.

'By order of the Commander-in-Chief.'

The ferocious governor of this little State, while refusing to permit his 'coloured' brethren to be enlisted promiscuously in the ranks of the patriotic white soldiers, announces his own willingness as an individual to lead them up to the cannon's mouth. The question here suggests itself, if the Africans are not considered worthy to stand side by side upon the field of battle with white Yankees, why are they not permitted to fight under the leadership of officers of their own colour? These Rhode Island negroes have enjoyed half a century of freedom under Northern auspices, and surely within so long a period they ought to have acquired capacity sufficient to lay some claim to the right of being killed under officers of their own race. It is something to be noted, that while the Rhode Island governor remembered the flattering terms in which Washington referred to the services of the black regiment from that State, during the revolutionary war, he omits the important fact, that this regiment consisted entirely of slaves, led by their masters. They were fighting for their protectors and their homes, while the miserable freed African of to-day has no friend or home among that hard-hearted people, who now ask him to come forward and sacrifice his life in their cause.

The little State of Rhode Island, in the past and the present, illustrates the utter insincerity of Northern pretensions in favour of the African. The slave trade was during a long series of years the chief occupation of its citizens who were engaged in commerce. It is safe to assume that no other State of similar population introduced half the number of slaves into the South as were brought from Africa by the ships of this miniature sovereignty. Between the years 1804 and 1808, there were fifty-nine ships containing 8,233 slaves, belonging to Rhode Island, entered the single harbour of Charleston. They were the last to surrender the 'lucrative traffic,' and only abandoned it when the South refused any longer to furnish a market for their human cargoes. As if to revenge themselves against the South for putting a stop to their favourite branch of commerce, their governor now proposes to engage these same Africans to murder those to whom they sold them. Are there those amongst and make merry in the halls where they had previously served as domestics. Their fears have been stimulated by threats of vengeance if they refused to join in the slaughter of the Southerners; but all in vain! Up to this moment the whites themselves have been scarcely more loyal to the South than the Africans. It may be that continued familiarity and association with bad men may in time make the negroes as savage and ferocious as their tutors. It may be that by promises and by threats a certain number may be induced to turn upon their masters and their mistresses, and slay them; but history will record the fact that no population of the same class, in any other country, bond or free, have ever resisted to the same extent the temptations to pillage and to murder.

Thanks to the Africans, our usual crops of cotton, and tobacco, and rice will be ready in due time for any purchaser who will come and take them, or who will bring to us in exchange the manufactures which we require. If none are so bold as thus to dare the frowns of the North, we can readily convert our cotton plantations into grain fields, and divert a portion of the labour hitherto employed in planting, to the developement of our great manufacturing

the disinterested speculators of this terrible conflict, who can believe that the North is actuated by any wish to improve the condition of the Africans, or that the condition of the slaves can be ameliorated by any result which may be brought about through such instrumentality?

resources. Under the stimulant of a present necessity, we can produce everything within ourselves which is important to our happiness, our daily wants, and even our luxuries. When the war is over all things will flow back into their old channel, or continue in the direction which they shall have received under the impulse of necessity.

The freemen of the South have entered upon their great struggle with a unity of feeling and purpose which has struck terror into the hearts of their enemies, and amazed even their friends; but their glorious work is not yet finished. The clouds are over our heads, my fellow-countrymen, and the storm is still raging around us, and many a heart will yet mourn the loss of dear ones, and many a tear of bitter anguish will fall, as the eye wanders over the desolated track of the ruthless invader; but behind the clouds we can, with the eye of hope, see the dawning of the bright and glorious sunlight, and above the roarings of the storm of battle we can hear the glad shouts of victory! And our soldiers will come back again to make joyous the homes which have been made solitary by their absence, and the tears of grief will be changed to tokens of rejoicings, and throughout our borders will ring forth the joyous cry of the people, 'We have fought, we have conquered, we are free.'

PRINTED BY SPOTTISWOODE AND CO., NEW-STREET SQUARE, LONDON.

70

Emily's Adventures
in Wonderland

Ryan & Julia